CULTURE AND INTERPERSONAL COMMUNICATION

Sage's *Series in Interpersonal Communication* is designed to capture the breadth and depth of knowledge emanating from scientific examinations of face-to-face interaction. As such, the volumes in this series address the cognitive and overt behavior manifested by communicators as they pursue various conversational outcomes. The application of research findings to specific types of interpersonal relationships (e.g., marital, managerial) is also an important dimension of this series.

SAGE SERIES IN
INTERPERSONAL COMMUNICATION
Mark L. Knapp, Series Editor

CULTURE AND INTERPERSONAL COMMUNICATION

William B. Gudykunst
Stella Ting-Toomey
with Elizabeth Chua

Sage Series

Interpersonal Communication 8

SAGE PUBLICATIONS
The Publishers of Professional Social Science
Newbury Park   Beverly Hills   London   New Delhi

For information address:

SAGE Publications, Inc.
2111 West Hillcrest Drive
Newbury Park, California 91320

SAGE Publications Inc.   SAGE Publications Ltd.
275 South Beverly Drive   28 Banner Street
Beverly Hills   London EC1Y 8QE
California 90212   England

SAGE PUBLICATIONS India Pvt. Ltd.
M-32 Market
Greater Kailash I
New Delhi 110 048 India

Printed in the United States of America

Library of Congress Cataloging-in-Publication Data

Gudykunst, William B.
    Culture and interpersonal communication.

    (Sage series in interpersonal communication ;
v. 8)
    Bibliography: p.
    Includes indexes.
    1. Interpersonal relations. 2. Interpersonal
communication. 3. Culture. 4. Intercultural
communication. I. Ting-Toomey, Stella.
II. Chua, Elizabeth. III. Title. IV. Series.
HM132.G83   1988   302.3'4   88-3159
ISBN 0-8039-2944-7
ISBN 0-8039-2945-5 (pbk.)

FIRST PRINTING 1988

CONTENTS

LIST OF TABLES

LIST OF FIGURES

SERIES EDITOR'S INTRODUCTION

This book marks a critical point in the maturation of scholarship focusing on the relationship of culture and communication. In the 1960s you could probably count on one hand the number of books in this area. In contrast, the 1970s was an explosion of activity and interest. The concept of the global village had captured the imagination of communication scholars and work began on many fronts. Interest groups and divisions focusing on communication and culture were formed in professional communication associations; textbooks and readers were published; scholarly journals and college courses were established. The study on intercultural communication and cross-cultural communication were characterized by a developing diversity of interests and activities.

But there were few active and ongoing research programs to give the field depth. In addition, the role of communication theory in individual research publications was not always clear. Scholarly respectability, it was argued, was directly related to the future development of theory-driven programs of research. The publication of *Culture and Interpersonal Communication* signals a new phase of scholarly development in this area. It is distinguished by the following features:

First, the clear and driving force throughout this book is the desire to understand and explicate the nature of interpersonal communication as it affects and is affected by culture. Interpersonal communication from this perspective, then, has an element of group identification that manifests itself in the verbal and/or nonverbal messages exchanged. The ability to identify "culture" and/or "group identification" in face-to-face transactions is often elusive, but the authors of this book provide us with useful guidelines for this important undertaking.

Second, this book is distinguished by its ability to synthesize a diverse and complex literature clearly. For example, our ability to understand the influence of culture on communication is dependent on our ability to understand a myriad of studies that profess to identify basic dimensions along which cultures vary. Gudykunst and Ting-Toomey have, gratefully, sifted through the semantic overlap and different methodologies in order to provide us with a manageable list of factors associated with cultural variations in communication. In addition, this volume contains a synthesis of six years of research by the authors themselves—including a number of studies focusing on the role of communication and culture in the development of interpersonal relationships.

Third, this book is theory-driven. It integrates theoretical perspectives from those who study culture and those who study communication. The authors show how an understanding of communication theory is critical for an understanding of the role of culture in human transactions.

Finally, this book sets a scholarly agenda for the study of interpersonal communication and culture. It identifies the major methodological problems and research needs. In my opinion, it is a major sourcebook that should act as a stimulus for improved scholarship in this area and for attracting new scholars.

This is a book that encourages a reader to ask questions; to look for new connections; to open one's mind to alternative perspectives. Most interpersonal communication scholars agree that, in one way or another, culture is an inherent part of all interpersonal transactions. In practice, however, culture and interpersonal communication are often talked about and studied as separate entities. *Culture and Interpersonal Communication* is a valuable exception to this hopefully short-lived and unfortunate trend.

Mark L. Knapp

PREFACE

Most research on interpersonal communication ignores culture. There are, however, at least two reasons theorists and researchers in interpersonal communication should be interested in culture. First, culture is, by definition, a boundary condition for all interpersonal research not conducted cross-culturally (i.e., the conclusions of studies must be limited to the culture—and ethnic group—in which they were conducted) and a scope condition for all theories that do not include culture as one of the concepts in the theory. Research must be conducted and theories must be tested in other cultures in order to establish generalizability. Second, culture is, in and of itself, a powerful and an interesting theoretical variable vis-à-vis interpersonal communication. There is tremendous variability in interpersonal processes across cultures that is not considered when doing research in only one culture. When culture is included in a study or treated as an explanatory variable in a theory, the scope of the study or theory is increased.

Our purpose in writing this book is to examine the theoretical influence of culture on interpersonal communication. The book is an attempt to summarize the work we have conducted on culture and communication over the past six or seven years, as well as to provide a theoretical framework for guiding future research and the interpretation of past research related to interpersonal communication. We contend that cross-cultural comparisons of interpersonal communication must be theoretically based. This implies that culture must be conceptualized in such a way that it can be treated as a variable in research. We present such a conceptualization in the first two chapters and apply it to specific areas of research in the remainder of the book.

There is extensive cross-cultural research on interpersonal processes in the communication, anthropology, and social psychological literature. Most of these studies, however, have not treated culture as a "theoretical" variable. Throughout the book we must, therefore, reinterpret previous research that has revealed cultural differences using the conceptualization of culture (as a theoretical variable) presented in the first two chapters. In so doing, we provide post hoc explanations as to how culture influences situational factors (Chapter 3), self-conceptions (Chapter 4), verbal communication styles (Chapter 5), nonverbal dimensions (Chapter 6), self-conceptions (Chapter 6), personality (Chapter 7), social cognitive processes (Chapter 8), affective processes (Chapter 9), interpersonal relationships (Chapter 10), and intergroup relationships (Chapter 11).

The chapters are ordered so that explanatory frameworks used in later chapters are presented in earlier chapters. The self-conceptions chapter, for example, comes before the verbal communication styles chapter because the facework theory presented in the self-conceptions chapter is used to explain differences in verbal communication styles. Deciding where to discuss some issues was problematic. To illustrate, conflict styles involve verbal communication, but they also are a function of social cognitive processes and, therefore, could have been examined in either Chapter 5 or Chapter 8. In deciding where to discuss issues like this, we emphasized the topic in the chapter in which the greatest conceptual overlap with other material appeared to exist.

It would be impossible for us to review all cross-cultural research on interpersonal processes. Summarizing the anthropological literature alone would require several books. Further, Harry Triandis and his associates recently completed a review of cross-cultural research in psychology that filled six volumes (*The Handbook of Cross-Cultural Psychology*). Our review of the research, accordingly, is selective.

We have attempted to cite the majority of the communication research of which we are aware (the references include many studies not cited in the text) and selected representative anthropological and social psychological studies to supplement in areas in which little or no communication research has been conducted. In some areas in which no cross-cultural research exists, we present a theoretical/conceptual argument regarding the relationship between cultural variability and the specific process involved. There is no research, for example, on face-negotiation across cultures. We, therefore, present Ting-Toomey's (1988) theory of face-negotiation in Chapter 4. The way we discuss the effect of culture on specific interpersonal communication processes across chapters, accordingly, is a function of previous research, or lack of research, on the topic.

The studies discussed in detail throughout the book are those in which we have confidence that the effects observed are due to culture and not other variables such as age, sex, social class, or rural-urban differences. We have not discussed studies in detail that used international students in the United States as respondents or studies that were not conducted in the respondents' native language. We have, in other words, tried to focus on those studies that, in our opinion, controlled for other explanatory variables (Note: sample equivalence is discussed in the final chapter). Where other plausible explanations exist, we point them out.

The specific research discussed is important, but it is not the main focus of the book. Rather, as indicated above, the objective of the book is to illustrate how scholars can theoretically explain cultural differences in interpersonal communication that have been observed in the past to proffer hypotheses about cultural variability in future research. The specific studies included, therefore, should be viewed only as examplars.

Before concluding, we want to express our gratitude to friends and colleagues who contributed their time and expertise in bringing the book to fruition. To begin, we owe an intellectual debt to Harry Triandis. He has influenced our thinking and approach to the study of culture and communication. The model presented in Chapter 1 (and used throughout the book) draws on his work and he graciously provided advice on the development of the model. Michael Bond and Geert Hofstede also have influenced our approach to the study of culture and interpersonal communication. Michael Bond has commented on drafts of several studies included and has provided many of the studies cited in the book. He has been a constant source of support for our work. Geert Hofstede's theory of cultural differentiation provides the basis of much of our work and we emphasize it throughout the book. Without his pioneering work, this book would not have been possible.

Charles Berger, Donald Cushman, David Johnson, Felipe Korzenny, and Tsukasa Nishida also commented on an earlier version of our model of culture and communication (as presented in Gudykunst, 1987a) and made valuable suggestions for improvement. Several colleagues—Young Yun Kim, Sandra Sudweeks, Paula Trubisky, Karen Schmidt, Dean Scheibel, Louise Eckel—and the series editor, Mark Knapp, read a complete draft of the book, commenting on coherency, style, and form. Even though we did not incorporate all of their suggestions, their critiques and suggestions were invaluable. We also want to thank Tsukasa Nishida, Mitchell Hammer, Karen Schmidt, Seung-Mock Yang, Tae-Seop Lim, Young-Chul Yoon, Lori Sodetani, Hiroko Koike, and Nobuo Shiino, coauthors on several of the studies reported herein. The writing of this book would not have been possible without their collaboration over the past several years.

We also want to thank the staff of the Auxiliary Resource Center of the College of Public Programs at Arizona State University. Marian

Buckley, Coralie Rose, and Mary Cullen typed and proofread numerous drafts. They corrected spelling and grammatical errors, as well as pointed out missing, incorrect, and inconsistent references. Their assistance was invaluable and we are grateful for all of their help. The errors that remain are ours.

The Department of Communication at Arizona State University provided a supportive environment in which to write the book. We want to thank our colleagues and graduate students for their encouragement. Last, but not least, Sandy, Charles, and Adrian helped us to keep the book in perspective and "take flight" when it was necessary.

1

Culture and Communication

Communication and culture reciprocally influence each other. The culture from which individuals come affects the way they communicate, and the way individuals communicate can change the culture they share. Most analyses of interpersonal communication, however, virtually ignore this relationship and study communication in a cultural vacuum. Our goal in this book is to emphasize one side of the reciprocal relationship between communication and culture by examining the influence of culture on interpersonal communication. We, therefore, are interested in variations in patterns of communication across cultures, not communication between members of different cultures (e.g., intercultural communication) or how communication influences the development of culture.

The purpose of this chapter is to specify what we mean by the terms "interpersonal communication" and "culture." We begin from a social cognitive approach to interpersonal communication. Next we examine uncertainty reduction, the theoretical perspective that guides our research. Following this, we define culture and present a model that specifies how culture influences interpersonal communication, integrating situational and affective responses.

INTERPERSONAL COMMUNICATION

There is disagreement over the boundaries for the study of interpersonal communication. Some argue that the boundaries are a function of the situation, that is, the number of communicators, the degree of physical proximity between communicators, the available sensory channels, and the immediacy of feedback (Miller, 1978).

Interpersonal communication also can be conceptualized as a developmental process, a law-governed process, and a rule-governed process (Miller, 1978). We cannot resolve the disagreements here, but it is necessary to outline the conceptualization of interpersonal communication that we use throughout the book. We borrow Miller and his associates' (Miller & Steinberg, 1975; Miller & Sunnafrank, 1982) conceptualization for two reasons. First, it is consistent with the theoretical perspective (uncertainty reduction theory; e.g., Berger & Calabrese, 1975) that has guided most of our research. Second, Miller's conceptualization is compatible with the distinction we draw between interpersonal and intergroup communication.

A Perspective on Interpersonal Communication

Miller and Steinberg (1975) assume that "when people communicate, they make predictions about the effects, or outcomes, of their communication behaviors; that is, they choose among various communicative strategies on the basis of predictions about how the person receiving the message will respond" (p. 7; italics omitted). Of course, when people communicate, they are not always highly aware of making predictions. Awareness of making predictions varies with the degree to which people are aware of alternative outcomes of the communication situation. In making predictions (consciously or unconsciously), communicators must rely on their knowledge of past events and expectations about future events.

There are two types of factors that influence the nature of the predictions communicators make. The first are "situational" factors. Situational factors are those features of the communication setting that are given and unalterable, for example, the time, place, or physical setting in which the communication takes place. "Dispositional" factors, the second type, are influenced by past experiences and expectations that dispose individuals to perceive certain behaviors and interpret them in selected ways (Miller & Steinberg, 1975).

Miller and Steinberg (1975) argue that "cultural," "sociological," and "psychological" data can be used in making descriptions, predictions, and explanations. People in any culture generally behave in a regular way because of their norms, rules, and values, and this regularity allows for making predictions on the basis of cultural data. Miller and Sunnafrank (1982) elaborate:

> Knowledge about another person's culture—its language, dominant values, beliefs, and prevailing ideology—often permits predictions of the

> person's probable response to certain messages. . . . Upon first encoun-
> tering . . . [another person], cultural information provides the only
> grounds for communicative predictions. This fact explains the uneasiness
> and perceived lack of control most people experience when thrust into an
> alien culture: they not only lack information about the individuals with
> whom they must communicate, they are bereft of information concerning
> shared cultural norms and values. (pp. 226-227)

Sociological predictions are based on memberships in or aspirations
to particular social groups or social roles. Miller and Sunnafrank (1982)
argue that sociological data are the principal kind used to predict the
behavior of people from the same culture. Students communicate with
professors, patients communicate with physicians, and customers
communicate with clerks, to name only a few interactions, based on
roles rather than on the people occupying those roles.

At the psychological level, predictions are based on the specific
people with whom individuals are communicating; individuals are
concerned with how others are different from and similar to other
members of the culture and of the groups to which they belong. Stated
differently, predictions made using psychological data are based on the
unique characteristics of the person with whom one is communicating.
The other person is individuated, as opposed to deindividuated.
Psychological predictions, therefore, involve stimulus discrimination
rather than stimulus generalization.

When interacting with others, rules emerge that govern communication. If the interaction is based on the cultural or sociological
data, the rules generally are understood by the members of the same
culture or group. When predictions are based on psychological data, in
contrast, an "idiosyncratic rule structure" emerges; that is, "the rules are
known only to the participants and seem ambiguous, perhaps inex-
plicable, to outsiders" (Miller & Steinberg, 1975, p. 21).

Miller and Steinberg (1975) differentiate between noninterpersonal
and interpersonal communication based on the type of data used.
Noninterpersonal communication takes place when the predictions are
based *primarily* on the cultural and/or sociological levels of data.
Interpersonal communication, in contrast, occurs when predictions are
based *primarily* on psychological data. It should be noted, however, that
no value judgment is made with respect to noninterpersonal and
interpersonal communication; both are necessary and valuable forms of
communication. The term "intergroup" communication, in fact, can be
substituted for the term "noninterpersonal" communication (for ratio-

nale, see our discussion of interpersonal versus intergroup communication below).

Noninterpersonal communication can be likened to "stimulus generalization," looking for sameness when making predictions about other communicators. Stimulus generalization does not take into consideration how objects or events differ. Seeking differences in making predictions in interpersonal communication, on the other hand, can be likened to "stimulus discrimination." By basing predictions on stimulus discrimination, communicators greatly reduce the amount of errors in assessing other communicators' responses.

Following from the above perspective, Miller and Steinberg (1975) "stipulate that *communication involves an intentional, transactional symbolic process*" (p. 34; italics in original). Although this definition is concise, each concept in it has implications for how interpersonal communication is viewed.

In analyzing the various definitions of communication, Dance (1970) found that one of the major areas of disagreement involved the "intention" to communicate. Miller and Steinberg's (1975) perspective assumes that there is no message if there is no intent. The intent to send a message may be perceived by the person receiving the message, an outside observer, or the person who sent the message. Scott (1977) takes a somewhat similar position, arguing that the concept of intent needs reconstituting:

> We may distinguish between intentionality, a constant state of consciousness, and having intentions, particular focuses of this state. Or, to put the matter a little differently, when we are aware of having intentions, we begin to account for our own intentionality. By such an accounting, we are in a position to understand our behaviors as the actions of agents and to understand the behavior of others as like actions, and herein lies the generating force of human communication. (p. 263)

It should be noted that the sender and receiver of the communication do not always agree on the issue of intentionality. Two potential communication problems result when the intended receiver of a message fails to attribute meaning to the sender's message or the receiver attributes meaning to a behavior when the sender did not intend to communicate (Miller & Steinberg, 1975). Even though these problems exist, they should not necessarily be labeled "communication." As Scott (1977) points out, "the intentional systems that we recognize as jointly creating meaning" should be called "communication" because they are consistent with our sense of "entering into" communication (p. 267).

The second term in the definition that needs attention is "transactional." In using the term transactional to define communication, the argument is that the data communicators collect and use in making predictions are a product of both environmental objects ("stimuli") and internal mental states. Further, transactional implies that when people communicate, they have an impact on each other. This view of communication is consistent with Stewart (1977) when he points out that "every time persons communicate, they are continually offering definitions of themselves and responding to definitions of the other(s) which they perceive" (p. 19). The major advantage of such a transactional view of communication is that it forces the focus of attention on what is going on between the communicators, rather than on the internal states of the communicators.

The third term in the definition, "process," is characterized by Berlo (1960) as follows:

> If we accept the concept of process, we view events and relationships as dynamic, on-going, ever-changing, continuous. When we label something as process, we also mean that it does not have a beginning, an end, a fixed sequence of events. It is not static, at rest. It is moving. The ingredients within a process interact: each affects all of the others. (p. 24)

Miller and Steinberg (1975) point out that adopting a process point of view implies that individuals cannot see the totality of a communication situation and the communication situation will exist even after the specific communicators leave.

The final aspect of the definition stipulates that communication behaviors are "symbolic." "A symbol is anything that, by convention, is used to stand for, or represent, something else" (Miller & Steinberg, 1975, p. 43). In the study of any form of communication, it is important to remember that "symbols are symbols only by convention" (p. 43). There is no natural connection between any one symbol and its referent—these relationships are totally arbitrary and vary from culture to culture and group to group.

To summarize, we are suggesting that interpersonal communication is a function of the way one person deals with others, that is, the nature of the predictions made. Given this general perspective, we will summarize the theoretical perspective that guides our research and the model of culture and communication presented later in the chapter.

Uncertainty Reduction

Language often is used synonymously for *speech* and *communication*. There are, however, important differences in these three concepts. Language is an abstract system of rules (phonological, syntactic, semantic, and pragmatic). As such, it is a medium of communication. The abstract rules are translated into a channel (spoken, written, or sign language) in order to create messages. When the channel is the spoken word, speech occurs. "Communication," however, "is a more general concept involving the exchange of messages which may or may not be spoken and linguistic in form" (Berger & Bradac, 1982, p. 52). The primary function of the exchange of messages is the reduction of uncertainty (Berger & Calabrese, 1975). Uncertainty in this context refers to two phenomena: (1) individuals' inability to predict their own and others' beliefs and attitudes (cognitive uncertainty); and (2) their inability to predict their own and others' behavior in a given situation (behavioral uncertainty). Uncertainty reduction, therefore, involves the creation of proactive predictions and retroactive explanations about our own and others' behavior, beliefs, and attitudes.

The major assumption of uncertainty reduction theory is that individuals try to reduce uncertainty about others when they can provide rewards or punishments, behave in a deviant fashion, or may be encountered in future interactions (Berger, 1979). The desire to reduce uncertainty, however, does not stop with initial encounters with strangers. Rather, as Berger (1979) argues, "the communicative processes involved in knowledge generation and the development of understanding are central to the development and disintegration of most interpersonal relationships" (p. 123). Berger and Calabrese's (1975) initial formulation of the theory posited seven axioms and 21 theorems specifying the interrelations among uncertainty, amount of communication, nonverbal affiliative expressiveness, information seeking, intimacy level of communication content, reciprocity, similarity, and liking. Berger's (1979) elaboration outlined three general strategies individuals use for reducing uncertainty: passive—strategies that involve unobtrusive observations of others (reactivity search, social comparison, and disinhibition search); active—strategies that involve exerting effort to obtain information (asking others about the target and environmental structuring); and interactive—strategies that involve direct interaction with those about whom information is sought (interrogation, self-disclosure, and deception detection). More recently, Berger and Bradac (1982) extended the theory emphasizing the influence of language and the general similarity construct on uncertainty reduction processes.

Parks and Adelman (1983) elaborated the theory arguing that shared networks and support from these networks influence uncertainty reduction.

When uncertainty is reduced, understanding is possible. Understanding involves perceiving meaning, knowing, comprehending, interpreting, and/or obtaining information. Three levels of understanding can be differentiated: description, prediction, and explanation (Berger, Gardner, Parks, Schulman, & Miller, 1976). Description involves delineating what is observed in terms of physical attributes (i.e., to draw a picture in words). Prediction involves projecting what will happen in a particular situation. Explanation involves stating why something occurred. Understanding, therefore, is the ability to make accurate descriptions, predictions, and/or explanations.

Uncertainty reduction theory has been criticized on several grounds. First, many critics point out that it is limited to initial interaction contexts. Recent research, nevertheless, has demonstrated that the theory is applicable in developed relationships (e.g., Gudykunst, Yang, & Nishida, 1985; Parks & Adelman, 1983). Second, concern has been raised over whether certainty is desirable and/or necessary for communication (e.g., Planalp & Honeycutt, 1985). Third, the assumptions underlying the theory have been questioned (e.g., Kellerman, 1986; Sunnafrank, 1986). Sunnafrank, for example, argues that the major concern in initial interactions is with the predicted outcome value of the relationship, rather than with uncertainty. At least one study, however, suggests that predicted outcome value and uncertainty may both be important issues in interpersonal relationships (Gudykunst, Nishida, & Schmidt, 1988).

Differentiating Interpersonal and Intergroup Communication

Miller and Steinberg (1975) argue that interpersonal communication occurs when predictions are made using psychological data. When cultural and/or sociological data are used to make predictions, "noninterpersonal" communication occurs. Another way of referring to what Miller and Steinberg call noninterpersonal communication is to think about it as intergroup communication. The distinction between these two "types" of communication is important and deserves further elaboration. Interpersonal and intergroup communication are differentiated in social identity theory (Tajfel, 1978; Tajfel & Turner, 1979; see Turner, 1987, for a recent statement of the theory).

One of the major cognitive tools individuals use to define themselves vis-à-vis the world in which they live is social categorization, "the ordering of social environment in terms of groupings of persons in a manner which makes sense to the individual" (Tajfel, 1978, p. 61), for example, men and women, Blacks and Whites. Because of social categorization, individuals perceive themselves as belonging to certain social groups and attach positive and negative values to these groups. A social group is "two or more individuals who share a common social identification of themselves or . . . perceive themselves to be members of the same social category" (Turner, 1982, p. 15). Once individuals become aware of belonging to one or more social groups, their social identities begin to form. Social identity, according to Tajfel (1978), is defined as "that *part* of an individual's self-concept which derives from his [or her] knowledge of his [or her] membership in a social group (or groups) together with the value and emotional significance attached to that membership" (p. 63). The part of the self-concept not accounted for by social identity is personal identity (Turner, 1982).

When social identity predominates, intergroup behavior occurs. Sherif (1966) argues that "whenever individuals belonging to one group interact collectively or individually, with another group or its members *in terms of their group identifications,* we have an instance of intergroup behavior" (p. 12). Intergroup behavior, therefore, differs from interpersonal behavior in that its locus of control is social, not personal, identity. The differences in social behavior due to its locus of control are outlined by Tajfel and Turner (1979) when they describe behavior as varying along a continuum from purely interpersonal to purely intergroup:

> At one extreme . . . is the interaction between two or more individuals which is *fully* determined by their interpersonal relationships and individual characteristics and not at all affected by various groups or categories to which they respectively belong. The other extreme consists of interactions between two or more individuals (or groups of individuals) which are *fully* determined by their respective memberships of various social groups or categories, and not at all affected by the interindividual personal relationships between the people involved. (p. 34)

The purely interpersonal extreme does not exist, but some cases (i.e., communication between two lovers) come close. Pure intergroup behavior, in contrast, does exist; for example, an air force bomber crew dropping bombs on an enemy population would be "pure" intergroup behavior, while labor-management negotiations over a new contract are very close to pure intergroup behavior.

Recent conceptualizations suggest that the interpersonal-intergroup continuum oversimplifies the nature of the communication involved (Giles & Hewstone, 1982; Stephenson, 1981). Stephenson (1981), for example, argues as follows:

> It is difficult to think of any social situation which may not have both intergroup and interpersonal significance. . . . In any interaction with another, our apparent membership in different social groups—be it male, female, young, English, black or European—is at least a potential allegiance which may be exploited by the other, such that we act in some sense as representatives of fellow members of those groups. When our nationality, sex, or occupation becomes salient in the interaction, this does not necessarily obliterate the interpersonal significance of the encounter; indeed it may enhance it. (p. 195)

Gudykunst and Lim's (1986) graphical representation of this view of interpersonal and intergroup relations is presented in Figure 1.1. The intergroup salience of an encounter is represented on the horizontal axis, while the interpersonal salience is on the vertical axis. The two axes yield four quadrants: (I) high interpersonal and high intergroup salience; (II) high interpersonal and low intergroup salience; (III) low interpersonal and high intergroup salience; and (IV) low interpersonal and low intergroup salience.

In his discussion of intergroup negotiations, Stephenson (1981) distinguishes between Quadrants I and III in terms of how negotiations take place. If they are conducted face-to-face, then they fall in Quadrant I, where there is high interpersonal and high intergroup salience. When negotiations take place over the phone, in contrast, they fall into Quadrant III (low interpersonal, high intergroup). The difference, according to Stephenson, is that in the face-to-face situation negotiators are aware of the interpersonal implications of their behavior, while they are much less aware of it when they negotiate over the phone. The remaining two quadrants involve encounters that typically are viewed as interpersonal. More specifically, Quadrant II (high interpersonal, low intergroup) includes most encounters between friends, lovers, mates, and so forth. Quadrant IV (low interpersonal, low intergroup) encompasses a large percentage of encounters between strangers, including strangers on public transportation, interaction between clerk and customer, and other encounters of this nature. Giles and Hewstone (1982) argue that this quadrant also involves occasions "when an individual is inattentive, distracted, fatigued, drugged, etc." (p. 208).

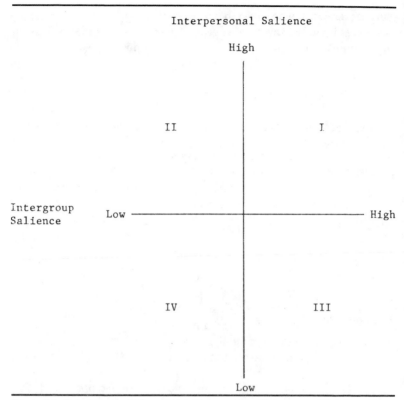

Figure 1.1:   **Interdependent Dimensions of Intergroup and Interpersonal Relations. From Gudykunst and Lim (1986, p. 5).**

Support for the distinction between interpersonal and intergroup salience can be found in Billig's (1987) analysis of "arguing and thinking." He contends that categorization alone cannot account for the way people think. Rather, thinking requires both categorization and particularization, with a constant give and take occurring between the categorization and the particularization in human thought. Categorization influences the level of intergroup salience in our interactions, while particularization affects the level of interpersonal salience in our encounters with others.

The focus of this book is interpersonal, rather than intergroup, communication. It is necessary at times, however, to discuss intergroup factors since both are salient in all encounters between individuals. A section of one chapter (8) on intergroup communication, therefore, also is incorporated in the book in order to address issues of communication that are relevant when interpersonal salience is low and intergroup salience is high. Before overviewing the remainder of the book, culture needs to be defined.

CULTURE AND SOCIOCULTURAL SYSTEMS

Given our conceptualization of interpersonal communication and how it differs from intergroup communication, we now turn our attention to the other major concept, culture. In this section, we define culture, differentiating it from society and social system, and overview the various areas of research that occur under the rubric communication and culture. Because of space limitations, our discussion of the conceptualization of culture is truncated (for more complete discussions the reader is referred to the sources cited below, as well as Griswold, 1987; Gross & Rayner, 1985; Wuthnow, 1987). Readers, therefore, are encouraged to consult the sources cited prior to applying the conceptualization presented in their research or theory construction.

Defining Culture

The conceptualization of culture has concerned social scientists for decades (e.g., Kroeber & Kluckhohn, 1952; see Shweder & LeVine, 1984, for recent conceptualizations). Numerous definitions exist, but to date no consensus has emerged within or across disciplines. Culture can be seen as consisting of everything that is human made (e.g., Herskovits, 1955), or as involving shared meanings (e.g., Geertz, 1973), to name only two possible conceptualizations. It also is equated with communication. Hall (1959), for example, believes that "culture is communication and communication is culture" (p. 169). Birdwhistell (1970) takes a slightly different position, suggesting that "culture and communication are terms which represent two different viewpoints of methods of representation of patterned and structured interconnectedness. As 'culture' the focus is on structure; as 'communication' it is on process" (p. 318).

Keesing (1974) reviewed theories of culture, concluding that the focus in anthropology is on two themes: culture as an adaptive system and culture as an ideational system. Those who see culture as an adaptive system tend to agree on several assumptions (Keesing, 1974). Theorists tend to assume that cultures link individuals to the ecological setting in which they live. Harris (1968), for example, contends that culture "comes down to behavior patterns associated with particular groups of people, that is, to 'customs' or to a people's 'way of life'" (p. 16). There also appears to be agreement that the adaptation process is similar to natural selection. Cultures tend to evolve toward equilibrium. Further, those aspects of the culture linked to production are viewed as the most central and adaptive part of cultural systems, but ideational components also have adaptive consequences.

Ideational theories of culture tend to view culture as a cognitive system, a structural system, or a symbolic system. Goodenough (1961) is one of the major proponents of culture as a cognitive system. He argues that culture "consists of standards for deciding what is . . . for deciding what can be . . . for deciding what one feels about it . . . for deciding what to do about it, and . . . for deciding how to go about doing it" (p. 522). Such a view makes culture unobservable and very similar to the cognitive systems of language. Lévi-Strauss (1971) suggests that cultures are "shared symbolic systems" that are "creations of the mind." He argues that the structuring of components of culture (e.g., myths) should be the focus of analysis. Geertz (1966, 1973) is the major advocate of the culture-as-symbolic-system school of thought. He uses the octopus as a metaphor for culture:

> The problem of cultural analysis is as much a matter of determining independencies as interconnection, gulfs as well as bridges. The appropriate image, if one must have images, of cultural organization, is neither the spider web nor the pile of sand. It is rather more the octopus, whose tentacles are in large part separately integrated, neurally quite poorly connected with one another and with what in the octopus passes for a brain, and yet who nonetheless manages to get around and to preserve himself [or herself], for a while anyway, as a viable, if somewhat ungainly entity. (1966, pp. 66-67)

Schneider (1972) takes a slightly different position differentiating cultural and normative systems:

> Where the normative system . . . is Ego centered and particularly appropriate to decision-making or interaction models of analysis, culture is system-centered. . . . Culture takes *a* man's [or woman's] position vis-à-vis the world rather than a man's [or woman's] position on how to get along in this world as it is given. . . . Culture concerns the stage, the stage setting, and the cast of characters; the normative system consists of the stage directions for the actors and how the actors should play their parts on the stage that is so set. (p. 38)

Taken individually, there are problems with each approach. Keesing (1974) argues, for example, that viewing culture as an adaptive system can lead to cognitive reductionism, while the view of culture as a symbolic system can lead to seeing the world of cultural symbols as spuriously uniform. To overcome the dilemmas in both definitions, he borrows the distinction between "competence" and "performance" from linguistics to explain culture:

> Culture, conceived as a system of competence shared in its broad design and deeper principles, and varying between individuals in its specificities, is then not all of what an individual knows and thinks and feels about his [or her] world. It is his [or her] theory of what his [or her] fellows know, believe, and mean, his [or her] theory of the code being followed, the game being played, in the society into which he [or she] was born. . . . It is this theory to which a native actor refers in interpreting the unfamiliar or the ambiguous, in interacting with strangers (or supernaturals), and in other settings peripheral to the familiarity of mundane everyday life space; and with which he [or she] creates the stage on which the games of life are played. . . . But note that the actor's "theory" of his [or her] culture, like his [or her] theory of his [or her] language may be in large measure unconscious. Actors follow rules of which they are not consciously aware, and assume a world to be "out there" that they have in fact created with culturally shaped and shaded patterns of mind. We can recognize that not every individual shares precisely the same theory of the cultural code, that not every individual knows all the sectors of the culture . . . even though no one native actor knows all the culture, and each has a variant version of the code. Culture in this view is ordered not simply as a collection of symbols fitted together by the analyst but as a system of knowledge, shaped and constrained by the way the human brain acquires, organizes, and processes information and creates "internal models of reality." (p. 89)

According to Keesing, culture must be studied within the social and ecological setting in which humans communicate, that is, sociocultural "performance" also must be studied.

Peterson (1979) reviewed the use of the concept "culture" in the sociological literature, concluding that the diverse conceptualizations share several elements:

> The focus on drama, myth, code, and people's plans indicates a shift in the image of culture. While it was once seen as a map *of* behavior, it is now increasingly seen as a map *for* behavior. In this view, people use culture the way scientists use paradigms . . . to organize and normalize activity. Like scientific paradigms, elements of culture are used, modified, or discarded depending on their usefulness in organizing reality. (p. 159)

Given the similarity of the conclusions, Keesing's and Peterson's explanations will be accepted as the working definition of culture.

Following Swidler (1986), we contend that culture independently influences behavior in "settled" cultural periods. In "unsettled" cultural periods, when a culture is undergoing massive change, actions are guided by explicit ideologies. Since we focus on "settled" periods here, this distinction is not critical for our analysis. For those interested in the influence of culture in periods in which a culture is "unsettled" (e.g., national development), the distinction is critical (see Swidler, 1986, for specifics of this argument).

Since culture cannot be studied in isolation from its social and ecological environment, it must be distinguished from the social system (the behavior of people who share a common culture, including networks of social relations and patterns of social interaction; Geertz, 1973; Parsons, 1951) and society (the population of humans who share a common culture and social system; Parsons, 1951). Rohner (1984) argues that "an individual is a *member* of society . . . individuals *participate* in social systems . . . and *share* cultures" (p. 132). Since society, social system, and culture are all interrelated and have an impact upon communication, the focus of the book is on the socio-cultural system, which is conceived as including all three.

Given the conceptualization presented, culture is a script or a schema shared by a large group of people. The "group" on which we focus throughout the book is the nation or society. More specifically, we technically are examining the influence of national sociocultural systems on interpersonal communication. We will, however, use the term "culture" because it is the shared culture that influences interpersonal communication, not membership in a society. The argument we make could be extended to "smaller" groups that share a specific culture (e.g., ethnic groups), but given the conceptualization of cultural variability presented in Chapter 2, we limit our analysis to "national cultures."

Areas of Research

The study of sociocultural systems and communication is not one unified area of research. Two dimensions differentiate the various areas of inquiry: interactive-comparative and mediated-interpersonal. These dimensions are defined by answers to two questions: Are patterns of communication being compared across systems (comparative) or are patterns of communication between members of different sociocultural systems being examined (interactive)? What channels of communication are used—interpersonal or mediated? Figure 1.2 combines the two dimensions, treating comparative-interactive as the horizontal axis and interpersonal-mediated as the vertical.

Quadrant I represents research conducted on intercultural communication. This area focuses on interpersonal communication *between* people from different sociocultural systems and/or communication between members of different subsystems (i.e., ethnic or racial groups) within the same sociocultural system. Quadrant II represents cross-cultural research in communication. The focus is interpersonal communication, as in Quadrant I, but research is comparative. Quadrants III and IV differ from the other two in that the phenomena studied are mediated communication. Research in Quadrant III focuses on mediated communication from one sociocultural system to another— research typically labeled international communication. Quadrant IV, in contrast, involves comparisons of media systems across sociocultural systems (comparative mass communication).

Extensive research exists in each of the four quadrants, but the quadrants are not rigid boundaries between areas of inquiry. Areas of research can and do overlap two or more quadrants. Issues surrounding the New World Information Order, for example, involve both international and comparative mass communication. While the four quadrants tend to represent different areas of inquiry, all share an interest in examining the influence of culture on communication. A review of research in each quadrant is beyond the scope of this book. The remainder of this chapter is devoted to outlining a theoretical framework for the study of cultural variability and communication that is applicable across the four quadrants. The remainder of the book, however, focuses on research that examines the influence of culture on interpersonal communication (Quadrant II). Where applicable, studies that look at cross-cultural differences in intercultural communication are included.[1]

AN ORGANIZING FRAMEWORK

In the preceding section we conceptually defined culture and stipulated that our focus is on cross-cultural communication. To explain past findings on cultural differences in interpersonal communication or posit predictions for future research, it is necessary to incorporate culture into a model of interpersonal communication. Our purpose in this section is to show why this is necessary and to proffer a

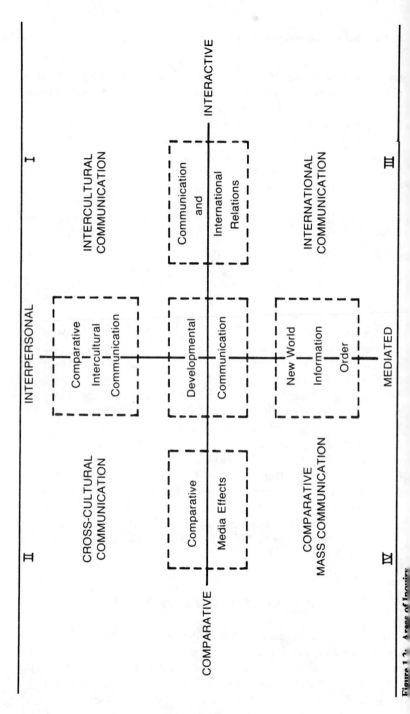

Figure 1.2: Areas of Inquiry

model for the study of cultural variability and interpersonal communication.

Need for a Framework

In recent years cross-cultural researchers have called for more attention to theory in the conduct of research (e.g., Malpass, 1977). Sechrest (1977), for example, argues that cross-cultural research constitutes "bits and pieces of knowledge that do not fit together in any particular way, that do not form any pattern and that more often than not fall far short of the aim of permitting a causal inference about the influence of culture on behavior and psychological processes" (p. 75). Theory is necessary for previous findings to be integrated. If theories of communication are to be developed that are not ethnocentric and limited to specific cultural contexts, research on cultural variability must be used to develop theory. Triandis (1976) outlines the role of research on cultural variability in constructing:

> We try to develop laws or relationships of the general form $y = f(x)$, in which x's are a characteristic, behavior, attitude or belief of a particular individual or group, or society and y's are responses of another individual to these characteristics, attitudes, or behaviors. Suppose that we find a particular function in one culture. It is legitimate to ask if a similar function might be obtained in other cultures. If the answer is that the function is invariant, across cultures, this is a piece of empirical information that is essential for the development of theories. If the function has parameters affected by culture, we want to know how much they are affected and why. Learning that a function f_1 is obtained in countries A, B, and C and a function f_2 is obtained in countries D, E, and F is an extremely valuable fact, which might allow, for instance, the development of some explanation about the way the two sets of cultures differ and hypothesize about the ecological basis of the difference. Conversely, finding that the same function applies in highly diverse cultures allows for the construction of a general theory. (p. 335)

Triandis, therefore, suggests that establishing generalities across cultures is essential in the development of comprehensive theories.

Foschi and Hales (1979) succinctly outline the issues involved in treating culture as a variable in developing theories:

> The uses of cultural differences can be classified in two groups: a theoretical use in which these differences serve to operationalize theoretical variables, and an atheoretical use in which they serve to explore variations in the experimental limitations of a study. In the first, or

> theoretical use, a culture X and culture Y serve to define operationally a characteristic *a*, which the two cultures exhibit to different degrees, and which is usually the independent variable in the study (e.g., level of economic development). The second, or atheoretical use, can be described as follows: the fact that the subjects are from culture X constitutes an experimental limitation, and the researcher is attempting to explore its effect on the dependent variable by also doing the experiment with subjects from culture Y. (pp. 246-247)

Cultural differences per se, therefore, are not of interest in theory construction. Rather, treating cultural differences as operationalizations of dimensions of cultural variation (e.g., individualism vs. collectivism; this dimension and others are discussed in Chapter 2) is of interest.

Cultural variations also can serve as scope or modifying conditions for theoretical hypotheses. Reynolds (1971) points out that all theories should include "a set of existence statements that describe the situations in which the theory can be applied" (p. 92). If a theory or hypothesis is tested initially in one culture (e.g., the individualistic culture of the United States), it may or may not be applicable in other cultures (e.g., the collectivistic culture in China). In initial tests, scope conditions should be stated narrowly and then relaxed in future tests until conditions are found in which the hypothesis or theory is invalid (see Walker & Cohen, 1985, for a discussion of the importance of scope statements). This procedure allows researchers to determine the generality of hypotheses or theories and the importance of the scope conditions and, therefore, increases their robustness (Foschi, 1980).

A Framework

Three major options for the development of a framework for explaining cultural variability and communication exists (Gudykunst, 1983d). First, one can be developed by extending communication theories designed to explain intracultural communication (e.g., rules theory, Pearce & Wiseman, 1983; cultural communication, Philipsen, 1975; uncertainty reduction theory, Gudykunst, 1985a, 1985c, in press b, in press c). Alternatively, a framework can be generated utilizing theory developed in other disciplines involving isomorphic social processes (e.g., attribution theory, Jaspars & Hewstone, 1982; constructivism, Applegate & Sypher, 1983; equity theory, Caddick, 1980; expectation states theory, Berger & Zelditch, 1985). These approaches are at times difficult to separate since many theories in communication are borrowed from other disciplines. Finally, a new framework can be developed based on research conducted specifically on sociocultural variability and communication (e.g., intercultural adaptation, Ellingsworth, 1983; cultural convergence, Barnett & Kincaid, 1983). The model proffered here combines the three methods (see Gudykunst, 1983c, for a discussion of the three perspectives).

Triandis's (1977, 1980a, 1984) model of behavior incorporates cultural variability and provides the starting point for the present framework. In order to focus on communication, rather than on behavior in general, a social cognitive perspective on communication is integrated with his model. The framework proffered, schematically depicted in Figure 1.3, is designed to provide a foundation for future research and theorizing on cultural variability and communication, not to present a formal theory.

The major premise underlying the framework is that culture interacts with language(s) to influence mediating processes (e.g., situational factors, social cognitive and affective processes, habits) that affect communication processes. Stated differently, cultural variability does not directly impact on communication per se, rather its influence is indirect through other processes.

Cultures vary along several definable dimensions (e.g., individualism-collectivism), and it is variance along these dimensions that affects the mediating processes (dimensions of cultural variability are examined in Chapter 2). Cultural variability is influenced by two major factors: history and ecology/resources. "Ecology refers to the relationship between organisms and the physical environment, including climate, physical terrain, prevailing fauna and flora, and the extent to which resources are limited or plentiful" (Triandis, 1980a, p. 212; see Berry, 1976, for a discussion of ecology). Resources include genetic and biological factors that affect particular populations.

The intrapersonal and interpersonal processes affected by cultural variability include social cognitive processes such as information processing, persuasive strategy selection, conflict management styles, personality, social relations, and self-perceptions, as well as affect (i.e., emotions and feelings) and habits (i.e., schemata, scripts). Cultural variability also has a major effect upon norms/rules, roles (including communication networks), language use, environmental settings (i.e., use of space, including territoriality, privacy, and crowding), the difficulties individuals have in communicating with others, and the skills that facilitate effective communication. Following Argyle, Furnham, and Graham (1981), these are considered to be elements of situations. Situational factors, therefore, are considered to be one of the major mediating processes between cultural variability and communication.

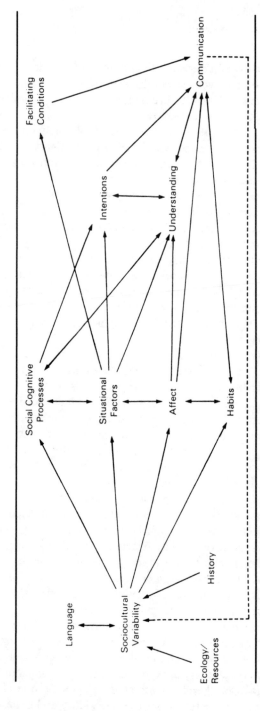

Figure 1.3: A Model for the Study of Cultural Variability and Communication

The situational factors, social cognitive processes, affect, and habits interact with each other, that is, each influences the others.

Social cognitive processes, situational factors, and affect in turn influence intentions and understanding (which reciprocally influence each other). Intentions are instructions individuals give themselves about how to communicate (Triandis, 1977, 1980a). Understanding involves the interpretation of incoming stimuli and the ability to describe, predict (including the perceived consequences of potential communicative behaviors; i.e., the perceived probabilities that certain types of consequences follow from certain patterns of communication), or explain these stimuli, including others' behavior. Understanding, in turn, feedbacks and influences social cognitive processes. Communication ultimately is based upon understanding and habits, intentions, or affect. The link between intentions and communication is affected by facilitating conditions, the "ability of the person to carry out the act, the person's arousal to carry out the act . . . and the person's knowledge" (Triandis, 1977, p. 10), which are a function of the situation.

PLAN FOR THE BOOK

The purpose of the remainder of the book is to examine each of the elements in the proposed framework. Dimensions of cultural variability are examined in Chapter 2. This chapter examines dimensions such as individualism-collectivism, uncertainty avoidance, power distance, masculinity-femininity, low- versus high-context, and numerous others. These dimensions of cultural variability lay the foundation for the theoretical interpretation of previous research on interpersonal communication across cultures that is reviewed throughout the book. Chapter 3 contains a discussion on cultural variations in selected situational factors—norms, rules, roles, and communication networks. In the fourth chapter, we look at cross-cultural variations in self-conceptions. Language and verbal style variations are discussed in Chapter 5, while Chapter 6 deals with the environment, space, touch, and time dimensions. The next three chapters look at how the implicit theories individuals hold vary across cultures. Implicit theories are divided into those dealing with personality (Chapter 7), social cognition processes (Chapter 8), and affective processes (Chapter 9). Chapter 10 examines interpersonal relationship development, while intergroup relationships are examined in Chapter 11. The book concludes with an evaluation of the framework proposed in the first chapter and an examination of the major methodological issues facing researchers doing cross-cultural research in Chapter 12.

NOTE

1. Areas of research peripheral to the study of interpersonal communication not directly discussed here, but reviewed elsewhere, include (reviews and/or representative studies are cited): bargaining (Fisher, 1983; Harnet & Cumming, 1980; Stephenson, 1981) bilingualism (Davey, 1982; Hammers & Blanc, 1982; Lambert, 1967; Segalowitz, 1980), Black-White communication (Ickes, 1984; Shuter, 1982), communication and change (Schramm & Lerner, 1976), diffusion of innovations (Rogers, 1983), diplomacy (Cioffi-Revilla, 1979; Fisher, 1979), interethnic discourse processes (Gumperz, 1982a, 1982b), foreigner talk (Varonis & Gass, 1985), intercultural friendships (Bochner et al., 1977; Bochner & Orr, 1979), international media appraisal (Johnson, 1983, 1984), language development (Bowerman, 1981), minorities and the media (Greenberg, Burgoon, Burgoon, & Korzenny, 1983), new world information order (McBride et al., 1980; McPhail, 1981; Nordenstreng, 1984), satellite broadcasting (Wigand, 1982), second language acquisition (Clément & Kruidenier, 1985; Gardner, LaLonde, & Pierson, 1983; Giles & Byrne, 1982), tourism (Cohen, 1984), and training (Brislin, Cushner, Cherrie, & Yong, 1986; Landis & Brislin, 1983). For reviews of research on intercultural communication, see Asante and Gudykunst (in press).

2

Cultural Variability

Cultural variability is examined in this chapter. Cultural variability has been discussed from many different vantage points. Dimensions of syntality (comparable to personality at the cultural level; e.g., Cattell & Brennan, 1984), dimensions of nations (e.g., Rummel, 1972), and national character (e.g., Inkeles & Levinson, 1969), for example, have been isolated. Variation also has been investigated from an evolutionary perspective. To illustrate, Naroll (1970) reviewed over 150 comparative studies identifying characteristics of cultural systems that tend to coevolve, including: (1) command of the environment (weak to strong); (2) organizational structure (simple to complex); (3) population patterns (rural to urban); (4) occupational specialization (general to specific); (5) leadership patterns (consensual to authoritative); (6) distribution of goods (wealth-sharing to wealth-hoarding); (7) behavior of elites (responsible to exploitative); and (8) function of war (vengeful to political). These schemas are useful, but their relationship to communication processes has not been articulated to date. Several schemas of cultural variability that influence communication more directly are reviewed in this chapter, beginning with the broadest and most widely used conceptualizations.

The focus of this chapter is on individualism-collectivism and low- and high-context communication. These dimensions are broader and more encompassing than other dimensions, such as uncertainty avoidance (Hofstede, 1980, 1983), human nature (Kluckhohn & Strodtbeck, 1961), affectivity-affective neutrality (Parsons, 1951), and structural tightness (Boldt, 1978), to name only a few of those discussed in this chapter. The dimensions of cultural variability examined in this chapter provide the foundation for the theoretical interpretations of past research on interpersonal communication across cultures that has revealed cultural differences.

INDIVIDUALISM-COLLECTIVISM

Individualism-collectivism is the major dimension of cultural variability isolated by theorists across disciplines (e.g., Bellah, Madsen, Sullivan, Swidler, & Tipton, 1985; Hofstede, 1980; Hsu, 1981; Hui & Triandis, 1986; Kluckhohn & Strodtbeck, 1961; Lebra, 1976; Marsella, DeVos, & Hsu, 1985; Parsons & Shils, 1951; Tönnies, 1961; Triandis, 1986; Westen, 1985; Yang, 1981a; Yum, 1987a). Emphasis is placed on individuals' goals in individualistic cultures, while group goals have precedence over individuals' goals in collectivistic cultures. Waterman (1984), for example, argues that individualistic cultures promote "self-realization" for their members:

> Chief among the virtues claimed by individualist philosophers is self-realization. Each person is viewed as having a unique set of talents and potentials. The translation of these potentials into actuality is considered the highest purpose to which one can devote one's life. The striving for self-realization is accompanied by a subjective sense of rightness and personal well-being. (pp. 4-5)

Saleh and Gufwoli (1982), in contrast, illustrate the collectivistic values in their discussion of management in Kenya:

> In Kenyan tribes nobody is an isolated individual. Rather, his [or her] uniqueness is a secondary fact. . . . First, and foremost, he [or she] is several people's contemporary. His [or her] life is founded on these facts economically, socially and physically. In this system group activities are dominant, responsibility is shared and accountability is collective. . . . Because of the emphasis on collectivity, harmony and cooperation among the group tend to be emphasized more than individual function and responsibility. (p. 327)

In individualistic cultures, "people are supposed to look after themselves and their immediate family only," while in collectivistic cultures, "people belong to ingroups or collectivities which are supposed to look after them in exchange for loyalty" (Hofstede & Bond, 1984, p. 419). The "I" identity has precedence in individualistic cultures over the "we" identity, which takes precedence in collectivistic cultures. The emphasis in individualistic societies is on individuals' initiative and achievement, while emphasis is placed on belonging to groups in collectivistic societies. People in individualistic cultures tend to be universalistic and apply the same value standards to all. People in collectivistic cultures, in contrast, tend to be particularistic and, therefore, apply different value standards for members of their ingroups and outgroups.

Members of individualistic cultures form specific friendships, whereas members from collectivistic cultures form friendships that are pre-determined by stable relationships formed early in life. Cushman and King (1986) illustrate the differences in friendships in individualistic and collectivistic cultures when they describe friendships in the United States and Japan:

> Japanese follow two types of friendship formation sequences: tsukiai, or interpersonal relationships cultivated and maintained as a result of social obligation; and personal friends, or class relationships that develop from mutual liking, attraction, interests or common values. Interpersonal relationships based on mutual liking, attraction, interests, values, or personal friends are usually among same sex schoolmates and usually last a lifetime. The number of close friends one has is small, but those friends serve the important function of allowing one to talk freely about a broad range of mutual interest while being at ease. . . . [North] Americans follow a single type of friendship formation sequence. When an [North] American meets another who has as part of his/her real self-concept some attribute that is admired, then one attempts to initiate a friend relation-ship. Such a relationship appears to have three underlying dimensions: trust, self-concept support, and helping behavior. Trust refers to a relationship based on authenticity; self-concept support refers to a relationship based upon respect for one's social and psychological identity; helping behavior refers to a relationship based on reciprocal assistance in time of need. (p. 48)

Triandis (1986) argues that collectivistic cultures focus on the ingroup and individualistic cultures do not. Collectivistic cultures em-phasize goals, needs, and views of the ingroup over those of the individual; the social norms of the ingroup, rather than individual pleasure; shared ingroup beliefs, rather than unique individual beliefs; and a value on cooperation with ingroup members, rather than maximizing individual outcomes. Triandis goes on to argue that the number of ingroups, the extent of influence for each ingroup, and the depth of the influence must be taken into consideration in the analysis of individualism-collectivism. He contends that the larger the number of ingroups, the narrower the influence and the less the depth of influence.

Since individualistic cultures have many specific ingroups, they exert less influence on individuals than ingroups do in collectivistic cultures, in which there are few general ingroups. Triandis also points out that ingroups have different rank-orders of importance in collectivistic cultures; some, for example, put family ahead of all other ingroups, while others put their companies ahead of other ingroups.

Triandis's (1986) conceptualization further suggests that members of collectivistic cultures draw sharper distinctions between members of ingroups (e.g., those with whom they go to school or work) and outgroups and perceive ingroup relationships to be more intimate than members of individualistic cultures. Ingroup relationships include brother/sister (family ingroup), coworker and colleague (company ingroup), and classmate (university ingroup), to name only a few, while outgroup relationships include, but are not limited to, interactions with strangers and/or members of different ethnic groups.

Triandis and his associates (1985, 1986) have argued that there is a personality dimension, idiocentrism-allocentrism, that corresponds to cultural variability in individualism-collectivism. Idiocentrism at the psychological level corresponds to individualism at the cultural level, while allocentrism at the psychological level is equated with collectivism at the cultural level. Triandis et al. (1985) found that allocentric tendencies involved three factors: subordinating individual goals to group goals, viewing the ingroup as an extension of the self, and strong ingroup identity. Allocentrics reported greater social support than idiocentrics, while idiocentrics reported being more lonely than allocentrics. This finding was collaborated by Triandis et al. (1986) in Puerto Rico.

Individualism also plays a major role in other theories of cultural variability. Parsons (1951) derived the pattern variable of self-orientation/collectivity-orientation. Self-orientation is the "pursuit of private interests" (Parsons, 1951, p. 60), while collectivity-orientation refers to the "pursuit of the common interests of the collectivity" (p. 60). The roles into which individuals are cast result in the same behavior that is collectivity-oriented in terms of the individual or is self-oriented in terms of a larger referent system. Parsons (1951) uses the example of a departmental executive whose actions may be aimed toward his or her own welfare, the department's welfare, the firm's welfare, or even the society's welfare.

One problem faced by members of all cultures discussed by Kluckhohn and Strodtbeck (1961) is defining humans' relations to other humans. Three possible definitions exist: the lineal, the collateral, and the individualistic. The lineal principle takes into consideration the fact that individuals are related to each other through time biologically and culturally. According to Kluckhohn and Strodtbeck, "continuity of the group through time and ordered positional succession within the group are both crucial issues when lineality dominated the relational system" (p. 19). Collaterality is found in societies in which individuals are not considered to be human except as they are part of a social order. One type of inevitable grouping that results is the laterally extended relationship. The typical relationship that is collateral is that between individuals who are biologically related: brother-sister, aunt-uncle, and so on. In individualistic societies, members' goals have primacy over the goals of groups. This does not mean, however, that individuals can selfishly pursue their own goals and disregard the interests of others. Individuals' goals and roles are autonomous or independent of other groups. Employees of a firm can cooperate with coworkers in accomplishing the goals of a company, but at the same time employees are also free to leave the firm if they are given a better offer elsewhere.

As indicated earlier, individualism-collectivism has been isolated in anthropology, comparative sociology, cross-cultural psychology, and philosophy. Further, it has emerged in Western and Eastern analyses of culture. Individualism-collectivism, therefore, is robust and provides a powerful explanatory framework for cultural differences in interpersonal communication. While individualism-collectivism defines broad differences between cultures, Hall's (1976) low- and high-context schema, discussed in the next section, focuses upon cultural differences in communication processes.

LOW- AND HIGH-CONTEXT COMMUNICATION

Hall (1976) differentiates cultures on the basis of the communication that predominates in the culture. A high-context communication or message is one in which "most of the information is either in the physical context or internalized in the person, while very little is in the coded, explicit, transmitted part of the message (Hall, 1976, p. 79). A low-context communication or message, in contrast, is one in which "the mass of the information is vested in the explicit code" (p. 79). While no culture exists at either end of the low-high-context continuum, the culture of the United States is placed toward the lower end, slightly above the German, Scandinavian, and Swiss cultures. Most Asian cultures, such as the Japanese, Chinese, and Korean, in contrast, fall toward the high-context end of the continuum.

Hall (1976) points out that the level of context influences all other aspects of communication:

> High-context cultures make greater distinction between insiders and outsiders than low-context cultures do. People raised in high-context systems expect more of others than do the participants in low-context systems. When talking about something that they have on their minds, a high-context individual will expect his [or her] interlocutor to know what's bothering him [or her], so that he [or she] doesn't have to be specific. The result is that he [or she] will talk around and around the point, in effect putting all the pieces in place except the crucial one. Placing it properly—this keystone—is the role of his [or her] interlocutor. (p. 98)

We believe that the dimensions of low-high-context communication and individualism-collectivism are isomorphic. All cultures Hall (1976, 1983) labels as low-context are individualistic, given Hofstede's scores, and all of the cultures Hall labels as high-context are collectivistic in Hofstede's (1980, 1983) schema. It, therefore, appears that low- and high-context communication are the predominant forms of communication in individualistic and collectivistic cultures, respectively. This position appears to be consistent with Levine's (1985) discussion of cultural variability in the use of directness versus indirectness and certainty versus ambiguity in communication. He describes communication in the Amhara culture (collectivistic) as follows:

> The Amhara's basic manner of communicating is indirect, often secretive. Amharic conversation abounds with general, evasive remarks, like *Min yeshallāl?* ("What is better?") when the speaker has failed to indicate what issue he [or she] is referring to, or *Setagn!* ("Give me!") when the speaker fails to specify what it is he [or she] wants. When the speaker then is quizzed about the issue at hand or the object he [or she] desires, his [or her] reply still may not reveal what is really on his [or her] mind; and if it does, his [or her] interlocutor will likely as not interpret that response as a disguise. (Levine, 1985, p. 25)

Levine goes on to describe communication in the United States (an individualistic culture) in this way:

> The [North] American way of life, by contrast, affords little room for the cultivation of ambiguity. The dominant [North] American temper calls for clear and direct communication. It expresses itself in such common injunctions as "Say what you mean," "Don't beat around the bush," and "Get to the point." (p. 28)

Levine (1985) also describes univocal and ambiguous communication more generally:

> Univocal verbal communication is designed to be affectively neutral. It aims for the precise representation of fact, technique, or expectation. Univocality works to strip language of its expressive overtones and suggestive allusions. Ambiguous communication, by contrast, can provide a superb means for conveying affect. By alluding to shared experiences and sentiments verbal associations can express and evoke a wealth of affective responses. The exploitation of ambiguity through wit and jokes can convey a wide array of feelings. The clandestine ambiguities of ironic messages have the capacity to transmit sentiments of enormous power. (p. 32)

These descriptions are consistent with Hall's (1976) conceptualization of low-high-context communication and Hofstede's (1980) discussion of the norms in individualistic and collectivistic cultures. Given the consistency, we assume throughout the remainder of the book that low-versus high-context communication and direct versus ambiguous communication are the predominant forms of communication in individualistic and collectivistic cultures, respectively. We do, however, use the terms low-context and high-context cultures whenever this is the conceptualization used in the work to which we refer. The labels "individualistic" and "collectivistic" can be substituted for low- and high-context whenever they are used in order to make higher-order generalizations.

Individualism-collectivism and low- versus high-context communication are broad dimensions of cultural variability that influence many different aspects of interpersonal communication. Given their breadth, we utilize these dimensions to explain many of the cultural differences isolated. It is not possible, however, to explain all cultural differences with these two dimensions. We, therefore, now turn our attention to other dimensions of cultural variability that have more limited scope, beginning with those isolated in Hofstede's (1980, 1983) theory of cultural differentiation.

HOFSTEDE'S DIMENSIONS

Hofstede (1980, 1983) derived four dimensions of cultural variability empirically from a study of multinational corporations in 53 countries and three regions (in the initial report, 1980, he analyzed data for 40 countries, while in the later, 1983, he added 13 countries and three regions). He describes his methodology as follows:

> The data . . . were extracted from an existing bank of paper-and-pencil survey results collected within subsidiaries of large multinational business organizations in 40 countries, and covering among others many questions about values. The survey was held twice, around 1968 and around 1972, producing a total of over 116,000 questionnaires; respondents can be matched by occupation, age, and sex. Additional data were collected among managers participating in international management development courses and unrelated to the first multinational business organization. The four main dimensions on which country cultures differ were revealed by theoretical reasoning and statistical analysis. They were labeled Power Distance, Uncertainty Avoidance, Individualism, and Masculinity. Each of the 40 countries could be given a score on these four dimensions. (Hofstede, 1980, p. 11)

The scores for the 53 countries and three regions reported by Hofstede (1983) are presented in Table 2.1 at the end of the chapter. The scores for each dimension were calculated from items on the questionnaires used in Hofstede's research. The specific method of calculation for each score is not of interest here, but it is important to note that we are assuming that Hofstede's scores are reliable and valid in our analysis.

Hofstede's (1980) theory of cultural differentiation has been criticized on several grounds. First, it was generated from data collected in a multinational corporation and personnel of the multinational may not be representative of other members of the culture. Hofstede argues, and we agree, that using personnel from the multinational corporation allows for the control of other variables that may confound the results (e.g., occupation, class, age) and, therefore, what actually is examined is culture. Second, the validity of the items used to construct one or two of the indices might be questioned. We contend that this is an empirical question and, if predictions derived from the dimensions are supported, the dimensions are valid. Finally, it might be argued that since the theory was developed on organizational communication, it is not applicable to interpersonal communication. Again, we believe this is an empirical question. Hofstede's dimensions have been used to explain the use of the equity and equality norms across cultures (Bond, Leung, & Wan, 1982), perceptions of interaction episodes (Forgas & Bond, 1985), perception of communication associated with relationship terms (Gudykunst & Nishida, 1986b), and cultural differences in affective communication (Gudykunst & Ting-Toomey, 1988)—all interpersonal phenomena. In general, we find Hofstede's dimensions useful in explaining previously observed cross-cultural differences in inter-personal communication. Since individualism was discussed above, it is omitted here.

Uncertainty Avoidance

In comparison to cultures low in uncertainty avoidance, cultures high in uncertainty avoidance have a lower tolerance "for uncertainty and ambiguity, which expresses itself in higher levels of anxiety and energy release, greater need for formal rules and absolute truth, and less tolerance for people or groups with deviant ideas or behavior" (Hofstede, 1979, p. 395). In high uncertainty avoidance cultures, aggressive behavior of self and others is acceptable, however, individuals prefer to contain aggression by avoiding conflict and competition. There is a strong tendency for consensus in cultures high in uncertainty avoidance, therefore, deviant behavior is not acceptable. High uncertainty avoidance cultures also tend to display emotions more than low uncertainty avoidance cultures. Low uncertainty avoidance cultures have lower stress levels and weaker superegos and accept dissent and taking risks more than high uncertainty avoidance cultures.

Hofstede (1980) compared scores on uncertainty avoidance with data from other large-scale cross-cultural studies. This comparison revealed that in comparison to members of low uncertainty avoidance cultures, members of high uncertainty avoidance cultures resist change more, have higher levels of anxiety, have higher levels of intolerance for ambiguity, worry about the future more, see loyalty to their employer as more of a virtue, have a lower motivation for achievement, and take fewer risks. In organizations, workers in high uncertainty avoidance cultures prefer a specialist career, prefer clear instructions, avoid conflict, and disapprove of competition between employees more than workers in low uncertainty avoidance cultures.

Power Distance

Power distance is defined as "the extent to which the less powerful members of institutions and organizations accept that power is dis-tributed unequally" (Hofstede & Bond, 1984, p. 419). Individuals from high power distance cultures accept power as part of society. As such, superiors consider their subordinates to be different from themselves and vice versa. High power distance cultures see power as a basic fact in society, and stress coercive or referent power, while low power distance cultures believe power should be used only when it is legitimate and prefer expert or legitimate power.

In comparing power distance scores with results of other cross-cultural studies, Hofstede (1980) found that parents in high power distance cultures value obedience in their children, and students value conformity and display authoritarian attitudes more than those in low power distance cultures. In organizations, close supervision, fear of disagreement with supervisor, lack of trust among coworkers, and directed supervision are all manifested more in high power distance cultures than in low power distance cultures. Further, in comparing this dimension with Triandis's (1972) data, Hofstede found that members of low power distance cultures see respect for the individual and equality as antecedents to "freedom," while members of high power distance cultures view tact, servitude, and money as antecedents to "freedom." Antecedents to "wealth" in low power distance cultures include happiness, knowledge, and love. Inheritance, ancestral property, stinginess, deceit, and theft, in contrast, are viewed as antecedents to "wealth" in high power distance cultures.

Masculinity-Femininity

High masculinity, according to Hofstede (1980), involves a high value placed on things, power, and assertiveness, while systems in which people, quality of life, and nurturance prevail are low on masculinity or high on femininity. Cultural systems high on the masculinity index emphasize differentiated sex roles, performance, ambition, and independence. Conversely, systems low on masculinity value fluid sex roles, quality of life, service, and interdependence.

Hofstede (1980) also compared masculinity-femininity scores with results of other cross-cultural studies. He found that, in comparison to people in feminine cultures, people in masculine cultures have stronger motivation for achievement, view work as more central to their lives, accept their company's "interference" in their private lives, have higher job stress, have greater value differences between men and women in the same position, and view recognition, advancement, or challenge as more important to their satisfaction with their work. He illustrates communication in a feminine culture by quoting Hall's (1959) description of emotion in Iran:

> In Iran . . . men are expected to show their emotions. Iranian men read poetry; they are sensitive and have well-developed intuition and in many cases are not expected to be too logical. They are often seen embracing and holding hands. Women, on the other hand, are considered to be coldly practical. They exhibit many of the characteristics we associate with men in the United States. A very perceptive Foreign Service Officer

... once observed "If you will think of the emotional and intellectual sex roles as reversed from [the United States] you will do much better out here." (p. 50)

To fully appreciate this illustration, it must be remembered that women are expected to be submissive in Iran (Hall, 1959).

Cross-Cultural Generalizability

Hofstede's (1980, 1983) theory of cultural variability was developed from a Western social science point of view. In order to determine if the potential bias influenced the dimensions generated, the Chinese Culture Connection (1987; the Chinese Culture Connection is a group of researchers interested in the Chinese culture organized by Michael Bond at the Chinese University of Hong Kong) tested the generalizability of the dimensions using a methodology with a Chinese bias. More specifically, a scale of 40 important Chinese values was constructed and administered to samples of at least 100 ethnic Chinese students in 22 different countries. Subjects rated each value on a nine-point scale from "no importance at all" (1) to "of supreme importance" (9).

Following Hofstede's procedures, the country mean scores for each item were submitted to an ecological factor analysis with four dimensions emerging: integration, Confucian work dynamism, human-heartedness, and moral discipline. Integration included values such as "tolerance of other," "harmony with others," "noncompetitiveness," and "a close, intimate friend." The Confucian work dynamism dimension involved values such as "ordering relationships," "thrift," "having a sense of shame," "reciprocation" (negative loading), and "protecting your face" (negative loading). Human-heartedness included values such as "kindness," "patience," "courtesy," and "sense of righteousness" (negative loading). Finally, moral discipline involved values such as "moderation," "keeping oneself disinterested and pure," " having few desires," and "prudence" (negative loading). The dimensional structure was verified with nonmetric multidimensional scaling because of the small number of cases (22 country scores) relative to the number of values (40).

Twenty of the 22 countries in the analysis overlapped with those reported in Hofstede's (1983) analysis. The country scores on the four Chinese dimensions, accordingly, were correlated with scores on Hofstede's four dimensions for the 20 countries. The Chinese dimension integration correlated positively with individualism-collectivism dimension, while moral discipline correlated with power distance and human-heartedness correlated with the masculinity-femininity dimension. Only the Confucian work dynamism did not correlate highly with any of Hofstede's four dimensions. It did correlate, however, with average growth in the Gross National Product over the past 20 years.

The Chinese Culture Connection (1987) concluded that power distance, individualism, integration, and moral discipline all tap "a basic dimension of cultural valuing. We propose that this underlying dimension be called collectivism in that each of the value groupings pit the maintaining of group integrity against narrowly defined self-seeking" (pp. 155, 158). They go on to argue that human-heartedness and masculinity-femininity can be combined to form a human- to task-centered dimension.

Because Hofstede (1980, 1983) isolated scores (see Table 2.1) for over 50 cultures, his dimensions can be used to make extremely specific predictions of cultural differences. Once a theoretical relationship between one of Hofstede's dimensions and an aspect of interpersonal communication has been established, specific predictions can be made as to which cultures should have highest, lowest, and middle scores vis-à-vis the aspect of interpersonal communication being examined (e.g., ordered predictions are possible). This, however, is not possible with the other dimensions of cultural variability to be discussed below. None of the other dimensions discussed (including Hall, 1976) allow for ordered predictions. Rather, they allow for qualitative predictions, that is, either two cultures should differ or they should be similar. Because Hofstede's theory of cultural differentiation (and the resultant scores for the various cultures on the four dimensions) allows for more sophisticated predictions and explanations, we rely on the four dimensions of cultural variability he isolated whenever possible. With this in mind, we will now examine Kluckhohn and Strodtbeck's (1961) variations in value orientations.

KLUCKHOHN AND STRODTBECK'S VALUE ORIENTATIONS

Value orientations are defined as "complex but definitely patterned . . . principles . . . which give order and direction to the ever-flowing stream of human acts and thoughts as these relate to the solution of 'common' human problems" (Kluckhohn & Strodtbeck, 1961, p. 4). The theory of value orientations is based on three assumptions: (1) People in all cultures must find solutions to a limited number of common human problems; (2) the available solutions to these problems are limited but vary within a range of potential solutions; and (3) while one solution tends to be preferred by members of any given culture, all potential solutions are present in every culture.

Kluckhohn and Strodtbeck (1961) posit five problems for which all cultures must find solutions. Posed as questions, these problems are as follows:

(1) What is the character of innate human nature? (human nature orientation)
(2) What is the relation of [hu]man to nature (and supernature)? ([hu]man-nature orientation)
(3) What is the temporal focus of human life? (time orientation)
(4) What is the modality of human activity? (activity orientation)
(5) What is the modality of [hu]man's relationship to other [humans]? (relational orientation) (p. 11)

As indicated above, every culture must find a solution to each of these problems. The solutions available, however, are limited for each of the problems. Since the relational orientation was discussed under individualism, it is omitted here.

Activity Orientation

The primary characteristic of the activity orientation is its emphasis on modes of self-expression in activity: being, being-in-becoming, or doing. In the being orientation, the kinds of activities that are performed are "spontaneous expressions of what are conceived to be given in the human personality" (Kluckhohn & Strodtbeck, 1961, p. 16). An excellent example is the Mexican fiesta, which, according to Kluckhohn and Strodtbeck, reveals "pure" impulse gratification.

The second activity orientation, being-in-becoming, is concerned with who we are, not what we can or have accomplished. The focus of human activity is on striving for an integrated whole in the development of the self. The best example may be Zen Buddhist monks, who spend their lives in contemplation and meditation to fully develop the self. This view was also manifested in the self-improvement movement of the 1960s and 1970s in the United States; Maslow's (1970) self-actualized person is in a constant state of being-in-becoming.

A prime example of the doing orientation is the United States. Its most outstanding characteristic is "a demand for the kind of activity which results in accomplishments that are measurable by standards conceived to be external to the acting individual" (Kluckhohn & Strodtbeck, 1961, p. 17). Activities must be measurable. In evaluating a person's worth, people in the United States tend to ask questions like "what did he or she do?" or "what has he or she accomplished?" According to this orientation, if someone is just sitting down daydreaming, he or she is not doing anything because his or her thoughts cannot be evaluated externally.

Human Nature Orientation

Another feature of Kluckhohn and Strodtbeck's (1961) value orientation is the assumption that the character of human beings is innately either good, evil, a combination of good and evil, or neutral. Human beings also can be assumed to be changeable (mutable) or unchangeable (immutable). The combinations of these six criteria result in human nature as being good and mutable, good and immutable, evil and mutable, evil and immutable, a mixture of good and evil, and neutral. Individuals who believe that they are basically evil but mutable will exercise control and discipline of the self to achieve goodness.

Human-Environment Orientation

The relation between humans and nature is subcategorized into mastery-over-nature, harmony-with-nature, and subjugation-to-nature orientations. Mastery-over-nature involves the perspective that all natural forces can and should be overcome and/or put to use by humans. This view in general is that it is the person's responsibility to overcome obstacles that may stand in his or her way (e.g., the U.S. culture). The harmony-with-nature orientation draws no distinction between or among human life, nature, and the supernatural—each is an extension of the others (e.g., traditional Chinese culture). Subjugation-to-nature involves the belief that nothing can be done to control nature. Individuals who believe that fate must be accepted, for example, may not consult a physician when they are dying (e.g., traditional Spanish-American culture).

Time Orientation

The temporal feature of human life concerns past, present, and future orientations (Kluckhohn & Strodtbeck, 1961). Cultural systems that value traditions highly are said to have past orientations (e.g., Chinese culture of ancestor worship and strong family tradition). Systems with present orientations pay relatively little attention to traditions and what might happen in the future (e.g., Spanish-American culture, the general belief of which is that the human being is a victim of natural forces). The future orientation predominates where change is valued highly (e.g., U.S. culture).

An alternative conception of cultural variability in dealing with time also has been proposed. Based on his work in several cultures (e.g., Pueblo Indians, New Mexico Spanish, Japanese), Hall (1983) differentiates between polychronic (P-time) and monochronic (M-time) cultures. Generally, people in cultures that use polychronic time do several things at once, while those in cultures that use monochronic time complete one thing before starting something else. Polychronic time stresses "involvement of people and completion of transactions rather than adherence to preset schedules" (Hall, 1983, p. 43). Appointments that are set up by members with polychronic orientation may not be as adhered to seriously, resulting in "no show" appointments. Being on time in a polychronic culture does not mean the same as it does in a monochronic culture. Future plans in a polychronic culture are changed as more important situations arise. In monochronic cultures, in contrast, people are so attuned to time that it determines and coordinates relations with others. Hall goes on to describe polychronic cultures as being oriented toward people, human relationships, and the family, while monochronic cultures are oriented toward tasks, schedules, and procedures. To illustrate, a hairdresser from a polychronic culture may cancel an appointment with a client when a member of the family requires the hairdresser's immediate attention, while a hairdresser in a monochronic culture would not change the schedule to take care of the family member.

Before examining the next dimension of cultural variability, a brief evaluation of Kluckhohn and Strodtbeck's (1961) schema is in order. Value orientations were used as an organizing framework for one of the first texts in intercultural communication (Condon & Yousef, 1975) and at least one explanation of intercultural relationships (Cronen & Shuter, 1983). Value orientations also have provided the conceptual framework for recent comparative studies (e.g., Nishida, 1981). We use value orientations as an explanation for cultural differences in the few cases in which Hofstede's (1980) and Hall's (1976) schemas are not applicable. Part of the reason value orientations are not more useful is that they initially were applied to explaining subcultural differences within the United States (e.g., explaining differences in Spanish American, Native American, Mormon, and Caucasian subcultures). Because the initial focus was on subcultures, the dimensions are rather narrow and, therefore, less useful than broader schemas in explaining differences in interpersonal communication across national cultural boundaries.

PARSONS'S PATTERN VARIABLES

A pattern variable is defined as "a dichotomy, one side of which must be chosen by an actor before the meaning of a situation is determinate for him [or her], and thus before he [or she] can act with respect to that situation" (Parsons & Shils, 1951, p. 77). In other words, pattern variables are mutually exclusive choices individuals make prior to engaging in action. These choices are made both consciously and unconsciously; however, they are generally made unconsciously since they are learned during the socialization process at an early age. Parsons's pattern variable self-orientation versus collective orientation was discussed under individualism and, therefore, is omitted here.

Affectivity-Affective Neutrality

This pattern variable is characterized by normative patterns that guide an actor to seek immediate gratification or restrain seeking gratification. The cultural aspect of affectivity grants the "permission of an actor, in a given situation, to take advantage of a given opportunity for immediate gratification without regard to evaluative considerations" (Parsons & Shils, 1951, p. 80). The affective neutrality "prescribes for actors in a given type of situation renunciation of certain types of immediate gratification for which opportunity exists, in the interest of evaluative considerations regardless of the content of the latter" (p. 80).

Ascription-Achievement

Whether an individual would treat an object or an individual because of what it is, what it does, or what response it produces makes up the ascription-achievement variable (Parsons, 1951). The cultural aspect of the ascription pattern prescribes that an individual should give priority to certain attributes that objects/individuals possess over any specific performances of objects/individuals. In contrast, the normative pattern of achievement prescribes that an individual in his or her selection and treatment of objects/individuals should give priority to their specific performances (past, present, future) over their given attributes.

Universalism-Particularism

This pattern variable pertains to modes of categorizing people or objects. A universalistic orientation is one in which people or objects are categorized in terms of some universal or general frame of reference. Universalistic interaction tends to follow a standardized pattern. In a particularistic orientation, people or objects are categorized in specific categories resulting in interactions unique to situations. Given this, we would expect low-context cultures like the United States to be characterized by a universalistic orientation, while a particularistic orientation tends to predominate in high-context cultures like those in the Orient. Individuals from universalistic cultures interact with strangers in the same way in different situations, while individuals from particularistic cultures interact with strangers differently in different situations.

Specificity-Diffuseness

While universalism-particularism is concerned with how we categorize people or objects, this pattern variable is concerned with how we respond to people or objects (Parsons, 1951). When a person or an object is treated in a holistic manner, a diffuseness orientation is displayed. When only aspects of a person or an object are responded to, a specificity orientation prevails. In collectivistic cultures, the tendency is for people to treat others as a whole person, while in individualistic cultures, the tendency is to treat people depending upon the unique identities they perform.

Like Kluckhohn and Strodtbeck's (1961) value orientations, Parsons's (1951) pattern variable schema initially was developed to explain variations within cultures. It has been used to explain variations across national cultural boundaries. Using combinations of the pattern variables, Lipset (1963), for example, was able to differentiate Great Britain, Canada, Australia, and the United States. While similar with respect to broader conceptualizations such as individualism-collectivism (e.g., all four are individualistic), these four cultures differ with respect to their underlying orientations toward actions. The pattern variable schema, therefore, may be useful in fine-tuning predictions and explanations when two cultures have similar scores on Hofstede's (1980) and/or Hall's (1976) dimensions.

BOLDT'S STRUCTURAL TIGHTNESS

The dimension of structural tightness arose as a response to inadequacies of earlier scales of cultural system complexity (Boldt, 1978). Accumulated findings suggest that cultural systems can be placed on a continuum from simple to more complex and differentiated (e.g., Naroll, 1970), as indicated earlier. The difficulty with the various evolutionary indices, however, is that cultural systems might come out as complex on one indicator, but simple on another. Witkin and Berry (1975) view tightness as the "degree of hierarchical structure among sociocultural elements in a society" (p. 11). They treat structural tightness as an antecedent variable in their review of differentiation in cross-cultural research, concluding that tight cultural systems display lower levels of differentiation than do loose cultural systems.

Boldt (1978) argues that role diversity (the number of roles and role relationships) and role relatedness (the nature of the bonds among roles), two distinct dimensions of social structure, must be distinguished when discussing structural tightness. Boldt and Roberts (1979) contend that role relatedness "bonds are defined by reciprocal role of expectations of individuals in a given social network, expectations which vary in the degree they are either 'imposed or received' or 'proposed and interpreted'" (pp. 225-226). Variation in role relatedness, not role diversity, defines a culture as relatively tight or loose. This dimension cuts across the complexity dimension, such that both simple and complex systems can display either tightness or looseness.

This final schema is not really a dimension of cultural variability per se. Rather, it is a dimension of variability in social systems, as defined in Chapter 1. We have included it here because it appears to offer plausible explanations for sociocultural differences in intergroup conflict that cannot be explained by any of the other dimensions discussed.

CONCLUSION

We have reviewed several of the major schemas of cultural variability in this chapter. These schemas provide dimensions on which cultures vary that can be used theoretically to explain cultural difference in interpersonal communication observed in past research. Throughout the remainder of the book, we will provide post hoc theoretical explanations whenever researchers have not provided them. We rely most heavily on Hofstede's (1980, 1983) dimensions of cultural variability because he provides "quantitative" scores for 50 cultures and three regions on each of the dimensions. These scores allow specific explanations and hypotheses to be proffered. We also use Hall's (1976) low- and high-context "theory" because this schema has been used extensively in previous cross-cultural research on interpersonal communication. As pointed out earlier, however, Hall's low- and high-context schema is isomorphic with Hofstede's individualistic and collectivistic cultures, respectively, in our opinion. In developing hypotheses for future research, investigators, therefore, could substitute individualistic for low-context and collectivistic for high-context.

Some dimensions of cultural variability are not used extensively throughout the remainder of the book (e.g., Kluckhohn & Strodtbeck's, 1961, value orientations; Parsons's, 1951, pattern variables) because the placement of cultures on these dimensions has not been clearly specified. No researcher, for example, has examined a large number of cultures to determine which human activity value orientation predominates in the cultures. Until such data exist, researchers/theorists must be familiar with the cultures under study in order to determine which value orientation or pattern variable predominates. It was necessary, however, to discuss these dimensions for two reasons. First, they offer alternative conceptualizations to those presented by Hofstede (1980) and Hall (1976) with which the reader should be familiar and we use them to explain some of the cultural differences observed in past research. Second, they are useful dimensions for making predictions in other areas of communication, that is, Kluckhohn and Strodtbeck's human-nature orientation could be used in studying the influence of the environment on communication.

TABLE 2.1
Scores on Hall's and Hofstede's Dimensions of Cultural
Variability for Selected Countries

Country	Power Distance	Uncertainty Avoidance	Individualism	Masculinity	Context
Afghanistan	—	—	—	—	high
Africa (East)[a]	64	52	27	41	high
Africa (West)[b]	77	54	20	46	high
Arab cultures[c]	80	68	38	53	high
Argentina	49	86	46	56	high
Australia	36	51	90	61	low
Austria	11	70	55	79	low
Bangladesh	—	—	—	—	high
Belgium	65	94	75	54	low
Bolivia	—	—	—	—	high
Brazil	69	76	38	49	high
Cameroon	—	—	—	—	high
Canada	39	48	80	52	low
Chile	63	86	23	28	high
China (People's Republic)	—	—	—	—	high
Columbia	67	80	13	64	high
Costa Rica	35	86	15	21	high
Cuba	—	—	—	—	high
Denmark	18	23	74	16	low
El Salvador	66	94	19	40	high
Equador	78	67	8	63	high
Finland	33	59	63	26	low
France	68	86	71	43	low
Germany (D.R.)	—	—	—	—	low
Germany (F.R.)	35	65	67	66	low
Great Britain	35	35	89	66	low
Greece	60	112	35	57	high
Guatemala	95	101	6	37	high
Honduras	—	—	—	—	high
Hong Kong	68	29	25	57	high
Hungary	—	—	—	—	low
Indonesia	78	48	14	46	high
India	77	40	48	56	high
Iran	58	59	41	43	high
Ireland	28	35	70	68	low
Israel	13	81	54	47	low
Italy	50	75	76	70	low
Jamaica	45	13	39	68	high

(*continued*)

TABLE 2.1 continued

Country	Power Distance	Uncertainty Avoidance	Individualism	Masculinity	Context
Japan	54	92	46	95	high
Korea (S.)	60	85	18	39	high
Malaysia	104	36	26	50	high
Mexico	81	82	30	69	high
Nepal	—	—	—	—	high
Netherlands	38	53	80	14	low
Nicaragua	—	—	—	—	high
Norway	31	50	69	8	low
New Zealand	22	49	79	58	low
Pakistan	55	70	14	50	high
Panama	95	86	11	44	high
Peru	64	87	16	42	high
Philippines	94	44	32	64	high
Poland	—	—	—	—	low
Portugal	63	104	27	31	high
Puerto Rico	—	—	—	—	high
Romania	—	—	—	—	low
Singapore	74	8	20	48	high
South Africa	49	49	65	63	low
Spain	57	86	51	42	high
Sri Lanka	—	—	—	—	high
Sweden	31	29	71	5	low
Switzerland	34	58	68	70	low
Taiwan	58	69	17	45	high
Thailand	64	64	20	34	high
Turkey	66	85	37	45	high
Uruguay	61	100	36	38	high
USA	40	46	91	62	low
USSR	—	—	—	—	low
Venezuela	81	76	12	73	high
Vietnam	—	—	—	—	high
Yugoslavia	76	88	27	21	high

SOURCE: Adapted from Hall (1976) and Hofstede (1980, 1983).

NOTE: The low/high designation for context is based on the cultures' score on individualism/collectivism (those below median are considered high-context, those above the median are considered low-context) or discussions of the culture in previous cross-cultural analyses.

a. Includes Kenya, Ethiopia, Tanzania, and Zambia.

b. Includes Ghana, Nigeria, and Sierra Leone.

c. Includes Egypt, Lebanon, Libya, Kuwait, Iraq, Saudi Arabia, and United Arab Emirates.

3

Situational Factors

Argyle, Furnham, and Graham (1981) argue that a situation is "a type of social encounter with which members of a culture or subculture are familiar" (p. 4). They isolate nine features of situations: (1) goals and goal structures, (2) norms/rules, (3) roles, (4) repertoire or elements, (5) sequences of behavior, (6) concepts, (7) environmental setting, (8) language and speech, and (9) difficulties and skills. Space does not permit a thorough examination of each feature, therefore the focus is on areas in which extensive research exists, including norms, rules, roles, and networks. Norms, rules, roles, and communication networks—all situational factors that influence interpersonal communication—are influenced by culture. Argyle et al. subsume networks under role, but we treat them as a separate feature.

Norms, rules, roles, and networks influence how we encode and decode both verbal and nonverbal messages. They also assert a strong influence on the patterns of interpersonal relationship development in different cultures. We begin our examination of situational factors by looking at norms.

NORMS

Norms are prescriptive principles to which members of a culture subscribe. The attributes of a norm include: "(1) a collective evaluation of behavior in terms of what ought to be; (2) a collective interpretation as to what behavior will be; (3) particular reactions to behavior including attempts to apply sanctions or otherwise induce a particular kind of behavior" (Gibbs, 1965, p. 590). While norms are culturally ingrained principles that are imparted systematically to children through the socialization process, cultural rules are situationally and interpersonally negotiable.

Olsen (1978) argues that norms assert both moral and ethical forces on an individual's behavior, but rules do not. Rules, according to Olsen, are developed for reasons of expediency, because they allow people to coordinate their activities. Noesjirwan (1978) takes the position that

> rules provide a statement of expected or intended behaviour and its outcome. As such, rules provide a number of related functions that serve to order social life and render it meaningful. Rules provide a set of mutual expectations, thus rendering the behaviour of each person predictable and understandable to the other. . . . The rules partly serve to define the meaning a situation has, and to define the meaning that any given action has within a situation. (pp. 305-306)

The violation of a cultural norm brings some form of overt or covert sanction on the individual committing the violation. The violation of a cultural rule in a particular situation may be subjected to different sets of interpretations and different sets of relational variable influences. Loose cultures (Boldt, 1978) assert less pressures on individuals to conform than do tight cultures, which assert high demands on individuals to adhere to the underlying norms and rules of the situation.

The two fundamental norms that influence cultural members' attitudes and behaviors in different interpersonal settings are the norm of justice and the norm of reciprocity. We begin by looking at the norm of justice.

Norm of Justice

There are two orientations toward the norm of justice: the "equity norm" and the "equality norm." The equity norm is followed when individuals perceive a favorable ratio between their input levels and reward outcome levels. This equity norm is tied closely with the notion of "deservingness." The equality norm is operating when the rewards are distributed evenly or equally regardless of the differential input levels of the individuals (Gergen, Morse, & Gergen, 1980; Lerner, 1974).

Cross-cultural research suggests that people in individualistic cultures tend to subscribe to the norm of equity, while people in collectivistic cultures tend to support the norm of equality. Mahler, Greenberg, and Hayashi (1981), for example, tested the norm of justice in Japan and in the United States, finding that Japanese students prefer the equality norm for reward distributions, while North American students prefer the equity norm for reward allocations. Leung and Bond (1982, 1984) examined the norm of justice in Chinese and North American subjects and found that Chinese subjects tend to favor the equality norm, while North American subjects tend to favor the equity norm. In addition, when subjects were asked to allocate to either ingroup or outgroup members, Chinese subjects used the equality norm more with members of the ingroup than with members of the outgroup. Further, Chinese males tended to favor the equality norm more than Chinese females, while Chinese females tended to favor the equity norm more than Chinese males. The reverse patterns held true for the North Americans.

Compatible findings were obtained in Mann, Radford, and Kanagawa's (1985) study with 12-year-old children in Japan and Australia, and with Polynesian and European subjects in Wetherell's (1982) study. Both studies found that members of the collectivistic cultures (Japan and Polynesian cultures) tend to select the equality norm more often than the equity norm, while members of individualistic cultures (Australia and Europe) tend to select the equity norm more often than the equality norm. The equity norm, in one sense, is based on a self-oriented calculation of what one thinks one deserves in accordance to one's personal contribution to a relationship or toward a task. The equality norm, in contrast, is based on an other-oriented evaluation of what everyone should gain on the ground of fairness to the group. The equity norm, therefore, serves individualistic self-interest, while the equality norm serves collectivistic other-interest. Cultures that value the equity norm foster the importance of individual contributions, individual ideas, and individual rights and needs. Cultures that value the equality norm foster the importance of group harmony, group consensus, and group rights and obligations. Cultures that value the equity norm also encourage individuals to stand out from their surroundings, while cultures that value the equality norm encourage individuals to "blend in" and pay close attention to others.

In interpersonal relationships in an individualist culture, "fairness" means people should get what they deserve based on their input and commitment level in the relationships. "Fairness," in the context of interpersonal relationships in collectivistic cultures, means everyone should be rewarded evenly regardless of their contributions. While "fairness" is viewed from a self-oriented, short-term perspective in the individualistic cultures, "fairness" is interpreted from an other-oriented, long-term perspective in the collectivistic culture. Every act, in collectivistic cultures, has larger group and social implications that influence the individuals that form the basic network of that person. While the norm of justice influences how one implicitly evaluates the outcome of the relationship, it is the norm of reciprocity that provides the turning points to an interpersonal relationship development process.

Norm of Reciprocity

The norm of reciprocity, according to Gouldner (1960), contains two interrelated minimal conditions: "(1) people should help those who have helped them, and (2) people should not injure those who have helped them" (p. 171). The norm of reciprocity is an implicit moral contract that binds and ties people together. The implicit maxim is: "Thou shalt not hurt those who have helped thee." On the behavioral level, the reciprocity norm is a transactional concept whereby "B's service to A is contingent upon A's performance of positive functions for B" (Gouldner, 1960, pp. 163-164).

Ting-Toomey's (1986a) ethnographic interview study with members of individualistic cultures (Australia, France, and the United States) and collectivistic cultures (China and Japan) indicated that members of collectivistic cultures emphasize the importance of the *obligatory* reciprocity norm and members of individualistic cultures stress the importance of the *voluntary* reciprocity norm. According to the Japanese informants, the concept of *on-giri* binds and ties people together in an interlocked, interdependent system. According to Lebra (1976), *on* is a "relational concept combining a benefit or benevolence given with a debt or obligation thus incurred. . . . From the donor's point of view, *on* refers to a social credit, which from the receiver's point of view, it means a social debt" (p. 91). On the other hand, the word *giri* refers to the feeling of indebtedness by the debtor toward his or her creditor and the reciprocal process of repaying and canceling out the debt.

While the concept of *on-giri* is of paramount importance in the Japanese culture, the concept of "face" is the underlying key that unlocks the inner psyche of the Chinese culture (Hu, 1944; Ting-Toomey, 1988; Yutang, 1968. Face is discussed in detail in Chapter 6). The "face" is an outer image that a person claims for him- or herself. It is the sense of being approved of or disapproved of, being included or excluded, and being appreciated or rejected. "Face-giving" and "face-repaying" are the terms equivalent to the *on-giri* concept. Both the "face-giving" and "face-repaying" concepts, and the *on-giri* concept follow an obligatory pattern of the norm of reciprocity. The more one gives face to another person, the more debt and obligations donors incur from their debtors. The debtors, in turn, have to engage in an active repayment process of face-honoring and face-compensating rituals toward their donors on a long-term give-and-take basis.

Johnson's (1977) study of kinship patterns among Japanese-American families in Honolulu supports the above observation. This research revealed that the majority of Japanese-American families follow an obligatory reciprocity norm pattern. This pattern includes: (1) sociocentricity—behaviors related to the concern for others, humility, and compassion; (2) obligation to parents—behaviors related to filial piety, respect for elders, and obedience; (3) regulation of debts and repayments—behaviors related to gift-giving and favor-exchange; and (4) dependence—behaviors related to integrative family and kinship activities. The reciprocity pattern in the Caucasian families, in contrast, included idiocentricity, voluntary respect toward parents, free form of gift-giving or favor-exchange, and independence.

While members of individualistic cultures practice a voluntary reciprocity norm, members of collectivistic cultures practice an obligatory reciprocity norm. A voluntary reciprocity norm is based on one's free will and one's free choices and an obligatory reciprocity norm is based on group's orientation and group's inclination. Based on monochronic values (or linear time values) toward the time dimension (Hall, 1983), people in individualistic cultures are also likely to practice the immediate (or short-term) reciprocity norm more than people in collectivistic cultures. Members of collectivistic cultures, which value polychronic time rhythm (fluid time values), are likely to practice the eventual (or long-term) reciprocity norm more than members of individualistic cultures.

Beyond the form and the time dimensions of the reciprocity norm, Gouldner (1960) proposed that individuals typically engage in two types of reciprocity: symmetrical reciprocity and complementary reciprocity. Symmetrical reciprocity means the exchange of resources between two individuals that are both equivalent in kind and in value. Complementary reciprocity means the exchange of resources between two individuals that are different in kind but approximately equal in value. While no study to date specifically has tested the symmetrical versus the complementary reciprocity pattern in a cross-cultural setting, it can be predicted that members of low power distance, individualistic cultures are more likely to follow the symmetrical pattern of reciprocity, while members of high power distance, collectivistic cultures are more likely to follow the complementary pattern of reciprocity. As Okabe (1983) noted in commenting on the characteristics of the U.S. culture and the Japanese culture:

> In the [North] American model, each individual asserts himself or herself to other individuals who are presumed to be his or her equals. This creates

symmetrical relationships, based as they are on an assumption of likeness, or similarity. The interaction between equals is predominantly the [North] American value assumption. Japanese culture, however, values the contrastive pattern of complementary relationships based on assumptions of differences, which complement each other to make a whole. (p. 27)

While members of low power distance, individualistic cultures value symmetrical exchange, members of high power distance, collectivistic cultures value complementary exchange. People in low power distance cultures shun the formal codes of reciprocity exchange, but people in high power distance cultures engage in complementary reciprocity norms that appropriately reflect their role, status, and power in the exchange process.

In terms of the types of resources for exchange, Foa and Foa (1974) developed a theory of social interaction based on the various resource exchange principles (this theory also is discussed in Chapter 10). They propose that social interaction is based on the exchange of six resources: love, status, information, money, goods, and services. Three dimensions govern the resource exchange process: (1) particularism-universalism, (2) concreteness-abstractness, and (3) giving-denying (Adamopoulos, 1984; Foa & Foa, 1974; Lonner, 1980).

Based on these three dimensions, it can be predicted that members of individualistic cultures are more likely to engage in target-specific exchanges, while members of collectivistic cultures are more likely to engage in target-general exchanges in interpersonal relationship development process. Target-specific exchanges emphasize the unique qualities of a relationship itself, while target-general exchanges emphasize the common bonding of a relationship with other relationships in a network. Target-specific exchanges emphasize the unique culture of the dyadic pair as separate from other types of relationships, while target-general resource exchanges emphasize a relationship that is embedded in multiple relationships in the network.

In relating the concreteness-abstractness dimension with the cultural variability dimensions, it appears that differences in Hofstede's (1980) masculine-feminine dimension influence concrete (e.g., goods and services) versus abstract (e.g., information and love) exchange. Masculine cultures place heavy emphasis on material goods, while feminine cultures place a high emphasis on nurturance and quality of life. The concrete exchange of material goods and services reflects the underlying values of masculine cultures, while the exchange of love and information is indicative of the values of feminine cultures.

Finally, in relating the giving-denying dimension with the cultural variability dimensions, it appears that Hall's (1976, 1983) low- and high-context dimension can explain the differential styles of giving-denying dimension in a resource exchange process. Members of low-context cultures (such as the United States)—which value line logic, the direct mode of verbal communication, and individualistic nonverbal interaction—are more likely to practice direct giving-denying style, while members of high-context cultures (such as Japan)—which value spiral logic, the indirect mode of verbal communication, and con-textualistic nonverbal interaction—are more likely to engage in an indirect style of giving and denying of symbolic resources of exchange.

Many cross-cultural studies (Gudykunst & Nishida, 1983, 1986b; Gudykunst, Yoon, & Nishida, 1987; Won-Doornink, 1979, 1985) have tested the disclosure exchange norm in relation to social penetration theory (Altman & Taylor, 1973; Knapp, 1978). Won-Doornink (1985), for example, examined the relationship between self-disclosure and the reciprocity norm, finding that Korean cross-sex dyads engage in lower rates of topical reciprocity than North American cross-sex dyads. In addition, Koreans are less likely than North Americans to reciprocate self-disclosures by discussing the same topic as that initiated by the other person.

In testing for disclosure exchange in same-sex friendships in Japan and the United States, Gudykunst and Nishida (1983) found that only 3 (own marriage and family; love, dating, and sex; emotions and feelings) out of 10 disclosure topics revealed significant differences between Japanese and the North Americans, with North Americans more willing to self-disclose than Japanese. Finally, Gudykunst and Nishida (1986b), in testing the dimension of individualism-collectivism on the social penetration process in Japan, Korea, and the United States, found that while members of collectivistic cultures (Japan and Korea) tend to perceive greater amounts of penetration and synchronization with their classmates than members of individualistic cultures (United States), they also perceive less difficulty in communicating with their classmates than their individualistic counterparts.

Overall, the patterns of reciprocity norm and synchronization process between nonintimates and intimates appears to vary in ac-cordance with the individualism-collectivism and power distance di-mensions of cultural variability. While members of collectivistic cultures tend to reciprocate and synchronize their communication patterns more in nonintimate interactions than intimate interactions, members of individualistic cultures tend to reciprocate and synchronize their communication patterns more in intimate interactions than nonintimate interactions. It appears that people who come from collectivistic, high power distance cultures are willing to spend more time to cultivate social relationships, to reciprocate social exchange information, and to stay on safe topics of exchange than people who come from individualistic, low power distance cultures. People in individualistic, low power distance cultures, in contrast, are willing to spend more time to develop personalized relationships, to reciprocate deep-level self-disclosure, and to take more risks in exchanging information concerning the more vulnerable areas of private self when interacting with in-group members than people in collectivistic, high power distance cultures.

The discussion thus far reveals that, overall, members of collectivistic cultures adhere to an obligatory pattern of reciprocity and engage in eventual or long-term reciprocity exchange, and that the reciprocity exchange entails exchange between family members, kinship ties, and friends. Conversely, members of individualistic cultures follow a voluntary pattern of reciprocity and typically engage in immediate reciprocity exchange, and the reciprocity exchange is much more salient in intimate relationships than nonintimate relationships. Finally, it is also predicted that members of individualistic, low power distance cultures engage in symmetrical reciprocity exchange, while members of collectivistic, high power distance cultures tend to engage in complementary reciprocity exchange processes.

RULES

In defining the basic characteristics of rules, McLaughlin (1984) commented: (1) "Rules can be followed; therefore, they can be broken." (2) "Rules have no truth value." (3) "Rules are conditional, but more general than the circumstances they cover." and (4) "Rules are 'indeterminable and negotiable'" (pp. 18-20; italics omitted). While norms are culturally ingrained principles, rules are codetermined principles that are affected by the dimensions of cultural variability. To verify the existence of rules for behavior, Shimanoff (1980) suggested researchers should look for three types of rule evidence: (1) that the behavior is controllable, (2) that the behavior occurs with regularity, and (3) that the behavior is prescribed and proscribed. Argyle and Henderson (1985) concurred with Shimanoff's conceptualization, and defined rules as "prescriptive rules, saying what ought or ought not to be there" (p. 64). Rules frame the expectational levels of the interactants in terms of what constitute appropriate or inappropriate behaviors in a situation.

Dimensions of Rules

Rules vary along four dimensions: (1) level of understanding, (2) rule clarity, (3) rule range, and (4) rule homogeneity or consensus (Cushman & Whiting, 1972). The greater the need for coordination in human activity, the greater the degree of accuracy and understanding of the rules. Given Hall's (1976) description of low- and high-context cultures, it can be argued that there is greater need for coordination of activity in high-context cultures than in low-context cultures and, therefore, there should be a correspondingly greater degree of accuracy in the implicit understanding of the rules in high-context than in low-context cultures. The variations in rules also appear to follow the tight-loose social structure (Boldt, 1978) dimension of cultural variability, with high-context and tight structures and low-context and loose structures tending to covary together with respect to rules.

In addition to varying with respect to level of understanding, rules vary with respect to the specificity of the actions required or permitted in a situation in which a rule applies (rule clarity), and in terms of the span of situations in which particular actions are permitted or required (rule range). When rules have a low degree of specificity and a large range, Cushman and Whiting (1972) contend that habitual communication behavior emerges. Given Hall's (1976) distinction between low- and high-context cultures, it can be inferred that rules are more specific and have more range in high-context than in low-context cultures.

Rules also vary with respect to the degree of consensus. "The homogeneity of a rule system refers to the degree to which accurate understanding and standard usage are evenly distributed among participants in a communication system" (Cushman & Whiting, 1972, p. 233). High-context cultures tend to be more homogeneous than low-context cultures (Hall, 1976). Because of the homogeneity of their system, members of high-context cultures are more likely to exhibit coordinated activity than members of low-context cultures.

Cross-Cultural Studies of Rules

Based on their test of rule emergence behaviors in 25 situations with over 800 subjects in the British culture, Argyle and Henderson (1984) concluded that all relationships are characterized by a structure of strongly endorsed rules, and certain rules are endorsed more strongly by interactants in more than half the settings (such as husband-wife relationship, doctor-patient relationship, etc.) than by others. These commonly held rules are labeled as "universal rules" by the researchers. These "universal rules" are (1) one should respect other's privacy, (2) one should look the other person in the eye during conversation, (3) one should or should not discuss that which is said in confidence with the other person, (4) one should or should not indulge in sexual activity with the other person, (5) one should not criticize the other person in public, and (6) one should repay debts, favors, or compliments no matter how small. In testing these six rules in Hong Kong, Japan, Italy, and Britain, Argyle, Henderson, Bond, Iizuka, and Contarelo (1986) found that the "respect privacy" rule receives the strongest endorsement from subjects in all four cultures. The "keeping confidence" rule receives strong endorsement from subjects in Hong Kong, Italy, and Britain, but not in Japan. The "public criticism" rule is endorsed more strongly by Hong Kong and Japanese subjects than by British subjects, and Italian subjects are least likely to endorse this rule.

The overall results of Argyle and his associates' (1986) study indicate that collectivistic cultures such as Hong Kong and Japan endorse the "public criticism" rule by avoiding public confrontations and negative criticisms of another person, while individualistic cultures such as Britain and Italy are less stringent in following the "public criticism" rule. Collectivistic cultures emphasize group harmony, individualistic cultures emphasize the importance of verbal self-assertion. While not examined in the Argyle et al. study, it can be predicted that high uncertainty avoidance cultures (such as France, Japan, and Greece) endorse rule-conforming behaviors, while low uncertainty avoidance cultures (such as Denmark, Jamaica, and Sweden) tolerate rule-violation behaviors. Members of high uncertainty avoidance cultures are threatened easily by uncertainty and ambiguous situations. They, therefore, need formal rules and rituals to foster a sense of social order and equilibrium. Members of low uncertainty avoidance cultures, in contrast, accept dissent and are willing to take risks. They, accordingly, tolerate behaviors that deviate from the formal rules and rituals of everyday interaction.

In another set of studies (Collier 1986; Collier, Ribeau, & Hecht, 1986; Hecht & Ribeau, 1984), rules have been found to vary within different ethnic groups in the United States. These researchers found that behaviors that conform to mutually shared rules are more rewarding and more self-concept affirming (Collier, 1986). In testing for the differences and similarities in the rules for intercultural interactions among Mexican-Americans, Blacks, and Whites, Collier et al. (1986) found that these three domestic groups differ in terms of five rule categories (politeness, role prescriptions, expression, content, and relationship climate) and five outcome categories (self-validation, relational validation, cultural validation, being understood, and goal accomplishment). The key findings in the study revealed that Blacks and Whites prefer verbal politeness rules, while Mexican-Americans prefer nonverbal politeness rules. In addition, while both Blacks and Whites prefer the enactment of personalized role prescriptions, Mexican-Americans prefer to perform in accordance to professional role labels. Among the outcomes, self-validation (i.e., confirmation of self-concept and acceptance of feelings and opinions) is the most frequently mentioned category with relational validation (i.e., confirmation of the development or maintenance of the dyad) second.

The verbal politeness rules of Blacks and Whites in the Collier et al. (1986) study can be attributed to the low-context characteristics of those two groups, while the Mexican-American nonverbal politeness rules can be attributed to the high-context characteristics of their ethnic culture. The differences of role prescriptive expectations can be explained by Hofstede's (1980) power distance dimension. Comparatively speaking, both Black and White domestic cultures are concerned with equalization of power distance, while Mexican-Americans continue to subscribe to unequal power distributions. Equal power distance cultures tend to emphasize a personal style of carrying out role prescriptions, while unequal power distance cultures tend to value a ritualistic style of carrying out professional role prescriptions. Rules and roles are to a large degree two interdependent constructs. We now turn our attention to roles.

ROLES

Cultural norms and rules affect role development processes. A role is a set of behavioral expectations associated with a particular position in a group. According to Sarbin and Allen (1968), the concept of role, "a term borrowed directly from the theater, is a metaphor intended to denote that conduct adheres to certain 'parts' (or positions) rather than the players who read or recite them" (p. 489). Positions include—but obviously are not limited to—professor, student, father, mother, physician, lawyer, judge, police officer, clerk, and customer. The behaviors you expect professors, for example, to perform are considered their role.

Dimensions of Role Relationships

There are four interrelated dimensions of role relationships that differ across cultures: (1) the degree of personalness of the relationship,

(2) the degree of formality expected in the participants' behavior, (3) the degree of hierarchy present in the relationship, and (4) the degree of deviation allowed from the "ideal" role enactment (Gudykunst & Kim, 1984a). Research to date has not linked variations in role behavior to specific dimensions of cultural variability, but differences along the four dimensions appear to be related to the dimensions of cultural variability isolated in Chapter 2.

Differences in expected degree of personalness are illustrated by a study of North Americans in Athens and their Greek coworkers completed by Triandis (1967a). Triandis found that Greeks perceive North American behavior in organizations as "'inhumanly' legalistic, rigid, cold, and overconcerned with efficiency" (p. 21). Even though Greek organizations are highly complex bureaucracies, "decisions are often taken on the basis of friendship and following strictly personal norms. . . . Greeks cannot understand the distinction between 'work behavior' and 'friendship behavior'" (p. 21). Thus Greeks tend to place a high degree of importance on personalness in role relationships. A similar tendency is described for Mexican bank employees by Zurcher (1968).

The degree of personalness in Japanese role relationships is illustrated by the *sempai-kohai* relationship. Although the direct translation of this relationship is senior-junior (or boss-subordinate), it really corresponds to a mentor-protege relationship. Pascale and Athos (1981), for example, compare superior-subordinate relationships in the United States and Japan as follows:

> Extensive research into the nature of boss-subordinate relationships in the West . . . reveals that an [North] American boss wants to know three things about those who work for him [or her]: (1) can they be trusted?; (2) are they competent?; and (3) are they consistent, or dependable? . . . The subordinate likewise weighs the clues that provide him [or her] data on his [or her] boss: (1) does he [or she] have integrity?; (2) is he [or she] competent?; and (3) is he [or she] open?—does he [or she] tell subordinates what they need to know in order to get the job done? . . . In Japan, the *sempai* (senior) expects the *kohai* (junior) to understand *him* [or her]. If the *sempai* doesn't always perform well, the *kohai* is expected to compensate for him [or her] and not to judge him [or her] except as a total human being. The *sempai,* in turn, is expected to display a wider breadth of understanding than normally exists in Western enterprises. (p. 138)

Thus there is a relatively high degree of personalness present in Japanese role relationships.

The degree of personalness expected in role relationships is related directly to Parsons's (1951) pattern variable of diffuseness or specificity. Specifically, an expectation of impersonalness, stems from a specificity orientation, the tendency to respond to specific aspects (i.e., the role) of another person. In contrast, an expectation of personalness stems from a diffuse orientation, the tendency to respond to others as total persons.

Role relationships also differ considerably with respect to the degree of formality expected in the relationship. Feig and Blair (1975) illustrate this by quoting a Turkish woman talking about the student-teacher relationship; she says, "You're supposed to fear the teacher like you fear Allah. When he comes into the class, all stand up. When you meet him on the street, you bow" (p. 39). Iranians display a similar attitude, according to Feig and Blair: "A professor who allows [her- or] himself to be treated without the utmost respect or one who confesses ignorance on a subject is not generally taken seriously by Iranian students. 'The average student,' said one man, 'loses respect for a teacher when he [or she] is too friendly and common with his [or her] pupils'" (p. 83). The degree of formality appears to be related to the low-high-context dimension, that is, more formality is expected in high-context than low-context cultures.

The third dimension of roles that differs across cultures is the degree of hierarchy in the relationship. The "clientship" relationship of the Kanuri culture in the Bornu province of Nigeria involves a wide-ranging hierarchical relation between a "patron" and a "client." Tessler, O'Barr, and Spain (1973) describe the relationship as follows:

> The term clientship refers to the diffuse relationship between two individuals (adult males), one of whom is considered the superior or patron and the other the subordinate or client. It is a diffuse relationship because the patron may demand a wide range of services from the client, while the client may expect a wide range of considerations from his patron. . . . These relationships are established explicitly to foster the immediate and long-term ambitions of both individuals involved. . . . Theoretically, each person in Bornu is the client of someone else. . . . However, in the common day-to-day perceptions of Kanuri, some people are simply not thought of as being clients; rather they are seen as having clients. . . . In general two types of client relationships may be distinguished: the apprentice-master relationship and the "simple" dependence relationship. For both, the relationship is entered into on a voluntary basis after initiation by the subordinate and with the agreement of the superior . . . they both "agree with" or are satisfied with the behavior of the other. The stress on behavior in such agreements reflects their mutual trust in the willingness and ability of each to meet the role expectations of the other. (pp. 144-146)

The degree of hierarchy appears to be related to power distance, that is, more formality is expected in high power distance cultures than in low power distance cultures.

The final dimension of roles that vary across cultures is the degree that discrepancies between the ideal role enactment and the actual behavior engaged in by people performing the role are tolerated. Some cultures allow more deviance from the ideal role than do other cultures. Consistent with Boldt (1978), Mosel (1973) suggests that cultures that allow a lot of deviance from the ideal role have "loose" social structures. Cultures that do not allow much deviance, in contrast, have "tight" social structures. Mosel points out a relationship between the looseness or tightness of the social structure and the predictability of behavior. He contends behavior is much more predictable in a tight social structure than in a loose social structure. The degree of certainty about how others behave, therefore, is higher in a culture with a tight social structure than in a culture with a loose social structure. If there is little variation from the ideal role enactment, as is true in a tight social structure, then the behavior of the people occupying roles should be predictable with a relatively high level of accuracy.

Tight versus loose social structure appears to be related to Hall's (1976) high- and low-context cultures. In high-context cultures most of the information is found in the context and not in the communication message transmitted. In low-context cultures, on the other hand, most of the information is found in the communication message rather than the context. High-context cultures require more conformity in behavior and, therefore, allow less deviation in role performance (i.e., have a tight social structure in Mosel's, 1973, terminology). Since most of the information is in the message in low-context cultures, more deviance from the ideal role enactment is permissible. Low-context cultures thus tend to have looser social structures. We do not mean to imply that it is impossible for a low-context culture to have a tight social structure or for a high-context culture to have a loose social culture. We believe, however, that the general patterns of loose social structure and tight social structure are reflective of the low-context system and the high-context system.

Cross-Cultural Studies of Sex Roles

Given Hofstede's (1980) theory of cultural variability, differences in sex roles are expected based on the degree of sex-role differentiation (masculinity dimension). While there is not extensive research in this area, a few related studies have been conducted. Buck, Newton, and Muramatsu (1984), for example, examined the concepts of independence and obedience in relation to sex roles in Japan and the United States. They used multidimensional scaling and had subjects provide similarity ratings for paired comparison of 20 concepts. Of the five gender-related concepts included in the study, "men" was the closest concept to "independence" for both males and females and "men" was also the closest to "obedience" for males and females in the United States. Both sexes in the Japanese sample, in contrast, rated "men" as closest to "independence" and "women" as closest to "obedience."

The concepts most closely associated with being independent in Buck et al.'s (1984) United States' male sample were "me," "men," "taking responsibility," and "having an education," while "being obedient," "marriage," and "taking care of children" were the farthest away. For females in the United States, "me," "having a job," "intelligence," and "taking responsibility" were closest to "being independent," while "being obedient" and "housework" were farthest away. Japanese males perceived "men," "having a job," "me," and "ideal man" as closest to "being independent," while they viewed "being obedient," "taking care of children," and "housework" as farthest away. Japanese females perceived "having a job," "men," "ideal man," and "having an education" as closest to "being independent," and "me," "being obedient," and "housework" as farthest away.

Buck et al.'s (1984) study further revealed that the U.S. male sample reported "me," "marriage," and "having a job" as closest to "being obedient," while they saw being "independent," "intelligence," "ideal man," and "having an education" as farthest away. Women in the United States perceived "me," "having a job," and "taking care of children" as close to "being obedient," and "being independent," "showing emotion," and "intelligence" as farthest away. Japanese men rated "showing emotion," "women," and "marriage" as closest to "being obedient," and "ideal man," "intelligence," and "being independent" as most distant. Finally, Japanese women saw "showing emotion," "women," and "marriage" as nearest to "being obedient," and "ideal man," "having a job," and "men" as farthest away.

The findings of Buck and her associates' (1984) study suggest that people in the United States value independence over obedience for both men and women, while Japanese value independence over obedience only for men. The Japanese, however, also see the "ideal woman" as less obedient than "women," thereby suggesting a desire for change in women's roles (at least among the college students studied). These findings appear compatible with Hofstede's (1980) masculinity dimension of cultural variability. There are clear sex-role expectations regarding being independent in the highly masculine culture (Japan) and relative equality in expectations in the culture with a moderate masculinity score (United States).

In a related study, Best and Williams (1984) administered the Kalin Sex Role Ideology (KSRI) Scale (Kalin & Tilby, 1978) to samples in seven countries: Canada, England, Finland, Malaysia, the Netherlands, the United States, and Venezuela. High scores on the KSRI indicate an egalitarian attitude toward sex roles and lower scores indicate a male-dominant attitude. Their results were consistent with Hofstede's (1983) analysis: the Netherlands and Finland are low masculine countries (Hofstede, 1983) and their scores on the KSRI were much higher (reflecting sex-role equality attitude) than the other countries, which all have moderate masculinity scores on Hofstede's dimension. A follow-up study by Best, Williams, Edwards, and Giles (1985) indicated that the respondents in Canada, England, and the United States desired androgynous to slightly masculine sex roles for both males and females. All three cultures fall in the middle range of Hofstede's masculinity scores. These results, therefore, also appear consistent with Hofstede's theory.

In the context of family sex-role development, Salamon (1977) compared Japanese family interaction and West German family interaction findings that Japanese husbands and wives clearly adhere to a sex-role segregation model, while West German husbands and wives display less sex-role differentiation. Ting-Toomey (1987) analyzed relational pattern differences in France, Japan, and the United States. She found that both Japanese and U.S. respondents display clear sex-role differences in self-disclosure patterns and conflict style patterns, but her data indicated no sex-role differences in the French culture. Tomeh and Gallant (1984) obtained similar findings for their French sample, in which both French males and females take an egalitarian perspective toward the sharing of family duties and chores in comparison to their North American counterparts.

In examining the scores on Hofstede's masculine-feminine dimension, French culture has a low score, the United States has a moderate score, West Germany has a moderate score, and Japan has a high score. Low scores suggest low sex-role differentiation, while high scores suggest high sex-role differentiation. In comparison to Japan and the United States, French culture endorses fluid sex-role interchange patterns, androgynous ideals, and equal sex-role power. In comparison to Japan, West Germany still comes out ahead in terms of sex-role equality and sex-role exchange patterns.

Low power distance, low masculine cultures (such as Denmark, Finland, Norway, and Sweden) appear to have person-oriented families, while high power distance, high masculine cultures (such as Greece, Japan, Malaysia, and Mexico) appear to have position-oriented families (Bernstein, 1971). Person-oriented families value equal power distributions, encourage the unique development of each family member, and support active verbal participation from all family members. Position-oriented families value unequal power distributions and status hierarchy within the family system, and usually the parents are the authoritarian figures that have control over major decision-making activities. Person-oriented families result in an equal sex-role socialization process, while position-oriented families result in an unequal sex-role socialization process.

Moving beyond family sex-role development, Morse (1983) examined love relationships in Australia and Brazil, finding that both cultures value emotional involvement and relational dependence as the two central criteria for love. Brazilians, however, displayed stronger sex-role differences on the emotional involvement dimension than did Australians. In another study, Cushman and Nishida (1984) asked Japanese respondents for their preferred qualities in an ideal mate. They found that Japanese males listed "common values," "easy to talk to," and "sound health," while Japanese females listed "sound health," "honesty," and "easy to talk to." In testing for differences in romantic relationship roles and opposite-sex friendship roles, Ting-Toomey (1987) found that in the U.S. culture the romantic relationship group consistently reports a higher level of love commitment, self-disclosure, relational ambiguity, and relational conflict than the friendship group. For the French culture, the romantic relationship group reports a higher level of love commitment and self-disclosure than the friendship group, however, the friendship group claims a higher level of relational ambiguity and conflict than the romantic relationship group. Finally, in the Japanese culture the romantic relationship group consistently reports a higher level of love commitment, self-disclosure, ambiguity, and relational conflict than the opposite-sex friendship group. While the four relational dimensions function similarly in both the U.S. and the Japanese samples, the four dimensions have differential weightings in the enactment of opposite-sex friendships in the French culture.

NETWORKS

Albrecht and Adelman (1984) define a network as a "configuration of personal ties where affect and/or instrumental aid is exchanged" (p. 4). More specifically, communication networks are "sets of overlapping dyadic linkages involving a focal person or persons" (Albrecht & Adelman, 1984, p. 12). According to Albrecht and Adelman, there are four structural elements of a communication network: (1) size—the number of individuals included in the network, those with whom the focal person reports having contact; (2) reciprocity/symmetry—the extent to which the exchange between the two persons is on an equal basis; (3) multiplexity—the extent to which multiple message contents are exchanged in a relationship; and (4) density/integration—the extent to which members of the focal person's network interact with each other.

There is extensive research on networks in various cultures, however, very few studies have compared the structure of networks across systems. Early kinship studies by anthropologists (e.g., Evans-Pritchard, 1940) can be considered network analyses, even though the term network was not used (Foster, 1979). This research focused on the development of relationships at both the interpersonal and group levels. More recently, comparisons of communication networks across ethnic groups has begun. Garrison (1978), for example, compared Puerto Rican and Black networks, while Yum (1983) examined the network structure of ethnic groups in Hawaii.

The study of communication networks is a focus of much of the research on the diffusion of innovations and social change (see Rogers & Kincaid, 1981, for a summary of this research). In reviewing studies of communication networks and social change, Korzenny and Farace (1977) concluded:

> Communication is a significant factor for change to take place, but it is not a sufficient condition. When there are opinion leaders who link the parts of a social system whose norms favor change, and external communication travels from outside the social system through opinion leaders to the community, change is triggered. Heterophily of association is not conducive to change by itself, but when there are opinion leaders who bridge the heterophily gap from the outside to the inside of a social system, the possibility for change to occur is heightened. If the norms of a social system in general are negative toward change, then any effort toward change is likely to fail, since informal opinion leaders tend to adhere to the norms of the system. (p. 69)

In addition to these lines of research, communication networks play a major role in the study of rural-urban migration (e.g., Mayer, 1961) and communication acculturation of immigrants (e.g., Kim, 1977b, 1978).

Most network research has been conducted on friendship network ties in immigrant cultures (Kim, 1977a, 1979; Yum, 1983). Overall, it has been found that heterogeneous friendship networks promote favorable immigrants' attitudes toward the host culture, while homogeneous friendship networks promote alienation and isolation in the host culture. Min (1984) studied the relationship between Korean immigrant families and kinship ties, finding that Korean immigrants typically turn to family members to seek help and support rather than turn outward for nonkin support. Salamon (1977) compared kinship ties and friendship ties in Japan and West Germany, discovering that Japanese families are likely to encourage individualized sets of friendship networks because of clear role differentiations within the system, while West German families favor overlapping network sets and a highly integrated system. More specifically, the Japanese are able to gather and spread out support through many sources, while West German families emphasize the exclusivity and togetherness of family relationships. Thus family ideology plays an important role in the formation of either individualized sets of friendship networks or overlapped sets of friendship ties.

Overall, it can be predicted that members of low power distance, low masculine cultures favor free-form, overlapped sets of friendship networks, while members of high power distance, high masculine cultures prefer segregated sets of friendship networks in accordance with role prescriptions and status hierarchy. In addition, members of low power distance cultures are likely to seek help and support from symmetrical equals, while members of high power distance cultures are likely to seek help from individuals that occupy higher authority positions. Finally, it can be predicted that members of low masculine cultures seek help and network support from both males and females, while members of high masculine cultures, because of sex-role segregation orientation, tend to seek help and comfort from same-sex networks and same-sex friendships.

CONCLUSION

In examining cultural research on norms, rules, roles, and networks, we found that Hofstede's cultural variability dimensions are useful constructs to explain the differences and similarities in rule developments and role enactments in diverse cultures. Specifically, the dimensions of individualism-collectivism, power distance, and uncertainty avoidance have been used to explain cultural norms and rules in interpersonal behaviors, while the dimensions of power distance and masculinity-femininity have been employed to explain and hypothesize about the possible differences in cross-cultural sex-role interactions and cross-cultural network linkages.

The research reviewed suggests that cultural variability does influence situational factors, such as norms, rules, roles, and networks, that affect interpersonal communication. The research in this area is, however, somewhat sporadic, and there are few lines of research underway. Further, few, if any, investigators have examined the influence of culture on the relationship between situational factors and other interpersonal processes. There is, for example, intracultural research on the influence of the type of situation on self-disclosure, but to date no cross-cultural research has been conducted on how culture influences the relationship between situation type and self-disclosure. Examining the influence of culture on the relationships between other variables is necessary to establish cross-cultural generalizability of research findings, as well as to specify cultural scope conditions for theories or to integrate culture into theories of interpersonal communication. Future research, therefore, is needed to address questions such as: Does following a norm of short-term reciprocity lead to greater communication satisfaction in individualistic cultures than collectivistic cultures? or, Does rule-violating behavior lead to greater increases in uncertainty in high uncertainty avoidance cultures than in low uncertainty avoidance cultures?

4

Self-Conceptions

Rosenberg (1979) defines the self-concept as "the totality of the individual's thoughts and feelings having reference to [her- or] himself as an object" (p. 7; italics omitted). As we indicated in Chapter 1, a further distinction can be made between social and personal identities, social identity being a function of group memberships. There also are differences between the public self and the private self (see Baumeister, 1986). The private self is that part of the self-concept of which only the individual is aware, while the public self is known to others. There is cross-cultural variability in self-conceptions in general (including public and private aspects), as well as in the use of facework and social identity in particular. We begin our analysis by examining general cross-cultural differences in self-conceptions.

THE SELF-CONCEPT

While there is disagreement over how to conceptualize the self in Western psychology, Johnson (1985) contends there also is agreement on defining the self

> as a *unitary phenomenon;* it is used to refer to a particular, individual person (or person-system) and not to a "personality" or to an aggregate of factors which "add up" to a person. The concept of self is typically separated into a nominative ("I") *self-as-subject,* and an accusative ("me") *self-as-object. Self-as-object* includes both the idea of *self as a social object to others* and that of *self as a social (and psychological) object unto itself.* (p. 93)

Johnson goes on to argue that the Western conception of the self is analytic, monotheistic, individualistic, and rationalistic. The most important characteristic for our present purposes is that the self is individualistic.

Viewing the self in individualistic terms implies that the self is conceived as being an entity unto itself and has existence apart from the groups to which the individual belongs. Geertz (1975) illustrates this view when he describes the conception of the person in individualistic (our term; he uses "Western") cultures "as a bounded, unique, more or less integrated motivational and cognitive universe, a dynamic center of awareness, emotion, judgment, and action organized into a distinctive whole and set contrastively both against other such wholes and against a social and natural background" (p. 48). Self-actualization and/or self-realization are viewed as important goals for individuals to pursue in individualistic cultures. When carried to the extreme, however, this leads to the "pathological" condition of narcissism (Lasch, 1979) and the decline of concern for others (Bellah et al., 1985). Self-esteem in individualistic cultures depends on how well the person can stand on his or her own feet. The inner self of people in individualistic cultures provides definition and guidance (Hsu, 1985).

Members of collectivistic cultures conceive of the self differently. In his analysis of culture and the self, Hsu (1985) suggests using the Chinese word *jen* to replace "personality," though his conceptualization also includes what Western writers normally label "self." He goes on to say:

> I suggest the term *jen* advisedly because the Chinese conception of [hu]man (also shared by the Japanese who pronounce the same Chinese word *jin*) is based on the *individual's transactions with his [or her] fellow human beings.* When the Chinese say of so-and-so "*ta pu shih jen*" (he [or she] is not a *jen*), they do not mean that this person is not a human animal; instead they mean that his [or her] behavior in relation to other human beings is not acceptable. Consequently terms like "*hao jen*" (good *jen*), "*huai jen*" (bad *jen*), etc., follow the same line of meaning. (pp. 32-33)

Self-esteem for members of collectivistic cultures is, therefore, linked to their relationships with other human beings and does not emerge from the individual alone, as it does in individualistic cultures. Being successful in collectivistic cultures like Japan requires the establishment of interdependencies with others in society (see, for example, Doi's, 1973, discussion of *amae*).

The relationship of one person to others is so important in collectivistic cultures that members of these cultures may deny the importance of the self. Minami (1971) and Doi (1973, 1986), for example, point out that Japanese deny their own self-importance, particularly in interactions with those of higher social status (when institutionalized it results in *enryo*, meaning "considerateness"). Such a view is the antithesis of the self-promotion that occurs in individualistic cultures. Some collectivistic cultures go a step further and do not have an *ethical* category for the person. Read (1955), for example, points out that the Gahuku-Gana of New Guinea do not "separate the individual from the social context and, ethically speaking, grant him [or her] an intrinsic moral value apart from that which attaches to him [or her] as the occupant of a particular status" (p. 257). He also points out that the value of people in this culture "does not reside in themselves as individuals or persons; it is dependent on the position they occupy within a system of inter-personal and inter-group relationships" (p. 250).

Some writers, however, question the conception of self in collectivistic cultures, as presented here (e.g., that it is embedded totally in group relationships). Befu (1980a, 1980b), for example, argues that there is a strong sense of "personhood" in Japan that is overlooked when the group model is used to analyze Japanese culture. In his discussion of *Shiroi Kyoto* by Toyoko Yamazaki, a novel about an ambitious Japanese professor trying to move up the academic power hierarchy, Befu (1977) states:

> A reexamination of empirical cases of the so-called "group orientation" in Japan would probably reveal that group orientation is more apparent than real, and that behind the appearance of group solidarity one will find each member being motivated more by personal ambitions than by his [or her] blind loyalty to the group. Put another way, in many cases Japanese are [or anyone is, for that matter] loyal to their groups because it pays to be loyal. (p. 87)

Befu (1980a, 1980b) argues that the Japanese concept of *seishin* deals with "individuals qua individuals." "*Seishin* has to do with one's spiritual disposition, one's inner strength, which results from character building and self-discipline" (Befu, 1980b, pp. 180-181; see Rohlen, 1973, for a detailed discussion of this concept). By including *seishin* in a conceptualization of self in Japan, Befu argues that the behavior of individuals who do not follow the group can be explained.

Befu (1980b) goes on to argue that the concepts of *tatemae* and *honne* also must be considered in explaining personhood in Japan. *Tatemae* refers to the principle or standard by which a person is bound, at least outwardly, while *honne* means the person's "real" or inner wishes

(Lebra, 1976). The distinction between *tatemae* and *honne* corresponds to differentiating public and private self, respectively. As Tedeschi (1986) points out, private self refers to "mental events in one person that are inherently unobservable by another person," while the public self entails behavior that "is open to the observations of anyone" (p. 2). Befu contends that descriptions of Japanese culture tend to focus on the Japanese "public" performance (*tatemae*) and not to what is really going on inside the individual (*honne*). Given Befu's (1980b) analysis of the roles of *tatemae* and *honne* in Japan, it could be argued that the public self is more important in collectivistic cultures than in individualistic cultures.

Triandis (1977) contends that the situation (e.g., public versus private) influences the "weights" given selected factors (i.e., norms/rules, roles) in predicting behavior. Research by Boyanowsky and Allen (1973), for example, found that when Whites' behavior toward Blacks is known to other Whites, responses to Blacks are less favorable than when the behavior is unknown to other members of the ingroup. Such a response is to be expected given the ingroup-outgroup distinction, but as indicated above, cultural variation also should be expected. To illustrate, Bond (1983) suggests that collectivism-individualism variations influence the impact of responses that are public or private (i.e., those that are known and unknown to members of the ingroup, respectively). Public responses should be affected more in collectivistic culture systems than in individualistic cultures.

Given this overview of self-conceptions in individualistic and collectivistic cultures, we now turn our attention to specific aspects of self-conceptions that vary across cultures. To begin, we examine an aspect of the public self that originated in "Eastern" cultures; namely, face.

FACEWORK

"Facework" is a ubiquitous concept that occurs in all cultures (Brown & Levinson, 1978; Goffman, 1959, 1967, 1971; Katriel, 1986; Hill, Ide, Ikuta, Kawasaki, & Ogino, 1986; Ide, Hori, Kawasaki, Ikuta, & Haga, 1986; Hu, 1944; Okabe, 1983; Ting-Toomey, 1985). The concept of "face" has been defined as "something that is diffusedly located in the flow of events" (Goffman, 1955, p. 214), "a psychological image that can be granted and lost and fought for and presented as a gift" (Yutang, 1968, p. 199), or "the public self-image that every member of a society wants to claim for himself/herself" (Brown & Levinson, 1978, p. 66).

Face, in essence, is a projected image of one's self in a relational situation. It is an identity that is defined conjointly by the participants in a setting. The degree to which one wishes to project an "authentic self" in a situation and the degree to which one chooses to maintain a "social self" in a situation, however, vary in accordance with the cultural orientations toward the conceptualization of selfhood. In other words, a different degree of selfhood is projected into the public self-image known as "face."

Ting-Toomey (1988) developed a theory on culture and facework. To begin, she argues that in some cultures (for example, individualistic cultures such as Australia, Germany, and the United States) maintaining consistency between the private self-image and a public self-image is of paramount importance. The public self-presentation of "face" should correspond to an invariant "core self" within an individual. In other cultures (for example, collectivistic cultures such as China, Korea, and Japan), the "self" is a situationally and relationally based concept. Tu's (1985) analysis of selfhood and otherness in Confucian thought in China suggests "a distinctive feature of Confucian ritualization is an ever-deepening and broadening awareness of the presence of the other in one's self-cultivation. This is perhaps the single most important reason why the Confucian idea of the self as a center of relationships is an open system" (p. 232).

In the Chinese cultural context, the self is defined through an intersecting web of social and personal relationships. The self in most collectivistic cultures, in fact, is maintained and codified through the active negotiation of facework, whereas in individualistic cultures such as the United States, the self often is defined as an intrapsychic phenomenon. The public "face" ideally, then, should correspond to individuals' internal states. Providing "face-support" to another person means lending support and confirmation to his or her idealized sense of self, which in turn ideally should be consistent with his or her core "authentic self" (McCall & Simmons, 1966, p. 75). Bellah et al.'s (1985) analysis of individualism and commitment in North American life suggests that "in the absence of any objectifiable criteria of right and wrong, good or evil, the self and its feelings become our only moral guidance. . . . There each individual is entitled to his or her own 'bit of space' and is utterly free within its boundaries" (p. 76).

From a collectivistic perspective, the self is never free. It is bounded by mutual role obligations and duties and structured by a patterned process of give-and-take reciprocal facework negotiations. Facework, in this context, is focused on lending role-support to other's face, while, at the same time, not bringing shame to one's own self-face. From an individualistic perspective, the self is ideally a free entity—free to pursue personal wants, needs, and desires. Facework, in this context, emphasizes preserving one's own autonomy, own territory, and own space, while simultaneously respecting the other person's need for space and privacy.

Brown and Levinson's (1978) theory of politeness contains two underlying assumptions concerning facework. First, all competent adult members of a society have (and know each other to have) "face"—the public self-image that every member wants to claim for herself or himself. The "face" has two related components: (a) negative-face—the basic claim to territories, personal reserves, rights to nondistraction, and (b) positive-face—the basic claim over this projected self-image to be appreciated and to be approved by others. Their second assumption is that all competent adult members of a society have certain rational capacities and modes to achieve these ends.

Negative facework is a negotiation process between two interdependent parties concerning the degree of threat or respect each gives to the other's sense of freedom and individual autonomy. Positive facework entails the degree of threat or respect each gives to the other's need for inclusion and approval. Negative facework (speech acts such as apology for imposition, prerequest ritual, and compliance-resistance) emphasizes the need for dissociation, while positive facework (speech acts such as self-disclosure, compliment, and promise) emphasizes the need for association. Both concepts (association and dissociation), in fact, are documented by cross-cultural researchers (Adamopoulos, 1984; Lonner, 1980; Triandis, 1972, 1977, 1978) as psychological universals that cut across cultural boundaries. While one might expect both negative facework and positive facework to be present in all cultures, the value orientations of a culture will influence cultural members' attitudes toward pursuing one set of facework more actively than another set of facework in a face-negotiation situation. Facework then is a symbolic front that members in all cultures strive to maintain and uphold, while the modes and styles of expressing and negotiating face-need would vary from one culture to the next.

In addition to the concepts of "negative-face" and "positive-face," Brown and Levinson (1978) identified five levels of facework strategies that potentially threaten either the negative-face or the positive-face of the involved parties in a politeness situation. These face-threatening acts (FTA) are arranged in different hierarchical levels of direct to indirect verbal speech acts. The direct FTA are viewed as posing the highest threat to the negotiators' faces, and the indirect FTA are viewed as posing the least threat, and hence are considered the most polite verbal acts. Again, the correlations between the direct mode and the perceived threat level, and the indirect mode and the politeness level vary from one culture to the next. In cultures that foster a direct mode of interaction in everyday life (such as low-context cultures, for example, Germany, Scandinavia, Switzerland, and the United States), a direct mode of behavior probably is perceived to be not as threatening as an ambiguous mode of interacting. In cultures that nurture an indirect mode of interacting (such as high-context cultures, for example, China, Japan, Korea, and Vietnam), a direct mode of communicating can be perceived as highly threatening and unsettling to one's own face. While Brown and Levinson (1978) focused mainly on the concept of "face-threat," the concept of "face-respect" was not explicitly dealt with in their politeness theory.

More recently, Shimanoff (1985, 1987) reconceptualized Brown and Levinson's (1978) FTA typology, identifying four types of affective strategies in terms of the degree they respect or threaten the face-needs of the negotiators in a problematic situation: (1) face-honoring (FH) type, (2) face-compensating (FC) type, (3) face-neutral (FN) type, and (4) face-threatening (FT) type. While the first three types represent respect strategies for other's face, the last type is viewed as a negative-face-confronting strategy. Shimanoff (1985, 1987) reported that marital partners tend to use more face-honoring, face-compensating, and face-neutral strategies than face-threatening strategies in the marital context. Baxter (1984) found that opposite-sex partners tend to use more face-politeness strategies in close relationships than in distant relationships.

In related research, Tracy, Craig, Smith, and Spisak (1984) tested discourse strategies in multiple "favor-asking" situations, discovering that favor-asking messages vary in the degree to which they acknowledge the hearer's desire to be liked and appreciated (positive-face need) and the hearer's desire for autonomy and freedom of action (negative-face need). In addition, they found that favor-asking messages vary in the attention they give to the speaker's own positive-face need. Finally, Leichty and Applegate (1987) analyzed individual differences in face-saving strategies, finding that actors are not overly concerned with intimate face wants on relatively small requests, but that they are when substantial autonomy threat is involved. Also, speaker power, request magnitude, and relational familiarity all influence the degree to which the persuadee's autonomy desire is attended to. A new theory of facework should make a clear distinction between strategies that threaten self-face and other-face, as well as strategies that gear toward negative-face maintenance and positive-face maintenance (Craig, Tracy, & Spisak, 1986; Leichty & Applegate, 1987).

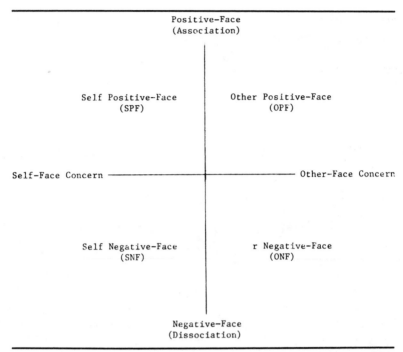

Figure 4.1: Two-Dimensional Grid of Facework Maintenance. From Ting-Toomey (1988).

In sum, work to date suggests that when two interdependent parties come together in a facework negotiation session, they negotiate over two implicit principles: (1) face-concern principle—self-face, other-face, or mutual-face; and (2) face-need principle—negative-face (concern for autonomy), and positive-face (concern for inclusion). Negative-face need can be translated as the need for autonomy or dissociation, and positive-face need can be viewed as the need for inclusion or association. These two principles are summarized in Ting-Toomey's (1988) two-dimensional grid presented in Figure 4.1.

Figure 4.1 consists of two conceptual dimensions: the self-concern and other-concern dimension and the positive-face and negative-face need dimension. The self-concern and other-concern dimension refers to the individual's orientation toward attention for self versus other. The positive-face and negative-face dimension refers to the individual's perceived need for association or dissociation. Self positive-face (SPF) maintenance means the use of certain communication strategies to defend and protect one's need for inclusion and association. Other positive-face (OPF) maintenance means the use of certain communication strategies to defend and support the other person's need for inclusion and association. Self negative-face (SNF) maintenance means the use of certain interaction strategies to give oneself freedom and space, and to protect self from other's infringement on one's autonomy. Finally, other negative-face (ONF) maintenance means the use of certain interaction strategies to signal respect for the other person's need for freedom, space, and dissociation. All four face types (SPF, OPF, SNF, and ONF) are subject to differential treatments by the hearer in the negotiation process. The hearer can defend, respect, threaten, or confront the speaker's concern for self- or other-image, and the speaker's need for either positive-face or negative-face maintenance.

To summarize, the basic assumptions of Ting-Toomey's (1988) theory of the facework negotiation process are: (1) members of all cultures negotiate over the concept of face; (2) the concept of face is especially problematic in uncertainty situations (for example, request situation, complaint situation, embarrassment situation, and conflict situation) when the situated identities of the interactants are called into question; (3) all face-negotiation entails multiple-goal orientations (self-concern and other-concern, negative-face and positive-face); (4) all negotiators express a concern for self-face protection or other-face support (or both) in problematic situations; (5) all negotiators express a need for dissociation (negative-face) and/or a need for association (positive-face) in problematic situations; (6) the self-other orientation dimension and the association-dissociation dimension would be influenced by the relational variables (such as low-high familiarity level, low-high intimacy level) and the situational variables (such as informal-formal level, public-private level) of the context, and the salience (such as topic magnitude, topic commitment) of the problematic issue; (7) the self-other dimension and the positive-face and negative-face need dimension would be influenced by the cultural interpretation and the cultural expectation levels of the context; and (8) while the four sets of suprastrategy—SPF, OPF, SNF, and ONF—are present in all negotiation settings in all cultures, certain sets of suprastrategies are preferred by members of a culture more often than others.

Ting-Toomey (1988) contends that to explain cultural differences in facework it is necessary to examine the individualism-collectivism and low-high-context distinctions. The terms "individualism" and "collectivism" refer to "a cluster of attitudes, beliefs, and behaviors toward a wide variety of people" (Hui & Triandis, 1986, p. 240). As indicated in Chapter 2, individualistic cultures focus on the "I" identity and collectivistic cultures focus on the "we" identity. Individualist cultures are concerned with the authenticity of self-presentation style. Collectivistic cultures are concerned with the adaptability of self-presentation image. This suggests that individualistic cultures are concerned with self-face maintenance and collectivistic cultures are concerned with self-face and other-face maintenance. Further, individualistic cultures value autonomy, choices, and negative-face need, while collectivistic cultures value interdependence, reciprocal obligations, and positive-face need.

Individualistic, low-context cultures (with the United States as the prime example) emphasize individual value orientations, line logic, direct verbal interactions, and individualistic nonverbal styles. Collectivistic, high-context cultures (with the Japanese culture as the prime example) emphasize group value orientations, spiral logic, indirect verbal interactions, and contextual nonverbal styles. Individualistic verbal and nonverbal communication style suggests that intentions are displayed clearly and have direct correspondence with verbal and nonverbal patterns. Contextual verbal and nonverbal style implies that intentions and meanings are situated within the larger shared knowledge of the cultural context. While meanings in low-context cultures are displayed overtly through direct communication forms, meanings in high-context cultures are embedded implicitly at different levels of the sociocultural context.

Hence, in low-context systems, face-negotiation is an overt communication process. The face-giving and face-protection moves and countermoves have to be overtly spelled out, and the arguments and the persuasions in a conflict situation would typically follow a linear logic pattern. Face-negotiation in the low-context system is based on an immediate cost-reward-comparison model, whereas in the high-context system, face-negotiation is an accumulative, long-term process. Since members of high-context systems are interlocked in a group value perspective, every face-support or face-violation act on another person has larger social and group implications. The arguments and disagreements in a conflict situation are expressed ambiguously and the face-giving and face-saving appeals typically follow a spiral logic pattern. Face-negotiation in high-context systems probably is based on a long-term, cost-reward-comparison model. In low-context systems, immediate reciprocity of face-giving and face-saving is important to the success of face-negotiation moves. In high-context systems, eventual reciprocity of face-honoring and face-compensating is important for the maintenance of both social and personal relationship developments.

Ting-Toomey (1988) summarizes the assumptions regarding culture and facework underlying her theory as follows: (1) low- and high-context systems have the concept of "face"—a public image that an interactant claims for him- or herself; (2) members of low-context systems project the "I" identity in facework negotiation, and members of high-context systems project the "we" identity in facework negotiation; (3) the "I" identity facework maintenance makes facework negotiation a competitive process, and the "we" identity facework maintenance makes facework negotiation a collaborative process; (4) the "I" identity orientation leads interactants to focus on self-face perseverance and other-face threat strategies, the "we" identity orientation leads interactants to focus on mutual-face perseverance and other-face honoring strategies; (5) members of low- and high-context systems negotiate negative-face and positive-face, with members of low-context systems focusing on negative-face maintenance process and members of high-context systems focusing on positive-face maintenance process; (6) members in low- and high-context systems use all four types of face-maintenance suprastrategy—SPF, OPF, SNF, and ONF—however, members of low-context systems tend to use SPF and SNF strategies, while members of high-context systems tend to use OPF and ONF strategies, in interpersonal problematic situations.

Based on the preceding analysis, Ting-Toomey (1988) developed the following propositions:

Proposition 1: Members of individualistic, low-context cultures express a greater degree of self-face maintenance than members of collectivistic, high-context cultures.

Proposition 2: Members of collectivistic, high-context cultures express a greater degree of mutual-face or other-face maintenance than members of individualistic, low-context cultures.

Proposition 3: Members of individualistic, low-context cultures use more autonomy-preserving strategies (negative-face need) than members of collectivistic, high-context cultures.

Proposition 4: Members of collectivistic, high-context cultures use more approval-seeking strategies (positive-face need) than members in individualistic, low-context cultures.

While privacy and autonomy are the trademarks of individualistic, low-context cultures, interdependence and inclusion are the hallmarks of collectivistic, high-context cultures. In a conflict uncertainty situation, face-threat attacks the need for autonomy and control over self and others in low-context systems. Face-threat attacks the need for inclusion and approval by others in high-context systems. Face-violation acts to members of low-context systems are communicative acts that violate their sense of independence and privacy. Face-violation acts to members of high-context cultures are communicative acts that violate their sense of interconnection and mutuality. Propositions 5 and 6 in Ting-Toomey's (1988) theory are:

Proposition 5: Members of individualistic, low-context cultures use more self-concern positive-face (SPF) and self-concern negative-face (SNF) suprastrategies than members of collectivistic, high-context cultures.

Proposition 6: Members of collectivistic, high-context cultures use more other-concern positive-face (OPF) and other-concern negative-face (ONF) suprastrategies than members of individualistic, low-context cultures.

Self-concern positive-face and other self-concern negative-face suprastrategies are defend-attack strategies that aim at protecting self-autonomy while attacking and assaulting the privacy and the self-integrity of the other conflict party. Other-concern positive-face and other-concern negative-face are camouflage-smoothing strategies that aim at protecting face from other's criticisms and rejections and at the same time smooth over the apparent conflicting interests. Members of low-context cultures use overt face-negotiation tactics, while members of high-context cultures use functionally ambiguous face tactics. Overt face-negotiation tactics promote competition, ambiguous face-negotiation tactics aim at preserving group harmony. Ting-Toomey's (1988) seventh and eighth propositions are:

Proposition 7: Members of individualistic, low-context cultures use a greater degree of direct face-negotiation strategies than members of collectivistic, high-context cultures.

Proposition 8: Members of collectivistic, high-context cultures use a greater degree of indirect face-negotiation strategies than members of individualistic, low-context cultures.

Ting-Toomey's (1988) analysis of culture and facework is summarized in Table 4.1. The propositions in her theory (not discussed here) specifically dealing with conflict negotiation are discussed in Chapter 8 when conflict is examined.

Thus far in this chapter we have looked at cultural variability in general self-conceptions and in facework, a specific aspect of the public self. We now turn our attention to another component of the self-concept, social identity.

TABLE 4.1
Summary of Low-Context and High-Context Face-Negotiation Processes

Key Constructs of "Face"	Individualistic, Low-Context Cultures	Collectivistic, High-Context Cultures
Identity	emphasis on "I" identity	emphasis on "we" identity
Concern	self-face concern	other-face concern
Need	autonomy, dissociation, negative-face need	inclusion, association, positive-face need
Suprastrategy	self-concern positive-face and self-concern negative-face	other-concern positive-face and other-concern negative-face
Mode	direct mode	indirect mode
Style	control style or confront style, and solution-oriented style	obliging style or avoidance style, and affective-oriented style
Strategy	distributive or competitive strategies	integrative or collaborative strategies
Speech Act	direct speech acts	indirect speech acts
Nonverbal Act	individualistic nonverbal acts, direct emotional expressions	contextualistic (role-oriented) nonverbal acts, indirect emotional expressions

SOURCE: From Ting-Toomey (1988).

SOCIAL IDENTITY

Social identity, according to Tajfel (1978), is "that part of an individual's self-concept that derives from his [or her] knowledge of his [or her] membership in a social group (or groups) together with the value and emotional significance attached to that membership" (p. 63). Social identity is based on shared social beliefs (Doise & Sinclair, 1973) and social representations (Hewstone, Jaspars, & Lalljee, 1982). McGuire and his associates' (1978) research reveals that ethnicity (group membership) is more likely to be mentioned as part of the spontaneous self-concept if ethnic group members are distinctive in the social environment than when they are not distinctive. This is consistent with Brewer's (1979a) argument that ingroup membership is more important for minority groups than for majority groups.

Tajfel (1978) focuses on social identity in explaining intergroup processes. Social identity theory begins from the assumption that individuals seek positive social identities in their interactions with others. Individuals compare their group(s) with other groups and interact with members of these groups in a way that creates a favorable distinction for their group on positively valued dimensions (e.g., economic position, power, etc.). When the ingroup is considered superior to the relevant outgroup, a positive social identity emerges for members of the ingroup (Tajfel, 1978).

There is evidence to suggest that group memberships are more important for self-conceptions in collectivistic cultures than in individualistic cultures (see Marsella et al., 1985). Gabrenya and Wang's (1983) research, for example, revealed that Chinese utilized more group-oriented self-conceptions than people in the United States. This suggests that collectivistic cultures emphasize social identity, while individualistic cultures focus on personal identity. This conclusion appears to be supported by cross-cultural studies of the spontaneous self-concept (Bond & Cheung, 1983; Driver & Driver, 1983). Bond and Cheung's research, however, suggests that a simple collectivistic-individualistic distinction may not fully explain the differences that emerge; that is, they found that Hong Kong Chinese and North Americans mentioned family roles more than Japanese, while Japanese mentioned sex and age more than the other two. These patterns correspond to Hofstede's (1980) masculinity dimension of cultural variability. Other social roles, such as ascribed group memberships (e.g., caste, social class), should be influenced by power distance.

Cross-cultural research also suggests that there is consistency in the emphasis placed on ethnic identity for majority and minority groups across cultures. Hofman (1985), for example, found that Blacks in the United States emphasize ethnic identity more than Whites and that Arabs in Israel place more importance on ethnic identification than Jews. This finding is consistent with both Brewer's (1979a) observation and Hewstone, Bond, and Wan's (1983) research in Hong Kong. Hofman also found greater cohesion in the subidentities of majority group members than in the subidentities of the minority group members in both cultures.

While social identity theory was developed in an individualistic culture, it appears to be generalizable to collectivistic cultures (Bond & Hewstone, 1986; Ghosh & Huq, 1985; Hewstone et al., 1983; Majeed & Ghosh, 1982). Majeed and Ghosh, for example, examined social identity in three ethnic groups in India, discovering differential evaluations of self, ingroup, and outgroups in High Caste Hindus, Muslims, and Scheduled Castes. Their research suggested also that the more that common attributes were shared, the less differentiation between ingroups and outgroups. Ghosh and Huq found similar results for Hindu and Muslim evaluations of self and ingroup in India and Bangladesh. Brewer and Campbell's (1976) research on ingroup-outgroup evaluations in Africa and Peabody's (1985) research in Europe supports these findings. Bond and Hewstone's (1986) research revealed that British high school students in Hong Kong perceived social identity and intergroup differentiation to be more important than Chinese high school students. Their study also indicated that the British students perceive group membership to be more important and have a more positive image of the ingroup than the Chinese. These results, however, do not contradict social identity theory, but they do suggest that social differentiation in Hong Kong is "relatively muted," according to Bond and Hewstone (see Bond, 1987, for a complete rationale).

In a more recent study, Brewer, Ho, Lee, and Miller (1987) tested four different explanations as to how different social identities operate in the same situation: category dominance, additivity, category conjunction, and hierarchical ordering. Brewer and her associates collected ratings of same- and opposite-sex Cantonese-speaking Chinese, Shanghai-speaking Chinese, North Americans, and Indian children from Cantonese-speaking children in Hong Kong. They found that sex is dominant over ethnicity in determining the desired level of intimacy of interaction (more of a desire for intimacy with same- than opposite-sex children), while ethnicity is dominant and sex subordinate when judging perceived similarity to self (member of the ingroups, other Chinese, were perceived as more similar than the two outgroups). These results support a hierarchical ordering model of social identity. The finding that sex predominates with respect to desired intimacy of interaction probably is related to Hong Kong having a moderate score on Hofstede's masculinity index. In cultures with moderate to high masculinity scores, there is sex-role differentiation between male and female intimacy interaction levels.

Closely related to work on social identity theory is research on ethnolinguistic vitality. Giles, Bourhis, and Taylor (1977) argued that ethnolinguistic vitality influences the degree to which members of a group will act as a group in intergroup situations. Three studies comparing different ethnic groups' perceptions within cultures have been conducted using Bourhis, Giles, and Rosenthal's (1981) measure of subjective ethnolinguistic vitality (see Allard & Landry, 1986, for an alternative approach). Bourhis and Sachdev (1984) examined Italian and English Canadians in both majority and equal situations. They found that both groups had more realistic perceptions in the majority than the equal setting. English Canadians, however, were more biased against the Italian language in the equal than in the major majority setting. Giles, Rosenthal, and Young (1985) studied Greek- and Anglo-Australian perceptions of ethnolinguistic vitality. Both groups agreed about some aspects of each other's vitality, but disagreed about each other's position in Australian society. The Anglos accentuated perceived differences between ingroup and outgroup vitalities, while the Greeks attenuated the differences. In a related study, Young, Pierson, and Giles (in press) found that perceptions of ingroup vitality are associated with the amount of exposure to the outgroup language in Hong Kong, while Young, Giles, and Pierson (1986) demonstrated that sociopolitical changes (i.e., Chinese takeover of Hong Kong) influenced the perceived vitality of languages (English in this case). Finally, recent research (Leclézio, Louw-Potgeiter, & Souchon, 1986) discovered that spoken language is the most salient feature of social identity of Mauritian immigrants in South Africa.

There is one additional study that examined cultural variability in ethnolinguistic identity. Gudykunst's (1987b) research revealed that three of Hofstede's four dimensions (individualism, uncertainty avoidance, and masculinity) have a significant multivariate effect on the five dimensions of ethnolinguistic identity (ingroup identification, other-group identification, group boundaries, intergroup comparisons, and ethnolinguistic vitality). Univariate tests indicated that individualism influences other-group identification and ethnolinguistic vitality; uncertainty avoidance affects intergroup comparisons and ethnolinguistic vitality; and masculinity is related to group boundaries, ingroup identification, and ethnolinguistic vitality. Specifically, Gudykunst found that (1) greater other-group identification occurs in collectivistic than in individualistic cultures; (2) stronger ethnolinguistic vitality exists in individualistic than in collectivistic cultures; (3) more secure intergroup comparisons are made in low than in high uncertainty avoidance cultures; (4) stronger ethnolinguistic vitality exists in high than in low uncertainty avoidance cultures; (5) softer group boundaries are found in masculine than in feminine cultures; (6) greater identification with the ingroup occurs in masculine than in feminine cultures; and (7) greater ethnolinguistic vitality exists in masculine than in feminine cultures.

CONCLUSION

We have examined cross-cultural variations in general self-conceptions, facework processes, and social identity in this chapter. The research suggests that individualism-collectivism influences general self-conceptions and facework processes, as well a selected aspects of social/ethnolinguistic identity. Work in this area, however, tends to be either exploratory research or initial theoretical propositions. Research obviously is needed to confirm the speculations presented here.

While the theoretical influence of culture on self-conceptions is relatively clear, little thought has been given to how culture influences the relationship of the self-concept to interpersonal communication processes. Research and theorizing on how the association between self-concept and interpersonal relationship development (e.g., using Cushman & Cahn's, 1985, perspective) varies as a function of individualism-collectivism, for example, is needed. Research such as this is necessary in order to integrate culture into theories of relationship development and/or to specify scope conditions for statements in the theories.

5

Verbal Communication Styles

Individuals learn the norms and rules of interaction through the language socialization process. As Ochs (1986) observes, children obtain "tacit knowledge of principles of social order and systems of belief (ethnotheories) through exposure to and participation in language-mediated interactions" (p. 2). Through verbal socialization processes, children learn (1) the norms and rules of appropriate interactional behaviors in specific contexts, as well as the fundamentals of communication competence; (2) to act appropriately and effectively to attain their goals and meet their needs; and (3) the verbal communication styles needed to express their intentions and wishes.

In commenting upon the relationship between language and context, Ochs (1986) argues that most cross-cultural differences in language are "differences in *context* and/or *frequency of occurrence*" (p. 10). She elaborates, pointing out that

> what is different across societies is the extensiveness of these routines in terms of the semantic-pragmatic content covered (e.g., politeness phenomenon, role instruction, teasing, shaming, insults, language correction), the number of interlocutors involved (dyadic, triadic, multiparty), the social relationship of the interlocutors (e.g., caregivers, peers, strangers), the setting (e.g., inside/outside household dwellings, private/public, formal/informal distinctions in setting), the length of the imitative routines (e.g., number of turns, length of time), and the frequency of occurrence in the experience of young children. (p. 10)

At different language acquisition stages, children do not learn language per se, rather they learn the various patterns and styles of language interaction that enable them to function as competent communicators in different situational contexts. Through the large socialization process, they learn an entire set of worldviews and beliefs that validate their sense of cultural identity and lend support to their role identities.

Stylistic mode of language, according to Katriel (1986), refers to the "tonal coloring given to spoken performance, their feeling tone" (p. 2). The "feeling tone," in turn, invokes the cultural ethos of a system. Cultural ethos is the "affective patterning, the moral and aesthetic 'tone' of a culture" (p. 1). Verbal interaction styles reflect and embody the affective, moral, and aesthetic patterns of a culture.

This chapter focuses on verbal communication styles. Four stylistic modes are isolated: direct versus indirect style, elaborate versus succinct style, personal versus contextual style, and instrumental versus affective style. Hofstede's (1980) dimension of cultural variability and Hall's (1976, 1983) low- and high-context schema are used to explain verbal stylistic variations across cultures.

Style is a meta-message that contextualizes how individuals should accept and interpret a verbal message. Verbal style carries the tonal coloring of a message. It is expressed through shades of tonal qualities, modes of nonverbal channels, and consistent thematic developments in the discourse process. Of the four stylistic modes of verbal interaction, the research evidence on the direct-indirect style dimension is the most extensive and persuasive.

DIRECT VERSUS INDIRECT STYLE

The direct-indirect style refers to the extent speakers reveal their intentions through explicit verbal communication. The direct verbal style refers to verbal messages that embody and invoke speakers' true intentions in terms of their wants, needs, and desires in the discourse process. The indirect verbal style, in contrast, refers to verbal messages that camouflage and conceal speakers' true intentions in terms of their wants, needs, and goals in the discourse situation. Okabe (1983) differentiates rhetorical style differences between Japan and the United States as follows:

> Reflecting the cultural value of precision, [North] Americans' tendency to use explicit words is the most noteworthy characteristic of their communicative style. They prefer to employ such categorical words as "absolutely," "certainty," and "positively." . . . The English syntax dictates that the absolute "I" be placed at the beginning of a sentence in most cases, and that the subject-predicate relation be constructed in an ordinary sentence. . . . By contrast, the cultural assumptions of

interdependence and harmony require that Japanese speakers limit themselves to implicit and even ambiguous use of words. In order to avoid leaving an assertive impression, they like to depend more frequently on qualifiers such as "maybe," "perhaps," "probably," and "somewhat." Since Japanese syntax does not require the use of subject in a sentence, the qualifier-predicate is a predominant form of sentence construction. (p. 36)

Johnson and Johnson (1975) make a similar observation, pointing out that "a child raised in a Japanese family learns that he [or she] should not call attention to himself [or herself] by being loud, conceited, or self-centered. Children who take verbal initiative are generally not rewarded, for the [Japanese American] subculture usually extols the quiet child as the good child" (p. 457). The language socialization process of Japanese children is aimed at fostering the norm of *enryo,* a ritualized verbal self-deprecation process for the purpose of maintaining group harmony. Johnson and Johnson also note that "the verbal styles of modal [North] Americans can be described as reflecting notions of individual worth, the positive value of assertiveness, and the tendency to conceptualize relationships as egalitarian" (p. 458). The language socialization process of North American children is cultivated toward the achievement of honesty. The norm of honesty reinforces the importance of using words and messages that reflect one's true intentions and values.

Clancy's (1986) observations of how verbal communication styles are learned by Japanese children supports the "intuitive, indirect communication" model concerning Japanese mother-child interaction. By using indirection in making and refusing requests, 2-year-olds are taught not to hurt the feelings of another person early in their lives, and they learn the subtleties of face-giving and face-threatening behaviors through modeling their mothers' behaviors. In addition, Japanese mothers typically use rhetorical questions to state their disapprovals and indicate disapproval mainly by their tone of voice and context. The norms of empathy and conformity are viewed as the primary reasons why Japanese children acquire the style of indirect verbal communication when interacting with other children and their mothers (Clancy, 1986).

Similar observations have been advanced by Hsu (1981) concerning the differences in communication styles between Chinese and North Americans. He notes that

the [North] American emphasis on self-expression not only enables the [North] American child to feel unrestrained by the group, but also makes him [or her] confident that he [or she] can go beyond it. The Chinese lack of emphasis on self-expression not only leads the Chinese child to develop a greater consciousness of the status quo but also serves to tone down any desire on his [or her] part to transcend the larger scheme of things. (p. 94)

Park (1979) argued that Koreans do not make "negative responses like 'no,' or 'I disagree with you,' or 'I cannot do it,' [Rather, they] like to use more frequently than [North] Americans circumlocutory expressions, such as . . . 'I agree with you in principle' . . . or 'I sympathize with you'" (p. 88). The importance of preserving group harmony and the importance of *nunchi* (an affective sense by which Koreans can detect whether others really are pleased or satisfied or not) are the two primary reasons why most Koreans opt for the indirect style of communication in their everyday lives, according to Park. The preference for indirect, ambiguous communication over direct, open communication is attributed to the importance of the face-honoring process whereby the concept of *kibun* (respect for the others' sense of selfhood that includes their morale, face, self-esteem, and state of mind) has a highly valued place in the Korean culture.

The value orientation of individualism propels North Americans to speak their minds freely through direct verbal expressions. Individualistic values foster the norms of honesty and openness. Honesty and openness are achieved through the use of precise, straightforward language behaviors. The value orientation of collectivism, in contrast, constrains members of cultures such as China, Japan, and Korea from speaking boldly through explicit verbal communication style. Collectivistic cultures like China, Japan, and Korea emphasize the importance of group harmony and group conformity. Group harmony and conformity are accomplished through the use of imprecise, ambiguous verbal communication behaviors.

Katriel (1986) examined direct and indirect style usage in Israeli Sabra culture. She argues that members of Israeli Sabra culture use the direct style of *dugri* speech (or "straight talk") to achieve the cultural functions of sincerity, assertiveness, naturalness, solidarity, and antistyle. According to Katriel (1986), *dugri* speech in Hebrew "involves a conscious suspension of face-concerns so as to allow the free expression of the speaker's thoughts, opinions, or preferences that might pose a threat to the addressee" (p. 11). To Hebrew speakers, the use of *dugri* speech implies the concern for sincerity in the sense of being true to oneself. To Arab speakers, the use of *dugri* speech implies the concern for honesty by stating the information truthfully without concealments and embellishments. As Katriel (1986) summarizes:

What stands in the way of truth-speaking in the Hebrew *dugri* mode is sensitivity to face concerns, interpreted as lack of courage and integrity. What stands in the way of truth speaking in the Arabic *dugri* mode is the high value placed on smoothness in interpersonal encounters as well as the ever-present temptation to embellish the facts for rhetorical purposes in the service of self-interest. (p. 12)

Israeli Sabra culture is a low-context, direct verbal style culture, while the Arab-speaking culture is a high-context, indirect verbal style culture.

In comparing Israeli verbal style with North American verbal style, Katriel (1986) borrows Gibson's (1966) term of "tough talk" style to characterize North American verbal interaction process. According to Gibson (1966), three speech styles can be found in contemporary North American prose: the "tough talk" style, the "sweet talk" style, and the "stuffy talk" style. He suggests that

the Tough Talker . . . is a man [or woman] dramatized as centrally concerned with himself [or herself]—his [or her] style is I-talk. The Sweet Talker goes out of his [or her] way to be nice to us—his [or her] style is you-talk. The Stuffy Talker expresses no concern either for himself [or herself] or for his [or her] reader—his [or her] style is it-talk. (p. x)

Building upon the "tough talker" concept, Katriel (1986) proposes that there are both similarities and differences between the North American "tough talker" and the Israeli Sabra culture's "straight talker." On the interactional level, both "tough talker" and "straight talker" are concerned more with preserving their own face than their addressee's face. They both share similar attitudes in terms of using the direct style to fulfill the "antistyle" function. They both are concerned with the faithful projections of their feelings concerning the issues being discussed. On the cultural-meaning level, however, Katriel observes that the form of "tough talk" is "to be read as a reaction against established cultural patterns after the First World War, whereas *dugri* speech . . . is part of the reaction to cultural patterns associated with Diaspora life and European tradition" (p. 101). While both "tough talk" and "straight talk" reflect the interactional patterns of individualistic, low-context cultures, the cultural underpinnings and the historical-cultural logics that give rise to such stylistic variations may vary from one culture to the next.

In contrast to "tough talk" and "straight talk," Arab-speaking communities can be characterized as engaging in "sweet talk." According to Katriel (1986), the cultural ethos of *musayra* (meaning roughly to go along, to humor, to accommodate oneself) characterizes Arab communication patterns. One of her informants reported that the concept of *musayra* "is in the blood of every Arab person" (p. 111). As Katriel summarizes:

> It seems that the indirectness of style associated with the ethos of *musayra* is shared by men and women alike, although differences are found in the contexts, manner, and norms of style enactment of the two genders. The high value placed on *musayra,* on metaphorically "going with" the other, on humoring, on accommodating oneself to the position or situation of the other, reflects a concern for harmonious social relations and for the social regulation of interpersonal conduct. (p. 111)

The verbal communication patterns of the Arab-speaking communities, therefore, are reflective of some of the fundamental norms and values in collectivistic, high-context cultures.

Cohen (1987) supports Katriel's (1986) observation. He identifies the dimension of direct-indirect style as the one of the four key dimensions that poses serious communication problems in diplomatic relations between Egypt and the United States. After analyzing several autobiographical accounts that produce dissonance between Egyptian and North American diplomats, Cohen concluded that the values of collectivism and conformity in Egyptian culture influence the use of indirect, smoothing style in Egyptian diplomatic relations, while the values of individualism and self-assertion in U.S. cultures influence the use of the direct, cut-and-dry style in U.S. diplomatic relations. According to Cohen, the former is a shame-oriented, mutual-face concern culture, while the latter is a guilt-oriented, individual-face concern culture.

Four implications can be drawn from the analysis of cross-cultural verbal direct and verbal indirect dimensions. First, the dimension of direct-indirect speech style is a powerful construct to tap possible differences and similarities in verbal interaction across cultures. Second, the use of direct verbal style in individualistic, low-context cultures is, overall, for the purpose of asserting self-face need and self-face concern, while the use of indirect verbal style in collectivistic, high-context cultures is, overall, for the purpose of preserving mutual-face need and upholding interdependent group harmony. Third, while the face-negotiation perspective provides a middle-range theory that may account for the reason one verbal style variation is preferred over another style, there may exist a set of deep-rooted historical-political logics that surround the use of one predominant style over another in different cultures. Fourth, the direct-indirect verbal style is subjected to context-specific interpretations.

The next step for future research is to map out the contextual parameters (e.g., formal-informal context, public-private context, male-female context) that foster or inhibit stylistic usage. Katriel's (1986) work on indirectness among Arab men and women, Keenan's (1974) work on Malagasy speech norms concerning male's indirect style and female direct style, and Rosaldo's (1980) account of Ilongot traditional oratory of "plain talk" versus "crooked talk" in public versus private contexts are some such examples. We will now turn our attention to a discussion of the verbal elaborateness and succinctness dimension.

ELABORATE VERSUS SUCCINCT STYLE

Different cultural assumptions underlie the dimension of verbal elaborate style and verbal succinct style. This dimension encompasses three verbal stylistic variations: elaborate style, exacting style, and succinct style. The dimension deals with the quantity of talk that is valued in different cultures. The elaborate style refers to the use of rich, expressive language in everyday conversation. The exacting style echoes the concept of Grice's (1975) "quantity maxim," which in effect states that one's contribution in language interaction ought to be neither more nor less information than is required. Finally, the succinct style includes the use of understatements, pauses, and silences in everyday conversation.

The linguistic patterns of people in Arab cultures reflect the use of an elaborate style of verbal communication. As Shouby (1970) comments on the Arab language, "fantastic metaphors and similes are used in abundance, and long arrays of adjectives to modify the same word are quite frequent" (p. 700). Wolfson's (1981) analysis of compliments supports this observation. According to Wolfson, Iranian and Arabic speakers' compliments typically are filled with metaphors, proverbs, and cultural idioms, while North American English speakers' compliments typically are very exacting and ritualized. To illustrate, an Arabic speaker in Wolfson's study complimented her friend's child by saying, "She is like the moon and she has beautiful eyes" (Wolfson, 1981, p. 120).

In analyzing the language style differences between Arab speakers and North American English speakers, Prothro (1970) concluded that "statements which seem to Arabs to be mere statements of fact will seem to [North] Americans to be extreme or even violent assertions.

Statements which Arabs view as showing firmness and strength on a negative or positive issue may sound to North Americans as exaggerated" (p. 711). Almaney and Alwan (1982) analyzed the forms of assertion (*tawkid*) and exaggeration (*mubalaqha*) in Arabic language, concluding that

> the built-in mechanism of assertion in language affects the Arabs' communication behavior in at least two ways. First, an Arab feels compelled to overassert in almost all types of communication because others expect him [or her] to. If an Arab says exactly what he [or she] means without the expected assertion, other Arabs may still think that he [or she] means the opposite. For example, a simple "No" by a guest to the host's request to eat more or drink more will not suffice. To convey the meaning that he [or she] is actually full, the guest must keep repeating "No" several times, coupling it with an oath such as "By God" or "I swear to God." Second, an Arab often fails to realize that others, particularly foreigners, may mean exactly what they say even though their language is simple. To the Arabs, a simple "No" may mean the indirectly expressed consent and encouragement of a coquettish woman. On the other hand a simple consent may mean the rejection of a hypocritical politician. (p. 84)

Cohen (1987) agrees with Almaney and Alwan's (1982) summary of the Arabic language. He argues that the Arabs' proclivity for verbal exaggerations and elaborations have done more to complicate Egyptian-North American international relations than almost anything else. The fact that Arabic is considered a "sacred and holy language" and that "Islam forbids the depiction of living beings in visual form" probably constitute the reasons why an elaborated style of language is the primary vehicle for both creative and political expressions (Adelman & Lustig, 1981; Almaney & Alwan, 1982).

Similar to the exaggerated style of Arabic language is the "crooked" style of Ilongot traditional oratory articulated eloquently by Rosaldo (1973, 1980). According to Rosaldo, the Ilongot oratory also employs abundant use of metaphors, flowery expressions, and elaborate rhythms in its language system. The purpose of using such an elaborate style of speech is to negotiate relational equality and social harmony, whereas the use of "plain talk" is reserved for power assertion and relational dominance.

At the opposite end of the continuum from the elaborate style is the succinct style. Johnson and Johnson (1975) compared Japanese-American and Caucasian language interaction in Hawaii. They contend that Japanese-Americans often use indirection, circumlocution, and silence in their everyday language interaction. This is consistent with

Hall's (1983) position that *ma,* or silence, is dominant in Japanese communication. According to Hall, *ma* in Japanese speech means that "it is the silences between words that also carry meaning and are significant" (p. 208). The concept of *ma*, however, is much more than pausing between words; it is rather a semicolon that reflects the inner pausing of the speaker's reflective state. Through *ma*, interpersonal synchrony is made possible.

Ting-Toomey (1980) studied language patterns in Chinese-American families. She found that members of tradition-oriented Chinese families use talk as a status resource while they use silence as an affiliative-power strategy. Members of modern-oriented Chinese families, in contrast, use talk as a distributional resource and use silence as a conversational-regulation strategy.

Wiemann, Chen, and Giles (1986) recently have begun a series of cross-cultural studies on the beliefs about talk and silence in different cultures. Based on their Beliefs About Talk Survey, they found that Caucasian-Americans perceive talk as more important and enjoyable than Chinese-Americans and native-born Chinese. Caucasian-Americans also perceive using talk as a means of social control, while native Chinese tend to perceive silence as a control strategy. Finally, native Chinese are more tolerant of silence in conversation than Caucasians or Chinese-Americans.

Similar to Asian cultures, Basso (1970) found that the concept of silence occupies a central role in the Apache culture in the United States. Silence is appropriate in the contexts of uncertain and unpredictable social relations. Silence is preferred over talk when the status of the focal participant is marked by ambiguity and the fixed role expectations lose their applicability. Basso also argues that members of the Navajo and Papago Indian tribes exhibit similar silent behavior under the same conditions as Apaches.

The use of an elaborate style characterizes many Middle Eastern communication patterns. The use of an exacting style is characteristic of people in many Northern European cultures and the U.S. culture, and the use of a succinct verbal communication style is characteristic of people in many Asian cultures and some American Indian cultures in North America. Middle Eastern cultures such as Egypt, Iran, Lebanon, and Saudi Arabia are moderate on Hofstede's (1980) uncertainty avoidance dimension and are high-context cultures. Denmark, Sweden, Germany, and the United States are low to moderate on Hofstede's (1980) uncertainty avoidance dimension and are low-context cultures. Finally, Korea, Japan, Taiwan, and Thailand are relatively high on

Hofstede's (1980) uncertainty avoidance dimension and are high-context cultures.

Given the preceding analysis, it can be argued that individuals in moderate uncertainty avoidance, high-context cultures tend to use an elaborate style of verbal communication; individuals in low uncertainty avoidance, low-context cultures tend to use an exacting style of verbal communication; and people in high uncertainty avoidance, high-context cultures tend to use a succinct style of verbal communication. Overall, members of moderate uncertainty avoidance, high-context cultures tend to use a fight-flight camouflaging verbal style to approach uncertainty situations. While they are not as overapprehensive about novel situations as members of high uncertainty avoidance, high-context cultures, they are, nonetheless, not as confrontative as members of low-context cultures in approaching new situations. Elaborate words and an exaggerated speech style are the best means for them to negotiate their self-face and the face of their conversational partners. The purpose of face-negotiation for them is to accomplish *musayra* (i.e., accommodating the wishes and needs of another person). Conversely, members of high uncertainty avoidance, high-context cultures have a high apprehension level of unpredictable situations. The more novel the situation, the more likely they will use understatements and silence to manage the situation. Understatements and silence are good ways to preserve the face of oneself and, at the same time, not to offend someone else's face in public. The purpose of face-negotiation for them is to maintain group harmony or *wa*.

Lastly, members of the low uncertainty avoidance, low-context cultures have the lowest apprehension level in unpredictable situations. They can, therefore, afford to be exacting and up-front in their verbal communication style. They can approach new situations confrontatively, without verbal elaborations or understatements, and they can afford to be "authentic" in their facework negotiation process. The cultural value of "honesty" may be the primary goal in their face-negotiations. In fact, Grice's (1975) conversational maxims of quantity (one should state no more or no less information than is needed), quality (one should state only that which one believes to be true), and manner (one ought to avoid obscure expressions, ambiguity, excessive verbosity, and disorganization), while applicable in low-uncertainty-avoidance, low-context cultures, may not be applicable in verbal communication styles in other cultures. Different cultural criteria and different cultural variations influence the use of one verbal style over another. We will now turn to a discussion of the personal-contextual dimension of language behaviors.

PERSONAL VERSUS CONTEXTUAL STYLE

Verbal personal style is individual-centered language, while verbal contextual style is role-centered language. Verbal personal style refers to the use of certain linguistic devices to enhance the sense of "I" identity, and verbal contextual style refers to the use of certain linguistic signals to emphasize the sense of "role" identity. In the verbal personal style, meanings are expressed for the purpose of emphasizing "personhood," while in the verbal contextual style, meanings are expressed for the purpose of emphasizing prescribed role relationships.

Gumperz, Aulakh, and Kaltman (1982) analyzed conversational styles in an East Indian English-speaking community and a British English-speaking community, observing that Indian English is very contextual-based, while British English is very individualistic-based. In British English, the use of personal pronouns and the use of temporal and spatial locatives (e.g., then, there) are vital in sentence constructions, whereas in Indian English, these linguistic devices are not emphasized. They concluded:

> In some cases explicit textual referents need not be present at all; where they are present and particularly where there are multiple possible referents, speakers use pragmatic rules very different from those of Western English. The general nature of the contrast is that Indian English users rely to a greater extent on shared assumptions about speakers' knowledge of the situation being talked about, rather than on structural features of the explicit textual context. (pp. 46-47)

Mishra (1982) concurs with the contextual nature of Indian English. She observes that speakers of Indian English like to provide many minor contextual points of a story before advancing the thesis of the story, while speakers of British English tend to first provide the topical thesis of the story, then proceed to provide relevant information.

Young (1982) analyzed Chinese discourse styles, making a similar observation. Rather than relying on a preview statement to orient the listener to the overall direction of the discourse, Chinese discourse relies heavily on contextual cues and tends to use single word items such as "because," "as," and "so" to replace whole clause connectives commonly used in English, such as "in view of the fact that," "to begin with," or "in conclusion" (Young, 1982, p. 79).

In commenting on the Japanese language, Okabe (1983) contends that English is a person-oriented language, while Japanese is a status-oriented language. The key distinction is that a person-oriented language stresses informality and symmetrical power relationships, while a status-oriented or contextual-oriented language emphasizes formality and asymmetrical power relationships:

> [North] Americans tend to treat other people with informality and directness. They shun the formal codes of conduct, titles, honorifics, and ritualistic manners in the interaction with others. They instead prefer a first-name basis and direct address. They also strive to equalize the language style between the sexes. In sharp contrast, the Japanese are likely to assume that formality is essential in their human relations. They are apt to feel uncomfortable in some informal situations. The value of formality in the language style and in the protocol allows for a smooth and predictable interaction for the Japanese. (Okabe, 1983, p. 27)

In other words, the Japanese language tends to put conversational members in the proper role positions and in the proper status hierarchical levels. The English language tends to emphasize the "personhood" of the conversationalists and aims for informality and symmetrical power distributions.

Similarly, Yum (1987b) notes that the Korean language accommodates the Confucian ethical rules of hierarchical human relationships; it has special vocabularies for different sexes, for different degrees of social status, for different degrees of intimacy, and for different formal occasions. The correct usage of the proper language style, for the proper types of relationships, and in the proper contexts are the sure signs of a learned person in the Korean culture (Yum, 1987b). She also argues that the Korean language is a context-based language because the cultural ethos of Korean communication style is based on the key concept of *uye-ri*. Three clusters of meanings define *uye-ri*. The first cluster includes justice, righteousness, a just cause, duty, morality, probity, and integrity. The second cluster refers to obligation, a debt of gratitude, loyalty, and faithfulness. The third cluster concerns the importance of proper relationships between people, such as the employer and employee relationship or friendship.

The philosophical orientation of *uye-ri* governs the contextual parameters of Korean language usage. The following three categories, for example, demand different degrees of formality in Korean verbal interaction: (1) those people who are from the same exclusive group and with whom one has developed close personal relationships over an extended period, (2) those whose background is such that they can draw upon *uye-ri* but who are not personally well-known, and (3) those who are unknown strangers (Yum, 1987b). The first category includes those who went to the same high school and were in the same class and have become close friends. The second category includes those who went to the same high school and with whom one has become acquainted but who are not necessarily close friends. Finally, the last group is the stranger group, the members of which one can ignore and bypass without necessarily engaging in active verbal communication. Formal language style is used when status differential is involved and relational distance is far. Informal language style is practiced when status differential is minimal and the relational distance is close. Park (1979) arrives at a similar conclusion, suggesting that the Korean language is a "situation-oriented" language in which propriety and harmony are preserved through status-oriented verbal communication style.

Status-oriented verbal style also has been uncovered as a major theme in Albert's (1972) study of the cultural patterning of speech behavior in Burundi. Based on fieldwork research, she finds that members in Burundi use different degrees of formal speech style in accordance to caste, age and sex, kinship, friendship, contiguous residence, or political-economic ties. She observes that

> distinctions are made according to the social roles of those present: the degree of formality, publicity or privacy, and the objectives of the speech situation. Together, social role and situational prescriptions determine the order of precedence of speakers, relevant conventions of politeness, appropriate formulas and styles of speech, including extralinguistic signs, and topics of discussion. Socialization and sanctions are also determined by the social role-situational complexes within which discourse occurs. (p. 86)

The style of speaking reflects the overall values and patterns of a culture. In the Burundi case, the contextual style of speaking is preferred over the personal style of speaking. Contextual style of speaking refers to the use of language to reflect hierarchical social order and asymmetrical role positions. The personal style of speaking refers to the use of language to reflect egalitarian social order and symmetrical relational positions. The Far East and the Southeast Asian cultures (such as Malaysia, India, and Indonesia) and many of the African cultures (such as Ghana, Nigeria, and Sierra Leone) have high scores on Hofstede's (1980) power distance dimension and are high-context, collectivistic cultures. The Australian culture, the North European cultures (such as Denmark, Finland, and Sweden), and the United States have low scores on Hofstede's power distance dimension and are low-context, individualistic cultures. Members of low power distance, low-context cultures tend to prefer a personal style of verbal interaction, while members of high power distance, high-context cultures tend to prefer a contextual style of verbal interaction. Individuals in low power distance cultures prefer informal codes of interaction, while people in high power distance cultures prefer formal codes of interaction. Members of low power distance cultures use personal style language to regulate relational control. Members of high power distance cultures, in contrast, use contextual style language to reflect the prescriptive nature of control that is inherent in the cultural patterning of speech. We will now turn to a discussion on the instrumental and affective styles of verbal interaction.

INSTRUMENTAL VERSUS AFFECTIVE STYLE

The instrumental verbal style is sender-oriented language usage and the affective verbal style is receiver-oriented language usage. The instrumental style is goal-oriented in verbal exchange, and the affective style is process-oriented in verbal exchange. The instrumental style relies heavily on the digital level to accomplish goal objective and the affective style relies heavily on the analogic level to negotiate relational definition and approval.

Ramsey (1984) commented on the Japanese interaction style, proposing that

> the Japanese value catching on quickly to another's meaning before the other must completely express the thought verbally, or logically. *Haragei (hara*—belly, and *gei*—sensitivity or subtleness) is referred to as the Japanese way of communication. *Haragèi* means heart-to-heart communication or guessing the inner thoughts of the other. *Ishin denshin* (intuitive sense) is an additional referent for this preference. (pp. 142-143)

The affective-intuitive style of the Japanese verbal communication pattern places the burden of understanding on both the speaker and the listener. While the Japanese speaker actively monitors the reactions of the listener, the listener is expected to display intuitive sensitivity toward meanings beyond words. Verbal expressions are presented only as hints to reality, but they never are expected to be perceived as accurate facts that capture the totality of reality.

Okabe (1983) uses the term *erabi* (selective) worldview to represent the instrumental nature of verbal communication style in the U.S. culture, while he uses the term *awase* (adjustive) worldview to represent the affective-intuitive nature of verbal communication style in the Japanese culture. *Erabi* worldview holds that "human beings can manipulate their environment for their own purposes as the speaker consciously constructs his or her message for the purpose of persuading and producing attitude change"; the *awase* worldview assumes that human beings will "adapt and aggregate themselves to the environment rather than change and exploit it, as the speaker attempts to adjust himself or herself to the feelings of his or her listeners" (Okabe, 1983, pp. 36-37). The *erabi* worldview segregates the roles of speaker and listener into distinct categories, while the *awase* worldview integrates the roles of speaker and listener into a highly interdependent relationship. Both speaker and listener are expected to use their "intuitive sense" to interpret the multifarious nuances that are being transmitted in the ongoing dialogue.

This "intuitive sense" also finds its way into the Korean language. According to Park (1979), the Koreans place a high emphasis on the concept of *nunchi* in everyday verbal communication. *Nunchi* refers to the intuitive sense by which Koreans can detect whether others are really pleased or are really satisfied concerning the ongoing dialogue. According to Kim (1975), *nunchi* is an "interpretation of others' facial expressions or what they say plus—mysterious 'alpha' hidden in the inner hearts" (p. 7). Similar to Japanese verbal communication patterns, the affective-intuitive style characterizes the Korean verbal communication pattern. As Park observes:

> In an instrumental communication pattern, like that of the [North] Americans, people assert themselves or make themselves understood by talking . . . whereas in a situation communication style like that of Koreans or Japanese, people try to defend themselves either by vague expressions or by not talking. [North] Americans try to persuade their listeners in the step-by-step process [regardless of] whether their listeners accept them totally. But a Korean or a Japanese tends to refuse to talk any further in the course of a conversation with someone once he [or she] decides that he [or she] cannot accept the other's attitude, his [or her] way of thinking and feeling in totality. (pp. 92-93)

Morris's (1981) ethnographic work on Puerto Rican discourse processes uncovered five key points concerning Puerto Rican language style that closely resembles both Korean and Japanese language style:

(1) In Puerto Rican society, one's place and one's sense of oneself depend on an even, disciplined, and unthreatening style of behavior. . . .

(2) In language one must take great care not to put oneself or others at risk, and one must reduce the risk of confrontation to the lowest degree possible. This implies a systematic blurring of meaning—that is, imprecision and indirectness. . . .

(3) This implies a constant problem of interpretation, testing, probing, second-guessing, and investigation, but conducted indirectly. . . .

(4) The personal value of the individual—and so the validity of his [or her] words—will be determined by what he [or she] actually *does,* not by what he [or she] says. . . .

(5) Information does not come in discrete "bits," but as complex indicators of fluid human relationships, the "bits" being inextricable from the constant, implicit negotiation of meaning. Information is sought in the flow of talk, the exchanging of clues, and the sharing and the referring. (pp. 135-136)

The predominant style of Puerto Rican discourse, therefore, is affective-intuitive in orientation. It is listener-oriented, and oftentime what is not said is as important as what is being said. Affective intuition is used to infer and interpret the hidden implications of the verbal message.

Moving beyond the subdued affective style, Adelman and Lustig (1981) notice that native Arab speakers in Saudi Arabia tend to use a dramatic affective style of verbal communication in their everyday discourse. They note that "Arabic intonation patterns carry unwanted affective meanings when used in speaking English. . . . The intonation for exclamatory sentences in Arabic is much stronger and emotional than in English. Further, the higher pitch range of Arabic speakers conveys a more emotional tone than does English spoken by a native speaker" (p. 353). Beyond paralinguistic style differences, Cohen (1987) comments on proxemic behavior differences concerning Arab speakers and North American English speakers:

> The Arab need for personal contact with his [or her] interlocutor is associated with an outlook that defines relationships in affective and familiar, not instrumental, terms. Once again we are back to the individual and the group. The [North] Americans' distaste for tactile intimacy with strangers is clearly linked with the cultural primacy of personal autonomy and "privacy." Close contact with someone who is, literately, not one's intimate, constitutes an invasion of one's living space. When Arab representatives meet, whether as friends or rivals, they do so as brothers. They embrace, hold hands, acquire a strong physical sense of the other's presence. Anything else leaves them "cold," uncomfortable and unable to relate to the issue at hand. Personal chemistry may not ensure a successful negotiation in the Arab world, but its absence makes life more difficult. (p. 41)

Arabs, therefore, use an affective style of verbal communication that emphasizes heavily on expressive nonverbal behavior. Whereas, for the

North Americans, the digital level of verbal communication is the prime concern for effective face-to-face communication.

Given the preceding analysis, it can be argued that members of individualistic, low-context cultures tend to engage in an instrumental style of verbal communication, while members of collectivistic, high-context cultures tend to engage in an affective style of verbal communication. An affective style of verbal communication may include two components: an "intuitive sense" component and a nonverbal expressiveness component. An instrumental style of verbal communication is concerned with self-face maintenance and is concerned with satisfying negative-face (dissociation) need. An affective style of verbal communication is concerned with mutual-face maintenance and is concerned with satisfying positive-face (association) need. Denmark, Netherlands, Switzerland, and the United States are some of the cultures in which people engage in an instrumental style of verbal interaction. Most Arab cultures, Latin American cultures, and Asian cultures are some of the cultures in which individuals engage in an affective style of verbal interaction. The former cultures are representatives of individualistic, low-context .cultures, while the latter cultures are representatives of collectivistic, high-context cultures.

CONCLUSION

Four verbal communication style dimensions have been discussed in this chapter: direct versus indirect style, elaborate versus succinct style, personal versus contextual style, and instrumental versus affective style. The four dimensions were selected because of the potential theoretical contributions they can offer to the study of language and culture. Most studies cited are based on qualitative research methods such as the ethnographic interview method, the participant observation method, and the discourse analysis method. In addition, theoretical analyses have been used to guide the conceptual development in this chapter.

The cultural variability dimensions of individualism-collectivism and low- and high-context were used to explain the use of direct and indirect styles of verbal communication, as well as the use of instrumental and affective styles of verbal interactions. The uncertainty avoidance dimension and low/high-contexts were applied to the elaborate-exacting-succinct verbal styles dimension. Finally, the power distance dimension was used to explain the personal versus the contextual styles of verbal communication. While all stylistic variations of communication exist in all cultures, each culture attaches its own significance and normative value on different verbal modes of interaction. More theoretically based studies are needed to explain why members of different cultures prefer one set of verbal stylistic modes over another. More data-based studies also are needed to tap language style usage in specific relational and situational contexts in different clusters of cultures. Multicultural research team effort is crucial to investigate systematically the effect of the cultural variability dimensions on the four stylistic modes of verbal interaction.

6

Nonverbal Dimensions and Context-Regulation

Nonverbal context provides the background in which verbal messages can be meaningfully encoded and decoded. A verbal message such as "don't touch me" can occur in the context of an angry tone of voice, an informative tone, and a teasing tone. The verbal message, in conjunction with the paralinguistic signals, can unfold in the context of dramatic or restrained kinesic movements, animated or controlling facial expressions, and close or distant proxemic interaction. Finally, both verbal and nonverbal messages occur in the context of environment, space, and time dimensions.

Context-regulation, in this chapter, refers to the regulation of the nonverbal aspects of environment, space, and time. Nonverbal communication is defined as the simultaneous multimodal, multilevel message transmission and message interpretation process. As indicated in Chapter 1, culture is the normative frame in which expectations concerning appropriate or competent nonverbal behaviors are defined consensually and interpreted in a given speech community. While variability along the dimensions of culture influence the display rules of nonverbal behavior in different cultures, Burgoon (1985) aptly observes that

> there is also considerable within-culture variability as a function of subgroup and contextual norms. In particular, such "people" factors as gender, age, socioeconomic status, race, and personality make a difference. So do contextual factors as the type of occupation in work settings and environmental constraints. (p. 360)

The overall purpose of this chapter is to map the possible relationship between dimensions of cultural variability and nonverbal signals. The focus is on aspects of nonverbal signals that may yield high theoretical and research values for analyzing interpersonal communication processes across cultures.

For general summaries of cross-cultural interpersonal nonverbal literature, see Burgoon (1985), Henley and LaFrance (1984), LaFrance and Mayo (1978a, 1979), Poyatos (1983), Ramsey (1979, 1984), Wiemann and Harrison (1983), and Wolfgang (1984). For nonverbal aspects of affective communication (e.g., facial expressions), the reader is directed to Chapter 9 of this book. This chapter is developed in four sections: environment; privacy-regulation, proxemics, and haptics; chronemics; and interpersonal synchronization processes.

ENVIRONMENT: A DIALECTICAL PERSPECTIVE

Kurt Lewin (1936) focused attention on the importance of environment in influencing human behavior, arguing that $B = f(P, E)$, where $B =$ behavior, $P =$ person, and $E =$ environment. In other words, Lewin believes that human behavior is defined by the persons interacting, as well as the environment in which the interaction takes place.

The Dialectical Perspective

Altman and Gauvain (1981) studied the relationship among culture, human behavior, and home environment, proposing a dialectical perspective to the study of the three constructs. The three theoretical assumptions that guided the development of the dialectical theory of the nonverbal environment are (1) the world, universe, and human affairs involve various oppositional tensions; (2) these oppositional processes function as a unified system—oppositional poles help define one another, and without such contrasts neither would have meaning; and (3) the relationships between opposites are dynamic—changes occur over time and with circumstances (Altman & Gauvain, 1981). While verbal communication is a digital communication process, nonverbal communication is a multilayered, multimodal, multidimensional, analogic process. The oppositional poles such as identity-communality and accessibility-inaccessibility govern the use of mixed nonverbal signals. The use of interaction space, for example, may signal the need for individual privacy or identity, while at the same time hand gestures and facial expressions may signal accessibility or openness for the purpose of minimizing relational distance or status difference.

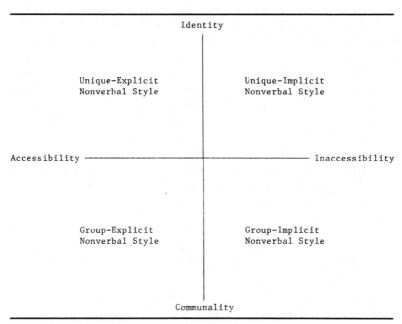

Figure 6.1: Two-Dimensional Grid of Interpersonal Nonverbal Styles

Altman and Gauvain (1981) suggest that the environment of a culture typically reflects the degree to which the culture and its members attempt to cope with two sets of dialectical opposites: the identity-communality dimension and the accessibility-inaccessibility dimension. The identity-communality dialectic reflects the "uniqueness and individuality of its occupants; that is, their personal identity as individuals and as a family, along with their ties, bonds, and affections with the communality and larger cultures of which they are part" (p. 288). The accessibility-inaccessibility dialectic involves the degree to which the home environment emphasizes the openness or closedness of occupants to outsiders. Figure 6.1 summarizes the dialectical perspective to the study of nonverbal human behavior.

The identity-communality dimension echoes the individualism-collectivism dimension, and the accessibility-inaccessibility dimension reflects the power distance and uncertainty avoidance dimensions. Individualistic cultures foster identity-type nonverbal behaviors and collectivistic cultures encourage communal-type nonverbal behaviors. In addition, people in low power distance, low uncertainty avoidance cultures tend to engage in an explicit nonverbal style that may create an impression of accessibility, while people in high power distance, high uncertainty avoidance cultures tend to engage in implicit nonverbal style that may create an impression of inaccessibility. The two-dimensional grid model includes four nonverbal style possibilities: unique- explicit nonverbal style, unique-implicit nonverbal style, group-explicit nonverbal style, and group-implicit nonverbal style. The degree of identity-communality continuum refers to the use of contexts (environment, space, time) to assert individual identity or communal identity, while the degree of accessibility-inaccessibility continuum refers to the use of specific nonverbal behaviors (such as parlinguistics or kinesics) explicitly or implicitly to regulate the nonverbal meanings of immediacy, potency, and responsiveness (Mehrabian, 1972). According to Mehrabian, immediacy refers to the like-dislike dimension, potency refers to the high-low-status dimension, and responsiveness refers to the active-passive energy dimension.

Unique-explicit nonverbal style refers to the use of nonverbal behavior to regulate individual privacy, as well as the use of expressive nonverbal gestures to signal immediacy, potency, and responsiveness. Unique-implicit nonverbal style refers to the use of nonverbal behaviors to protect individual privacy while simultaneously using subdued nonverbal gestures and movements to display relational liking and power distance. Group-explicit nonverbal style refers to the use of nonverbal behaviors to ensure group norms and regulate public face and the use of expressive nonverbal gestures to signal immediacy, potency, and responsiveness. Finally, group-implicit style refers to the use of nonverbal behaviors to uphold group norms and public face while at the same time using subdued nonverbal behaviors to display relational liking and power distance.

Overall, we may conclude that members of individualistic, low power distance, and low uncertainty avoidance cultures (such as Australia and the United States) are likely to engage in the unique-explicit nonverbal style of interaction, and members of individualistic, high power distance, and high uncertainty avoidance cultures (such as Belgium and France) are likely to engage in unique-implicit nonverbal style of interaction. Conversely, members of collectivistic, low (to moderate) power distance, and low uncertainty avoidance cultures (such as Hong Kong and Singapore) are likely to use a group-explicit style of nonverbal communication, while members from collectivistic, high power distance, and high uncertainty avoidance cultures (such as Japan and Korea) are likely to use a group-implicit style of nonverbal communication.

In fact, reviews of past cross-cultural nonverbal research (LaFrance & Mayo, 1978a, 1978b; Ramsey, 1979, 1984) point out clearly that members of individualistic cultures tend to engage in more privacy-regulation nonverbal behaviors, while members of collectivistic cultures tend to engage in more public face-regulation nonverbal behaviors. Further, while people in low power distance, low uncertainty avoidance cultures tend to use explicit nonverbal gestures to signal accessibility, people in high power distance, high uncertainty avoidance cultures tend to use implicit nonverbal gestures to regulate status positions and relational power.

Unfortunately, no study to date has yet examined the interaction effects among the various cultural variability dimensions on nonverbal communication processes. The dialectical perspective of the identity-communality dimension, and the accessibility-inaccessibility dimension on cross-cultural nonverbal styles lays the groundwork for further theorizing and systematical testing on cross-cultural nonverbal inter-action differences and similarities. The remainder of this section, therefore, is devoted to examining Altman and his associates' work on the dialectical theory of the nonverbal environment across cultures.

Home Environments

In applying the dialectical theory to the study of home environments across cultures, Altman and Gauvain (1981) found that the middle-class home environment in individualistic cultures is very different from the middle-class home environment in collectivistic cultures. In indi-vidualistic cultures, the middle-class home environment typically is separated from the community at large through the use of front yards, backyards, gates, and lawns. In collectivistic cultures, the middle-class home environment is developed in such a way that the architectural design of the home is integrated with a central plaza, a community center, or a neighborhood dwelling. Altman and his associates (Altman & Gauvain, 1981; Werner, Altman, & Oxley, 1985) further observe that the decor and furnishings of North American middle-class suburban homes symbolize the desire of the owners to differentiate themselves from one another, while the decor and furnishings of Indian, Japanese, and Mexican middle-class homes tend to express the communal desire of getting together, of interconnecting, and of group identity. Ramsey (1979) points out that while Northern European middle-class homes tend to emphasize edges, boundaries, and the segmentation of individual spaces and norms for each household member, Southeast Asian middle-class homes tend to emphasize communal spaces between objects in interior design. Finally, Altman and Gauvain (1981) found that while suburban North American homes can be identified by their individualized landscapes, by their locations in the middle or rear part of a lot, and by their separate entranceways, the Pueblo Indian homes are clusters of dwellings that surround a central courtyard or plaza where work, community activities, and religious events take place.

In sum, the dialectical opposites of individual identity and communal identity are present in all home environments, but the relative strength of individuality or communality is displayed in the exterior and interior layouts of home environments in different cultures. As Altman and Gauvain (1981) comment:

> In particular, we will suggest that dwellings reflect the degree to which cultures and their members must cope with common dialectic oppositions, namely, individual needs, desires, and motives versus the demands and requirements of society at large. Individual forces relate to the attempt of people to be unique and distinct—independent and free of the influences of others. These forces are associated with the satisfactions of individuals, and their families or primary reference groups. At the same time, there are forces operating to make the person part of and at one with society; to facilitate his or her identification with the community, and to increase susceptibility to influence and dependence on the larger community. (p. 287)

Tuan (1982), in relating individual consciousness with group life, concurs with Altman and Gauvain's (1981) observation:

> After the second world war, two of the desires to generate communal life in the city are the shopping plaza and the central-city neighborhoods. Europeans needed such places to replace those destroyed during the war. [North] Americans needed them to combat the diffuseness of the sprawling suburbs and either the glass-and-steel sterility or the decay of the urban cores. What steps must be taken to ensure that the new shopping centers combine bustling activity with intimacy, as in Old World Markets, but without the noise, confusion, and dirt? And how does one create complex, lively, and humane neighborhoods? Clearly the physical setting has an important role in the quality and extent of human intercourse. (p. 192)

Human behavior and nonverbal environment are intricately interwoven. While both individual and communal forces are present in the landscapes and architectures of all cultures, one theme typically predominates over another in terms of the overall scheme of cultural design. As Tuan (1982) concludes:

This ambiguity and equivocation of the modern [North] American house neatly mirrors the conflict between polarized [North] American ideals: individualism and communality, selfhood developed in the privacy of one's own space and democratic togetherness. But let it be said again, the communal ideal is one evoked deliberately by individuals. Communality of the kind that modern men and women can personally experience is an artifact of individualism. (p. 188)

Compartmentalization, personal space, and monochronic time pacing are some of the motifs that reflect the identity theme, while integration, collective space, and polychronic time pacing are some of the motifs that echo the communality theme. The conjoint dimensions of identity-communality and accessibility-inaccessibility are examined through a discussion of privacy-regulation, proxemics, and haptics.

PRIVACY-REGULATION, PROXEMICS, AND HAPTICS

Privacy-Regulation

Privacy-regulation is concerned with the identity expressiveness dimension and the information accessibility dimension. Altman (1975) defines privacy-regulation as the "selective control of access to the self or to one's group" (p. 18). Privacy-regulation can be achieved through both concrete and behavioral means. On the concrete level, the use of closed doors in the United States, the use of soundproof, double doors in the German culture (Hall, 1966), the use of large, carved doors in Norway, and the use of high shrubbery, trees, and fences to shield the home from public in Canada and England (Altman & Gauvain, 1981), all display the high need for personal privacy and individual identity in these cultures. Conversely, in Javanese (Geertz, 1973), Japanese, and many Southeast Asian cultures, population density and crowded environmental conditions make it virtually impossible for members of these cultures to manipulate the concrete environment to maintain and create personal privacy. Furthermore, personal privacy might not be as major a concern for people in collectivistic cultures as it is for people in individualistic cultures. A compensatory norm also appears to exist among privacy-regulation, environmental manipulation, and self-disclosure in collectivistic cultures. Many studies (Barnlund, 1975a; Gudykunst, Yang, & Nishida, 1985; Won-Doornink, 1985), for example, have found that members of individualistic cultures are more accessible in disclosing private information during initial interactions than members of collectivistic cultures. Conjointly, members of individualistic cultures also tend to engage in environmental control to assert their unique identity and to claim private space than do members of collectivistic cultures. Whereas in collectivistic cultures, individuals do not necessarily manipulate the environment to ensure individual privacy, they compensate by monitoring their self-disclosure process more judiciously and cautiously. As Derlega and Chaikan (1977) suggested, the reconceptualization of self-disclosure in the direction of nonverbal privacy-regulation may yield more fruitful avenues for future research into self-disclosure and interpersonal development process. In identity-based cultures, where people tend to use barriers and proxemic space to ensure individual privacy, the verbal self-disclosure process becomes more free-flowing, spontaneous, and accessible. In communal-based cultures, where people are less likely to use environmental space to assert individual privacy, the verbal self-disclosure process then becomes more regulated and inaccessible.

Proxemics

Claiming a space for oneself means injecting a sense of identity or selfhood into a place with clear boundaries surrounding it. According to Hall's (1966) proxemic theory, the use of interpersonal space or distance helps individuals regulate intimacy by controlling sensory exposure. Altman (1975) views the study of proxemics as the claiming of personal territory that includes the "personalization of or marking of a place or object and communication that it is 'owned' by a person or group" (p. 107). While members of all cultures engage in the claiming of space for self or collective effort, the experience of spaciousness and crowdedness and the perception of space-violation and space-respect vary from one culture to the next. The key mediating variable appears to rest with the need for sensory exposure and contact in different cultures.

Intimacy by sensory exposure (and therefore the need for close personal space) "is reported to be high among South Americans, Southern and Eastern Europeans, and Arabs, and low among Asians, Northern Europeans, and North Americans" (Sussman & Rosenfeld, 1982, p. 66). Andersen (1987) provides a further explanation by arguing that high-contact cultures, wherein members prefer to stand close and touch, tend to be located in warmer climates or regions; while low-contact cultures, wherein members prefer to stand further apart and touch little, tend to be located in cooler climates or regions. He concludes that cultures in cooler climates tend to be more task-oriented and interpersonally "cool," whereas cultures in warmer climates tend to be more interpersonally oriented and interpersonally "warm" (p. 10). In short, people in low-contact cultures have a low need for sensory exposure and people in high-contact cultures have a high need for sensory exposure.

Sussman and Rosenfeld (1982) tested the proxemic theory of sensory exposure by examining the use of interpersonal distance in Japanese, Venezuelan, and North American students. They found that (a) when speaking their native languages, Japanese sit further apart than Venezuelans, with North Americans at an intermediate distance; (b) females sit closer than males; and (c) when speaking English, respondents from other cultures use personal distances more closely approximating North American conversational distance norms than when speaking their native languages. While Venezuela is a high-contact culture, Japan is a low-contact culture. It seems that when individuals converse in their native language, the use of their native language also triggers a broader package of culturally appropriate behaviors.

Engebretson and Fullmer (1970) found that Japanese prefer greater interaction distances with their friend, father, and professor than do Japanese-Americans in Hawaii and Caucasian Americans. Little (1968) also found that members of Mediterranean cultures (such as Greeks and Southern Italians) prefer closer distances than do Northern Europeans. LaFrance and Mayo (1978a) commented that Argentineans make greater differentiations between the use of personal distance and relationship type, while Iraqis make little distinction between the use of personal space and relationship type. In terms of spatial violation behavior, a series of studies by Bond and Shiraishi (1974), Bond and Komai (1976), and Bond and Iwata (1976) suggest that members of individualistic cultures tend to take an active, aggressive stance when their space is violated, while members of collectivistic cultures tend to assume a passive, withdrawal stance when their personal space is intruded.

Burgoon (1978, 1983) developed a theory of spatial violation behavior based on the violations of expectations model. She argues that the manner in which one reacts to violations is dependent upon the characteristics of the perpetrator of the violations, whether the violation is closer or farther than expected, and its extremity. The process of arousal labeling, the message value of proximity shift, and competing privacy and affiliation needs also affect individuals' expectations (Burgoon, 1983). The model, however, has not been tested in cultures where status relationships may assert a stronger influence on the expectation violation model than in the North American setting (e.g., cultures high in power distance). The assumption that "given a rewarding initiator, optimal communication outcomes are achieved by violating the expected distance rather than conforming to it" (p. 105) may be applicable in individualistic, low power distance cultures (such as the United States), but not in other cultures. Different behavioral outcomes may occur in collectivistic, high power distance cultures (such as Japan), for example, when the rewarding initiator (defined as a high-status person) attempts to violate the personal space of a low-status person. A high-status person, in violating the personal space of a low-status person in collectivistic, high power distance cultures is acting totally out of his or her ascribed role performance, and in turn, will bring stress and anxiety to the asymmetrical relationship.

To summarize, it is expected that in low power distance, low uncertainty avoidance cultures, few rules and norms are used in regulating of proxemic behavior. In high power distance, high uncertainty avoidance cultures, many rules and norms are employed in regulating status proxemic behavior and relational proxemic behavior. Violations of proxemic distance in individualistic cultures evoke an aggressive mode of reaction, while violations of proxemic distance in collectivistic cultures evoke a withdrawal mode of reaction. Furthermore, low-contact cultures are reflective of individualistic cultures located along the cold weather regions, while high-contact cultures are reflective of collectivistic cultures that reside along the warm weather regions.

Haptics

Different cultures encode and interpret touch behavior in different ways. Low-contact cultures engage in less touch behavior than high-contact cultures. People in collectivistic cultures with high-intimacy sensory exposure need tend to engage in more tactile interaction than people in individualistic cultures with low-intimacy sensory exposure need. Hall (1983), for example, found that Arabs typically feel a strong sense of "sensory deprivation" and alienation at the lack of close, intimate contact with North Americans, while North Americans find Arabs' need for close personal space anxiety-provoking and disturbing. Almaney and Alwan's (1982) and Cohen's (1987) work supports Hall's observation concerning the nonverbal personalism and impersonalism dimension of Arab and North American cultures. As Almaney and Alwan (1982) conclude:

> To the Arab, to be able to smell a friend is reassuring. Smelling is a way of being involved with another, and to deny a friend his [or her] breath

would be to act ashamed. In some rural Middle Eastern areas, when Arab intermediaries call to inspect a prospective bride for a relative, they sometimes ask to smell her. Their purpose is not to make sure that she is freshly scrubbed; apparently what they look for is any lingering odor of anger or discontent. The Burmese show their affection during greeting by pressing mouths and noses upon the cheek and inhaling the breath strongly. The Samoans show affection by juxtaposing noses and smelling heartily. In contrast, the [North] Americans seem to maintain their distance and suppress their sense of smell. (p. 17)

The tendency for North Americans to remain outside the appropriate olfactory zone of Arabs often leads to Arabs suspecting the speakers' genuine intentions, whereas the close contact need of the Arabs often constitutes a violation of the personal space and privacy of the North Americans. Similar to the Arab cultures' need for sensory intimacy, studies (Engebretson & Fullmer, 1970; Mayo & LaFrance, 1977; Shuter, 1976; Watson, 1970) on touch behaviors in Latin American cultures and the U.S. culture reveal that people in Latin American cultures tend to engage in more frequent tactile behavior than people in the United States. In comparing touch behavior in Japan and the United States, Barnlund (1975a) found that Japanese tend to engage in same-sex touch behavior more often than North Americans, while North Americans tend to engage in opposite-sex touch behavior more often than Japanese. Further, Japanese females tend to touch more than do Japanese males. Conversely, in the Mediterranean cultures, LaFrance and Mayo (1978a) concluded that male-male touch behavior is used more frequently than female-female touch behavior.

Jones and Remland (1982) used the Touch Avoidance Measure (Andersen & Leibowitz, 1978) to analyze touch avoidance behaviors in Mediterranean, Near Eastern, Far Eastern, and U.S. cultures. They found that people in the Mediterranean are more touch-avoidant to opposite-sex touching than people in the United States. People in the Near East are less touch-avoidant to opposite-sex touching than both Mediterranean and Far Eastern groups. Finally, the Far Eastern group is the most touch-avoidant cultural group in opposite-sex touch behavior among the four groups. These findings support Watson's (1970) contention that the Far Eastern cultures are low-contact cultures, the North American culture is a moderate-contact culture, and the Arab and the Mediterranean cultures are high nonverbal contact cultures. Of course, variables such as gender, age, and relational distance will have an effect on the initiation and the receptivity levels of touch behavior, as well as on the variations of nonverbal touch forms.

The norms and rules employed regarding nonverbal touch behavior in high power distance, high-masculine cultures are more stringent than the norms and rules used in low power distance, low-masculine cultures. While tight relational norms and rules regulate tactile behavior in high uncertainty avoidance cultures, loose relational norms and rules govern tactile behavior in low uncertainty avoidance cultures.

To summarize, collectivistic high-sensory exposure cultures such as Arab cultures, Mediterranean cultures, and Latin American cultures tend to be nonverbal accessible cultures on the touch dimension, while individualistic and collectivistic low-sensory exposure cultures tend to be nonverbal inaccessible cultures on touch. Members of individualistic cultures do not engage in as much touch behavior as Arab and Mediterranean cultures, but they do place a heavy emphasis on verbal disclosure for regulating relational intimacy. In addition, while members of collectivistic low sensory exposure cultures do not engage in explicit nonverbal touch behavior, they do rely heavily on intuitive, implicit nonverbal behavior to convey sentiments and their emotions. The norm of privacy-regulation influences the restrictive use of tactile interaction in individualistic low sensory exposure cultures. The norm of propriety and public face-regulation, in contrast, influences the understated use of tactile communication in collectivistic low sensory exposure cultures. While members in different cultures may engage in similar types of nonverbal behaviors, the interpretations, the functions, and the end goals of each nonverbal signal may vary from one cultural system to the next.

CHRONEMICS

Beyond the use of space and touch, time is reflective of the psychological environment in which communication occurs (see Jones, 1988, and LeVine, 1988, for recent cross-cultural comparisons). Time flies when two friends are enjoying themselves and having a good time. Time crawls when two ex-friends stare at each other and have nothing to say to one another. Hall (1983) distinguished two patterns of time that govern different cultures: Monochronic Time Schedule (M-time) and Polychronic Time Schedule (P-time).

According to Hall (1983), the M-time and P-time are empirically quite distinct, "like oil and water, they don't mix" (pp. 45-46). He elaborates, arguing that

> each has its strengths as well as its weaknesses. I have termed doing many things at once, Polychronic, P-time. The North European system—doing one thing at a time—is Monochronic, M-time. P-time stresses involvement of people and completion of transactions rather than adherence to preset schedules. Appointments are not taken as seriously and, as a consequence, are frequently broken. P-time is treated as less tangible than M-time. For polychronic people, time is seldom experienced as "wasted," and is apt to be considered a point rather than a ribbon or a road, but that point is often sacred. (p. 46)

For Hall (1983), Latin American, Middle Eastern, Japanese, and French cultures are representatives of P-time patterns, while Northern European, North American, and German cultures are representatives of M-time patterns. People that follow M-time patterns usually engage in one activity at a time, they compartmentalize time schedules to serve self-needs, and they tend to separate task-oriented time from socio-emotional time. People that follow P-time tend to do multiple tasks at the same time, they tend to hold more fluid attitudes toward time schedules, and they tend to integrate task need with socio-emotional need. Members of individualistic cultures such as Denmark, Finland, Germany, and Norway tend to follow the M-time pattern, while members of collectivistic cultures such as Greece, Iran, Turkey, the Philippines, and Thailand tend to follow the P-time pattern. While members of individualistic cultures tend to view time as something that can be possessed, killed, and wasted, members of collectivistic cultures tend to view time as more contextually based and relationally oriented. People who follow M-time schedules tend to emphasize individual privacy, schedules, and appointments. People who follow P-time schedules, in contrast, tend to emphasize human connectedness, fluidity, and flextime.

Beyond M-time and P-time, Hall (1959) also differentiates five time intervals for arriving late for appointments: (1) mumble something time, (2) slight apology time, (3) mildly insulting time, (4) rude time, and (5) downright insulting time. For people who follow M-time schedules, if they are five minutes late for an appointment, they mumble something. If they are 10 to 15 minutes late, they would probably make a slight apology. For people who follow P-time schedules, it is not unusual for a person to be 45 or 60 minutes late and not even "mumble something," or to express a slight apology. While individualistic cultures are time-oriented, collectivistic cultures are relationally oriented. Members of individualistic cultures view time from a linear past-present-future perspective and members of collectivistic cultures tend to view time from a spiral, cyclical perspective. From the perspective of people in individualistic cultures, time can be controlled and wasted by individuals. From the perspective of people in collectivistic cultures, time regenerates itself without the necessary control and imposition by individuals.

In sum, people in individualistic cultures with high privacy regulation need tend to monitor their time closely, while people in collectivistic cultures with low privacy regulation need tend to be fluid in their use of time. Members of individualistic cultures tend to protect their individual identity and space more stringently through the conscientious regulation of the time dimension than members of collectivistic cultures, who tend to connect and assert their communal identities by placing relational orientation before the temporal dimension. People in individualistic cultures are into the privacy regulation of M-time patterns, while people in collectivistic cultures use the public face-regulation of the P-time patterns.

INTERPERSONAL SYNCHRONIZATION PROCESSES

According to Argyle (1979), the five basic nonverbal communication functions are (1) conveying interpersonal attitudes, (2) expressing emotional states, (3) managing conversations, (4) exchanging rituals, and (5) regulating self-presentation. One of the key concepts that may tie all these five nonverbal functions together is "interpersonal synchrony." According to Hall (1983), interpersonal synchrony refers to convergent rhythmic movements between two people on both the verbal and the nonverbal levels. Every facet of human behavior is involved in the rhythmic process. As Hall commented:

> It can now be said with assurance that individuals are dominated in their behavior by complex hierarchies of interlocking rhythms. Furthermore, these same interlocking rhythms are comparable to fundamental themes in a symphonic score, a keystone in the interpersonal processes between mates, co-workers, and organizations of all types on the interpersonal level within as well as across cultural boundaries. (p. 153)

Based on kinesic and proxemic film research, Hall (1983) found that conversational distances between individuals always are mentioned with incredible accuracy, that the process is rhythmic, and that the individuals are locked together in a "dance" that functions almost totally out of awareness. He also observed that people in Latin

American, African, and Asian cultures seem to be more conscious of these rhythmic movements than are people in Northern European and North American cultures. The fact that synchronized rhythmic movements are based on the "hidden dimensions" of nonverbal behavior might explain why people in African and Latin American cultures (as high-context nonverbal cultures) are more in tune and display more sensitivity toward the synchronization process than people in low-context verbal cultures, such as those in Northern Europe and the United States.

Members of high-context, collectivistic cultures that are relational and group-oriented tend to have a higher need to contextualize the rhythmic pattern of an event from beginning, middle, and ending. It takes people in collectivistic cultures a longer time to engage in greeting and goodbye rituals, a longer time to move the relationship level from a low degree of intimacy to a higher degree of intimacy, and a longer time to terminate the action chain of an event than it takes people in individualistic cultures. Conversely, members of individualistic cultures have a relatively low need to complete an action chain; approach greeting, maintenance, and goodbye rituals with a fast pace; and approach the initiation, maintenance, and termination of a relationship with a faster pace than do members of collectivistic cultures. Whatever members of individualistic cultures do not accomplish on the nonverbal level, they can rely on words to convey.

Interpersonal synchrony or convergence is achieved when the nonverbal behavior between two individuals moves toward broadness, uniqueness, efficiency, flexibility, smoothness, personalness, and spontaneity, and when overt judgment is suspended (Knapp, 1983). Interpersonal misalignment or divergence occurs when the nonverbal behavior between two individuals moves toward narrowness, stylized behavior, difficulty, rigidity, awkwardness, publicness, and hesitancy, and when overt judgment is given (Knapp, 1983). Interpersonal synchrony signifies increased liking, rapport, and attention, while interpersonal misalignment signifies increased disliking, rejection, and indifference. While members of individualistic, low-context cultures emphasize speech convergence, members of collectivistic, high-context cultures emphasize the importance of nonverbal convergence. People in individualistic, low-context cultures emphasize the assertion of individual identities in the manipulation of environment, space, touch, and time dimensions. People in collectivistic, high-context cultures, in contrast, emphasize the importance of communal identities in the use of environment, space, touch, and time dimensions. Finally, while members of low-context, individualistic cultures tend to be more accessible

through explicit verbal self-disclosure, members of high-context, collectivistic cultures tend to be more accessible through either explicit or
implicit means of nonverbal interaction.

The concept of communication competence (Hymes, 1972; Spitzberg
& Cupach, 1984) indeed takes on a cultural-specific meaning when the
norms and values of verbal and nonverbal patterns in different cultural
systems are examined. Researchers examining communication competence in individualistic, low-context cultures would place a higher
value on verbal communication competence. Researchers analyzing
communication competence in collectivistic, high-context cultures
would place a higher emphasis on the study of nonverbal communication
competence.

CONCLUSION

Research on differences in four nonverbal contexts—environmental,
proxemic, tactile, and temporal—across cultures were examined. A
two-dimensional grid of the identity-communality dimension and the
accessible-inaccessible dimension was used to facilitate the discussion of
the nonverbal environment construct and the privacy-regulation issue.
Extending the implications of the two-dimensional nonverbal grid, the
themes of proxemics, haptics, chronemics, and interpersonal synchrony
were traced. The nonverbal grid was posed as a starting point to think
about the disparate findings in cross-cultural nonverbal research and an
attempt to make sense of the divergent functions and interpretations of
nonverbal codes across cultures.

On the theoretical level, future cross-cultural work should pay extra
attention to (1) the theorizing level and the explanatory logic under the
different nonverbal findings, (2) the context that undergirds the
differences and the similarities of nonverbal signals and displays in
different cultures and the dimensions of cultural variability that are
related to those contexts, and (3) the relational contexts (for example,
relational type and gender type) that surround the display of nonverbal
expressions or affection. Methodologically, more nonverbal studies
need to be conducted (1) in the naturalistic setting rather than lab
setting, (2) on multiple units of analysis on combined nonverbal
channels and combined nonverbal codes, (3) on the multifunctional
dimensions of single nonverbal codes in different cultures, (4) on the
interpersonal synchronization process of different cultural members on
the nonverbal convergence dimension, and (5) on the synchronization

process of different cultural members on the verbal-nonverbal convergence dimension.

Overall, the knowledge base about nonverbal communication across cultures is mostly atheoretical and descriptive in nature, and most studies are cross-cultural nonverbal comparison studies that are conducted in lab settings without clear control of confounding variables such as personality styles, relational distance, native versus second language usage, degree of cultural similarity or dissimilarity, and so forth. While more naturalistic nonverbal descriptive studies are needed across cultures, researchers would be well advised to develop a theoretical frame that can systematically account for the nonverbal variations and the divergence that accompany the verbal repertoires of members of different cultures.

7

Personality

The concept of personality, in relation to culture, has received extensive treatment by anthropologists and psychologists (e.g., see LeVine, 1973, for an overview of the early work). The purpose of this chapter, however, is not to review research on psychological anthropology and/or personality and culture. Rather, the purpose is to examine cross-cultural variations in those aspects of personality that directly affect interpersonal communication.

Personality traits—"any distinguishable, relatively enduring way in which one individual differs from others" (Guilford, 1959, p. 6)—are related to interpersonal communication. Daly (1987) points out that personality traits "account for significant variation in communication behavior as well as communication-based perceptions" (p. 29). Communication-based perceptions are in large part a function of implicit personality theories (Daly, 1987). Personality traits that influence interpersonal communication and have been studied cross-culturally include self-monitoring (Snyder, 1974), self-consciousness (Fenigsten, Scheier, & Buss, 1975), communication apprehension (McCroskey, 1978), communicator style (Norton, 1983), and locus of control (Rotter, 1966). Space does not permit an examination of cross-cultural research on classic personality inventories, such as the Minnesota Multiphasic Personality Inventory (see Butcher & Pancheri, 1976; Butcher & Spielberger, 1985) and the Eysenck Personality Questionnaire (see Barrett & Eysenck, 1984, for data on 24 cultures, but also see Bijnen, Van Der Net, & Poortinga, 1986, for an argument against the cross-cultural comparability of this scale) or the extensive research on "national characteristics" (see Peabody, 1985, for a recent study). Before examining specific personality dimensions, we will look at implicit personality theories.

IMPLICIT PERSONALITY THEORY

Implicit personality theories focus on how information about others is selected, the processes by which information about others' personalities are generated, how the information is organized, and how conflicting pieces of information are combined (Wegner & Vallacher, 1977). How information is selected is a function of the observers' cognitive structure and the situation in which the observations occur. Cultural variations influence the attributes to which individuals attune in observing others. People from collectivistic cultures, for example, focus on factors that give an indication of others' background and social status, while members of individualistic cultures focus on individual attitudes, values, and beliefs (Gudykunst, Nishida, Koike, & Shiino, 1986).

Information about others is generated by inferences based on observations. Once observers select pieces of information about another, an impression of the whole person is made through inferences about expected relationships. The need to make inferences is greater when dealing with strangers than when dealing with those who are familiar (Koltuv, 1962). The information generated originates in stereotypes. Stereotypes emerge from the categorization process and refer to categorizations of people based on individual elements (e.g., race, ethnic group, religion, sex). Tajfel (1981b) differentiates social stereotypes from general stereotypes: "Stereotypes can become social only when they are 'shared' by large numbers of people within social groups or entities—the sharing implying a process of effective diffusion" (p. 145). Stereotypes are determined by (1) the degree of familiarity with the group being stereotyped, and (2) the amount and quality of contact with the other group (Triandis, 1977). The stereotypes individuals hold are related to intergroup attitudes such as prejudice and ethnocentrism (e.g., LeVine & Campbell, 1972) and, in turn, have an effect on discriminatory behavior toward members of outgroups (e.g., Rubovits & Maehr, 1973).

Stereotypes also influence other aspects of the communication process. Drawing on Hewstone and Giles's (1986) analysis of stereotypes, at least four generalizations appear to be warranted: (1) Stereotyping is the result of cognitive biases stemming from illusory correlations between group membership and psychological attributes; (2) stereotypes influence the way information is processed, that is, more favorable information is remembered about ingroups and more unfavorable information is remembered about outgroups; (3) stereotypes create expectancies (hypotheses) about others, and individuals try to confirm these expectancies; and (4) stereotypes constrain others' patterns of communication and engender stereotype confirming communication, that is, they create self-fulfilling prophecies. These generalizations are consistent with Hamilton's (1979) summary of stereotypes' effects:

> Stereotypic expectations can influence the perceivers' own behavior toward a member of the stereotyped group . . . that behavior, which has been affected by stereotypic beliefs, can have an influence on the nature of the behavior manifested by the target person . . . and the target's behavior can be modified by his or her perception of the stereotypic expectations held by the perceiver. . . . Finally, one's stereotypes, when used as a basis for judging others, can result in negative evaluations of one who manifests counterstereotypic behavior. (p. 79)

Information gathered through stereotypes must be organized. While there is little research on variations across cultures, Warr and Haycock's (1970) research with British and Tzeng's (unpublished; reported in Triandis, 1977) study of Japanese are illustrative of differences to be expected. Both studies revealed the dimensions of evaluation (e.g., good-bad), potency (e.g., strong-weak), and activity (e.g., fast-slow; i.e., these dimensions were isolated originally by Osgood, May, & Miron, 1975), but additional factors emerge in each study and there are differences in the activity dimension (i.e., British activity is related to fast and agile, Japanese to flexible and vivid). Studies drawing on Norman's (1963) dimensions of personality structure also are applicable. Norman found five dimensions of personality in the United States: extroversion, good-naturedness, conscientiousness, emotional stability, and "culture" (e.g., good manners, savoir faire). Guthrie and Bennett (1971) conducted comparable research in the Philippines, while Bond, Nakazato, and Shiraishi (1975) and Bond (1979) replicated the study in Japan and Hong Kong, respectively. The first three factors appear to be consistent across cultures, but the ordering of the factors vary (suggesting different weights to the factors across systems). Bond (1979) points out that these factors are associated with Osgood and his associates' (1975) three dimensions of affective meaning: Extroversion is similar to the activity dimension, good-naturedness and emotional stability are related to evaluation, and conscientiousness and "culture" are similar to potency. More recently, Eysenck (1986) found that similar factors (psychotricism, extroversion, neuroticism) emerge on his personality inventory in 24 different countries. Bond also believes that the factors from these studies are related to the dimensions of behavior isolated by Triandis (1977, 1978), which are discussed in Chapter 10.

Yang and Bond (1983; cited in Bond & Hwang, 1986) examined dimensions of personality using traits from the Chinese language. They used 150 descriptors from the 557 adjectives used in Yang and Lee's (1971) study. Yang and Bond had Chinese rate various target-persons (e.g., self, mother, father, most familiar friend, most familiar teacher, etc.) using these adjectives. Analyses of the data for all target-persons yielded a "large" first factor labeled "social morality." This factor included such items as "reliable," "kind," and "modest," among others. The items included on the factor are related to maintaining harmony in interpersonal relations and appear consistent with a collectivistic orientation.

The final concern of implicit personality theories is how information is combined. Wegner and Vallacher (1977) argue that individuals go to extreme lengths to achieve consistency in combining information about others. Triandis (1968) reviewed several cross-cultural studies of cognitive consistency, concluding that "people do utilize a number of judgment continuums that are related to each other in roughly comparable ways across the cultures studied so far. People from different cultures combine simple stimuli to make complex judgments in roughly similar ways. On the other hand, they do utilize different weights for different characteristics" (p. 729).

Given this overview of cultural variations in implicit personality theories, we will now turn our attention to specific personality factors that influence interpersonal communication. In the following two sections we will discuss cultural variability in self-monitoring and self-consciousness, personality factors included in uncertainty reduction theory. We will then look at communication apprehension, communicator style, and locus of control, three dimensions that are related to specific aspects of interpersonal communication.

SELF-MONITORING

Snyder (1974) characterizes self-monitoring as "self-observation and self-control guided by situational cues to social appropriateness" (p. 526). He goes on to argue that "the self-monitoring individual is one who, out of concern for social appropriateness, is particularly sensitive to the expression and self-presentation of others in social situations and uses those cues as guidelines for monitoring his [or her] own self-presentation" (p. 528).

Berger and his associates (Berger, 1979; Berger & Douglas, 1981; Berger & Perkins, 1978) have linked self-monitoring to uncertainty reduction. Their research suggests passive uncertainty reduction strategies are influenced by self-monitoring. Berger and Douglas, for example, discovered differences in the perception of how informative formal and informal situations are in reducing uncertainty by level of self-monitoring: Low self-monitors perceive formal situations as more informative, while high self-monitors see informal situations as more informative. This finding is consistent with Ickes and Barnes (1977), who reported high self-monitors initiate and regulate conversations more, initiate more conversational sequences, and have a greater need to talk than low self-monitors. Research by Tardy and Hoseman (1982) revealed that high self-monitors exhibit more self-disclosure flexibility than low self-monitors, while Gudykunst and Nishida (1984) discovered that self-monitoring has an impact upon two of the interactive strategies, intent to self-disclose and intent to interrogate in Japanese-North American communication. Self-monitoring also has been found to be related to the third interactive strategy, deception detection: High self-monitors are more accurate than low self-monitors in detecting deception (Brandt, Miller, & Hocking, 1980a; Siegman & Reynolds, 1983). Finally, Gudykunst, Yang, and Nishida's (1985) research revealed that self-monitoring is related to the use of uncertainty reduction strategies across cultures, while Gudykunst (1985a, 1985e) found that self-monitoring influences uncertainty reduction strategies in intercultural relationships.

Snyder (1974) developed a 25-item instrument to measure self-monitoring that includes true-false descriptive statements. His research revealed an internal reliability of .70 and test-retest reliability of .83 for the scale. To demonstrate construct validity, he presented research on peer ratings, stage actors, psychiatric patients, expressions of behaviors, and attention to social comparison information (see Snyder, 1979, for a review). In the study of peer ratings, for example, Snyder found that individuals with high scores on the self-monitoring scale are good at learning what is socially appropriate in new situations, have good self-control of their emotional expressions, and can use this ability effectively to create the impressions they want.

Snyder (1974) assumes that the self-monitoring scale is unidimensional. This assumption, however, has been called into question by several studies. Briggs, Cheek, and Buss (1980), for example, found three factors in the scale that they labeled acting, extroversion, and other-directedness. Tobey and Tunnel (1981) found three similar factors, but the items loading on the factors varied somewhat. Gabrenya and Arkin (1980), in contrast, discovered four factors when they examined the construct validity of the scale. They labeled these dimensions theatrical acting ability, sociability/social anxiety, other-directedness, and speaking ability. Dillard, Hunter, and Burgoon's (1984) research also revealed four factors: extroversion, sociability, other-directedness, and acting. These findings are consistent with Briggs and Cheek's (1986) argument that the self-monitoring scale is not unidimensional, but rather it has at least three factors.

Snyder and Gangestad (Gangestad & Snyder, 1985a, 1985b: Snyder & Gangestad, 1986) argued that studies that find more than one factor have used rotated factor structures, rather than unrotated structures, which they claim are more appropriate when the scale is unidimensional. They go on to suggest that by omitting items that discriminate poorly between low and high self-monitors, the low reliability of the total scale in previous studies can be overcome. Snyder and Gangestad (1986), therefore, proffered a "new" 18-item version of the self-monitoring scale that accounts for a majority of the common variance (62% with three factors extracted) and has higher reliability (.70 *alpha*) than the original 25-item instrument.

Gudykunst, Yang, and Nishida (1987) argued that individualism should influence self-monitoring. Cultures high on individualism focus on the self, not others. In individualistic cultures, knowing the context is not necessary to predict others' behavior. Cultures low on individualism (i.e., collectivist cultures), in contrast, value conformity to in groups and group memberships. In collectivistic cultures, knowing the context is essential to predicting others' behavior.

On the surface, it might appear that highly individualistic cultures would reinforce low self-monitoring, and collectivistic cultures would reinforce high self-monitoring (see Snyder, 1987, for a statement of this position). This, however, is *not* the case. Snyder (1979) reviewed research on self-monitoring, concluding that high self-monitors imagine what the prototypic person for the situation would be and try to be that person, while low self-monitors "draw upon an enduring self-image or self-conception that represents knowledge of her or his characteristic actions in the behavioral domains most relevant to the situation" (p. 103). Members of collectivistic cultures' self-conceptions include their relationships with others present in the situation (Doi, 1986; Marsella et al., 1985; Yum, 1987b) and the context influences how they define themselves. They, therefore, must take the context and status relationships into consideration when deciding how to behave in a particular situation. This suggests that they do not base their behavior on how a prototypic person would behave in the situation. In other words, they would not be high self-monitors given Snyder's conceptualization. (Note: If self-monitoring were conceptualized as to include the context and status relationships, members of collectivistic cultures would be high self-monitors. Since the conceptualizations developed in the United States do not include these components, the opposite must be predicted.) Gudykunst, Yang, and Nishida (1987) consequently predicted that individualism influences self-monitoring. Given the scores on this dimension, self-monitoring should be higher in the United States than in Japan and Korea, and the two collectivistic cultures should not differ significantly in levels of self-monitoring.

Results of Gudykunst, Yang, and Nishida's (1987) study indicated that the U.S. sample reported significantly higher levels of self-monitoring than both the Japanese and the Korean samples and that these two samples did not report significantly different levels of self-monitoring. Consistent with predictions derived from Hofstede's (1980) analysis, members of cultures high on the individualism dimension engaged in more self-monitoring than individuals from cultures low on this dimension (i.e., collectivistic cultures). While self-monitoring in individualistic cultures involves behaving as prototypic persons would behave in the situation at hand, members of collectivistic cultures must take into consideration the context, the specific individuals present in the situation, and their status relationship with them in deciding how to behave in a particular situation.

SELF-CONSCIOUSNESS

Self-consciousness, the "consistent tendency of persons to direct attention inward or outward" (Fenigstein et al., 1975, p. 522) is conceived as having three components or dimensions. Private self-consciousness is similar to Jung's (1933) conception of introversion and is concerned with attending to inner thoughts and feelings (e.g., "I reflect about myself a lot"). Public self-consciousness, in contrast, involves a general awareness of the self in relation to others and is related to Mead's (1934) analysis of the self as a social object (e.g., "I'm very concerned about the way I present myself"). The final dimension, social anxiety, is defined by a discomfort in the presence of others (e.g., "I feel anxious when I speak in front of a group"). Public and private self-consciousness, therefore, refer to the process of self-attention, while social anxiety involves a reaction to the process (Fenigstein et al., 1975).

Research indicates that the three dimensions of self-consciousness have an effect on behavior (e.g., Brockner, 1979; Buss, 1980; Fenigstein, 1979; Lloyd, Paulsen, & Brockner, 1983; Scheier, 1976; Scheier, Buss, & Buss, 1978; Scheier & Carver, 1977, 1981). Scheier and Carver (1977), for example, found that high private self-conscious persons react in a more extreme fashion than persons low on the dimension. Similarly, Scheier et al. reported that high private self-conscious persons are more attentive and knowledgeable about their own attitudes than are those low in private self-consciousness. Buss (1980) concluded that public and private self-consciousness produce different effects on aggression, dominance, and self-descriptions. Gudykunst, Yang, and Nishida's (1985) research, however, suggested that self-consciousness does not directly influence the strategies individuals use to reduce uncertainty across cultures.

Fenigstein et al.'s (1975) self-consciousness scale consists of 23 items that yield three factorially distinct dimensions: public self-consciousness (seven items), private self-consciousness (10 items), and social anxiety (six items). Their research reveals that the instrument has adequate test-retest reliability: .84 for public, .70 for private, .73 for social anxiety, and .80 for the total score. A substantial amount of evidence also has been presented to establish the scale's convergent and discriminate validity (see Carver & Scheier, 1981, for a review). Fromming and Carver (1981), for example, found that private self-consciousness correlates with overall compliance, while after controlling for the effect of private self-consciousness a significant but opposite correlation is displayed between public self-consciousness and compliance. This research and that reported by Carver and Scheier (1981) suggest that the two dimensions have independent and opposite influences on other variables. Correlations among the three subscales reported are low, fluctuating around .20 (Carver & Glass, 1976; Fenigstein et al., 1975).

In their study of self-consciousness across cultures, Gudykunst, Yang, and Nishida (1987) argued that since uncertainty avoidance influences the level of anxiety in a culture, this dimension of cultural variability should affect social anxiety. Specifically, they expected that Japanese and Koreans would exhibit higher levels of social anxiety than people in the United States. Their findings revealed that the differences in social anxiety were consistent with Hofstede's (1980) uncertainty avoidance dimension, as hypothesized. Uncertainty avoidance involves a lack of tolerance for ambiguity and uncertainty that results in higher levels of anxiety in cultures with high levels of uncertainty avoidance. Both Japan and Korea are near the top of the uncertainty avoidance scale, while the United States is relatively low. In addition to being consistent with Hofstede, the results for social anxiety are compatible with previous cross-cultural studies of communication apprehension (discussed in the next section). Social anxiety as defined by Fenigstein et al. (1975) appears to be related closely to communication apprehension.

Klopf and Cambra's (1979) research indicates that both Japanese and Koreans have higher levels of communication apprehension than do North Americans. Social anxiety correlated .50 to .70 with the short form of McCroskey's (1978) measure of communication apprehension in Gudykunst, Yang, and Nishida's (1987) study.

The focus of public self-consciousness is on the self as a context-free social object. The dimension of culture most relevant to the self is individualism. Cultures high in individualism place an emphasis upon the self, while cultures low in individualism (i.e., collectivistic) emphasize membership in ingroups and see the self as embedded in a context and social relationships. Gudykunst, Yang, and Nishida (1987), therefore, hypothesized that individualism influences public self-consciousness. Given the scores on this dimension for the three cultures, it was predicted that people in the United States exhibited higher levels of public self-consciousness than would Japanese and Koreans. Their results for public self-consciousness were consistent with the hypothesis. Fenigstein and his associates (1975) argue that public self-consciousness involves "a general awareness of the self as a social object that has an effect on others" (p. 523). The focus here is on the self, but the self outside of a context and specific social relationships. Given this focus, people in cultures high on individualism should have higher levels of public self-consciousness than people in cultures low on individualism (i.e., collectivist).

Private self-consciousness involves introspection about the self. The dimension of culture most directly relevant to introspection is masculinity. Cultures high on this dimension value performance and ambition, both of which require introspection about individual abilities. Hofstede also points out that members of masculine cultures tend to be field independent (i.e., rely on internal frames of reference), while members of feminine cultures tend to be field dependent (i.e., rely on external frames of reference). While field dependence tends to be associated with the degree of conformity in a culture (i.e., high uncertainty avoidance), DeVos (1980) has shown that Japanese do not fit this pattern, rather they are highly field independent. This is consistent with Hofstede's data, which reveal that the Japanese culture has the highest masculinity score. Gudykunst, Yang, and Nishida (1987), accordingly, suggested that masculinity influences private self-consciousness. More specifically, they anticipated that people in Japan are higher in private self-consciousness than those in Korea and the United States. Their results revealed that the Japanese report significantly greater private self-consciousness than Koreans, while the U.S. sample falls in between, but is not significantly different from either. The pattern of results is consistent with their hypothesis. High masculinity cultures (i.e., Japan) value performance and ambition, while cultures low in masculinity (i.e., Korea) value service and interdependence. Ambition requires that individuals are attentive to their own thoughts, feelings, and attitude (i.e., high private self-consciousness), while focusing on the values of service and interdependence requires less introspection. The results also appear to be consistent with recent discussions of self-consciousness in Japan (Doi, 1986) and Korea (Yum, 1987b).

COMMUNICATION APPREHENSION

McCroskey (1984) views communication apprehension as "a relatively enduring, personality-type orientation toward a given mode of communication across a wide variety of contents" (p. 16; italics omitted). Daly and Stafford (1984) reviewed research on the correlates of communication apprehension. Their review revealed that communication apprehension is related inversely to self-esteem, individuation, self-disclosure, self-monitoring, argumentativeness, assertiveness, responsiveness, attentiveness, and perceptiveness. It is associated positively with loneliness, public self-consciousness, social isolation, alienation, anomie, dogmatism, loss of control, and intolerance of ambiguity, to name only a few of the major relationships observed in previous research.

There have been several cross-cultural studies of communication apprehension. Klopf, Cambra, and Ishii (1983), for example, reviewed research on communication apprehension among several thousand Japanese (students and businesspersons). Their results clearly indicate that Japanese display higher levels of verbal communication apprehension than comparable samples in individualistic cultures such as the United States and Australia. Similarly, Klopf and Cambra (1979) report higher levels of communication apprehension in Korea than in the United States and Australia, with no difference between the Australian and U.S. samples (for a summary of the same data omitting Australia, see Ishii, Klopf, & Cambra, 1979). Other studies (e.g., Crocker, Klopf, & Cambra, 1978) also have not found significant differences between the United States and Australia (for related research see Fayer, McCroskey, & Richmond, 1982). Supporting data comes from studies of shyness across cultures, that is, Pilkonis and Zimbardo (1979) found that Chinese are shier than North Americans (see also Zimbardo, 1977).

The finding that Japan and Korea have higher levels of communication apprehension than Australia or the United States should not be taken to imply that communication apprehension or shyness are "problems" in these cultures. In fact, probably the opposite is true—it is valued. Elliot, Scott, Jensen, and McDonald's (1982) research illustrates this position. They found that Koreans are attracted more to individuals who do not engage in a lot of verbal activity than they are to those who engage in high levels of verbal activity. The opposite finding, however, emerges in the United States. This suggests that the behaviors that are associated with high communication apprehension are valued in Korea. A similar argument can be made for Japan (see Okabe, 1983). This line of argument is consistent with the view that high-context communication predominates in collectivistic cultures like Japan and Korea and, therefore, high scores on McCroskey's (1978) Personal Report of Communication Apprehension are to be expected in collectivistic cultures.

COMMUNICATOR STYLE

People perceive not only the content of verbal and nonverbal cues, but also the way cues are communicated. The latter provides information concerning how the former, the content, is to be interpreted. Norton (1978, 1983) refers to the way the content is communicated as communicator style. More specifically, he defines this construct as "the way one verbally and paraverbally interacts to signal how literal meaning should be taken, interpreted, filtered, or understood" (1978, p. 99).

The communicator style construct is conceptualized as including 10 "predictor" styles and one "dependent" variable (Norton, 1978, 1983). The predictor styles involve ways of dealing with people during interaction: (1) dominant—the strategies that lessen the roles of others during communication, (2) dramatic—the exaggeration and/or coloring of communication content, (3) contentious—the negative aspects associated with being aggressive or argumentative, (4) relaxed—a calm, collected, not anxious strategy, (5) impression leaving—the impact communicators have on those with whom they interact, (6) animated—the frequent and intense use of behaviors such as eye contact, body movement, etc., (7) precise—a concern for proof and accuracy in discourse, (8) attentive—social sensitivity as illustrated by listening and showing interest in what others are saying, (9) friendly—the tendency to encourage others and to acknowledge their contributions to interactions, and (10) open—the tendency to express opinions, feelings, and emotions and to reveal personal aspects of the self. The dependent construct, communicator image, is "a general assessment of a person's style of communicating" (Montgomery & Norton, 1981, p. 126).

Two kinds of expectations influence communicator style formation: cultural and idiosyncratic (Norton, 1983). Cultural expectations refer to a culture's norms or central tendencies concerning communication styles, while idiosyncratic expectations refer to individuals' tendencies regarding their way of sending messages. Individuals' communicator styles, therefore, are conditioned by their culture on the one hand, but they deviate from the central tendencies based upon their personal idiosyncratic experience.

Only one published report of cross-cultural comparisons of communicator style appears to exist. Klopf and Cambra (1981) present data comparing samples from Japan and the United States on Norton's (1978) version of the communicator style construct. They found significant differences on 8 of the 10 dimensions studied. The Japanese sample scored lower than the U.S. sample on attentive, contentious, animated, impression-leaving and communicator image. The U.S. sample scored lower than the Japanese sample on relaxed, dramatic, and open.

These findings appear to be consistent with Hofstede's dimensions of cultural variability. Specifically, it would be expected that members of high uncertainty avoidance cultures (e.g., Japan) would be more open and dramatic than members of low uncertainty avoidance cultures (e.g., the United States). It also would be predicted that members of individualistic cultures (e.g., the United States) would be more attentive to verbal communication, more contentious, leave stronger impressions based on verbal communication, and present a stronger individual communicator image than members of collectivistic cultures (e.g., Japan).

LOCUS OF CONTROL

There is extensive research on Rotter's (1966) locus of control construct (see Hui, 1982, for a recent review of cross-cultural research). Rotter's basic hypothesis can be summarized as follows:

> If a person perceives a reinforcement as contingent upon his [or her] own behavior, then the occurrence of either a positive or a negative reinforcement will strengthen or weaken the potential for that behavior to recur in

same or similar situations. If he [or she] sees the reinforcement as being outside his [or her] own control or not contingent, that is, depending upon chance, fate, powerful others, or unpredictables, then the preceding behavior is less likely to be strengthened or weakened. (p. 5)

When behavior is viewed as a function of the individual's own action, an internal locus of control exists. When behavior is not a function of the individual's own action, in contrast, it is an external locus of control.

Several studies report that Japanese are controlled externally more than people in the United States (Bond & Tornatzky, 1973; Krampen & Wieberg, 1981; Mahler, 1974). Similar results emerge for Chinese-U.S. comparisons (e.g., Hsieh, Skybut, & Lotsof, 1969). There is, however, contradictory evidence in two unpublished studies cited by Hui (1982). Reitz and Groff (1972) found that Thais are more external with respect to leadership than people in the United States, but there are not significant differences in other areas. In a follow-up study, Reitz and Groff (1974) discovered that respondents in Thailand and Japan are controlled externally more than respondents in Mexico and the United States. They attributed these differences to an "East-West" difference, .but research by Parsons and Schneider (1974) and McGinnies, Nord-holm, Ward, and Bhanthumnavin (1974) is inconsistent with Reitz and Groff's (1974) findings. Parsons and Schneider, for example, found that two Oriental cultures, Japan and India, are highest and lowest in terms of externality, and that all of the Western and Middle Eastern cultures studied fall between the two. McGinnies and associates similarly discovered that external locus of control is highest in Sweden, followed by Japan, Australia, the United States, and New Zealand. Both of the latter studies also revealed sex differences in locus of control.

Given Hofstede's (1980) theory of cultural differentiation, it would be expected that members of collectivistic cultures are controlled externally more than members of individualistic cultures. Much of the research is consistent with this argument (e.g., Bond & Tornatzky, 1973; Hsieh et al., 1969; Krampen & Wieberg, 1981; Mahler, 1974; Reitz & Groff, 1972, 1974). Parsons and Schneider (1974) and McGinnies et al. (1974), however, are inconsistent. The inconsistencies in these studies can be explained by incorporating other dimensions of cultural variability into the explanation. Specifically, it appears that when collectivistic cultures are also low in uncertainty avoidance, external locus of control does not operate and individuals are controlled more internally. Further, when an individualistic culture is low in masculinity, its members take others' opinions into consideration and, therefore, are controlled externally more than people in masculine, individualistic cultures. This argument, however, must be considered speculative until further research is conducted explicitly to test the predictions.

CONCLUSION

We examined cross-cultural variability in personality in this chapter. The research reviewed suggests that variations in personality (i.e., self-monitoring, self-consciousness, communication apprehension, communicator style, locus of control) can be linked to individualism-collectivism. Intracultural research suggests that personality factors differentially influence interpersonal communication processes (see, for example, McCroskey & Daly, 1987). When combined with the research on cross-cultural variability, this line of research clearly suggests that different personality variables may yield different relationships with other interpersonal communication variables across cultures. To date, however, there is virtually no research linking these variables to other interpersonal processes. Future research should, therefore, examine relationships between personality variables and other interpersonal communication variables across cultures in order to establish cross-cultural generalizability for relationships observed in intracultural research in order to integrate culture into current theories and/or to specify scope conditions for statements in theories. One personality factor that may be particularly useful in future research is Triandis and his associates' (1985, 1986) idiocentrism-allocentrism, the personality dimension that corresponds to the individualism-collectivism dimension of cultural variability (see Chapter 2 for a discussion of this personality dimension).

8

Social Cognitive Processes

Social cognition involves "how people think about people" (Wegner & Vallacher, 1977, p. viii). "There is no evidence . . . that any cultural group wholly lacks a basic process such as abstraction, or inferential reasoning, or categorization" (Cole & Scribner, 1974, p. 193). Rather, it appears that cultural variations influence which of the alternative processes are evoked in particular situations. It is impossible to discuss social cognitive processes en toto here. The focus, therefore, is on those areas of research that have been linked to cultural variations and that influence interpersonal communication, including information processing strategies, persuasive strategy selection, attributional processes, and conflict management styles.

INFORMATION PROCESSING

There is extensive research on information processing across cultures, but much of the work is strictly psychological, with little direct linkage to interpersonal communication. Deregowski (1980), for example, reviewed cross-cultural research on perception, while Pick (1980) looked at psychological perspectives and Price-Williams (1980) summarized anthropological perspectives on cognition. Further, Cole and Means (1981) reviewed cross-cultural research on how people think. To fully understand cross-cultural differences in information processing it is necessary to be familiar with this research. Since excellent reviews exist, we have omitted this work to conserve space. We, therefore, focus on research that has direct application to interpersonal communication in this chapter, including field independence-dependence, patterns of thought, persuasive strategy selection, and conflict management.

Field Independence—Field Dependence

Differentiation refers to the "complexity of a system's structure. A less differentiated system is a relatively homogeneous structural state; a more differentiated system is a relatively heterogeneous state" (Witkin, Dyk, Faterson, Goodenough, & Karp , 1962, p. 9). As differentiation increases, increased specialization and separation of psychological processes occur (i.e., cognition is separated from affect and behavior). Thought based on increased differentiation is field independent, while thought based on lower levels of differentiation is field dependent. Field independence, therefore, involves differentiated and analytical thinking, rather than diffuse and global thinking. Witkin and his associates (1962) suggest that field dependence is associated with forming impressions of people based on physical characteristics, conforming with authority, and showing relatively little interest in individual achievement. Witkin and Berry (1975) also contend that field-dependent people are less impersonal and more attentive in their interactions with others than are field-independent. Field-dependent thought tends to be associative, while field-independent thought tends to be abstractive.

Field independence and field dependence tend to be associated with cultural variations. Witkin and Berry (1975) conclude:

> The evidence from these studies together suggests that a relatively field-dependent cognitive style, and other characteristics of limited differentiation, are likely to be prevalent in social settings characterized by insistence on adherence to authority both in society and in the family, by the use of strict or even harsh socialization practices to enforce this conformance, and by tight social organization. In contrast, a relatively field-independent cognitive style and greater differentiation are likely to be prevalent in social settings that are more encouraging of autonomous functioning, which are more lenient in their childrearing practices, and which are loose in social organization. (p. 46)

Field dependence, therefore, appears to be associated with tight social structures (Boldt, 1978) and high power distance (Hofstede, 1980), while field independence is associated with loose social structures and low power distance.

Patterns of Thought

Glenn (1981) isolates two dimensions that can be used to describe patterns of thought across cultures: abstractive-associative and universalism-particularism. When knowledge is acquired through a direct experience with the environment, it is associative. When thought is codified into precise meanings, abstraction takes place. Associative patterns tend to be syncretic, diffuse, indefinite, and rigid, while abstract patterns tend to be discrete, articulated, definite, and flexible. Glenn (1981) points out that

> associative reasoning is marked by "arbitrary" ties between informational units. Abstractive reasoning is marked by (1) the definition of information that is relevant to a given situation, and (2) the definition of the relationship between informational units. . . . The primary process for the acquisition of knowledge appears to be associative. Abstraction appears as the primary process for the organization of knowledge. (p. 57)

The use of associative thought does not readily allow new or novel information to be integrated. While associative and abstractive thought both exist in all cultures, one tends to predominate.

An emphasis on associative versus abstractive thought is related to deriving identity from ascription and achievement in that assessing achievement requires abstraction. It also is related to specificity-diffuseness, with associative thought related to a tendency for diffuse response patterns and abstract thought associated with specific patterns. Triandis (1984) argues that people with associative patterns of information processing depend on oral, face-to-face communication and find it difficult to follow written instructions.

Universalism involves seeing the world through conceptualizations that are reflected in definitions of words. Universalistic processing does not take into consideration experiences that make individuals different; it is abstract. Particularism, in contrast, recognizes specifics; it tends to be associative, reflecting personal lives (Glenn, 1981). Particularistic information processing starts with specific observations and extracts generalizations, while universalistic begins with broad categories and determines how observations fit the categories. These correspond to inductive and deductive processes, respectively. Universalism and abstraction tend to go together, while particularism and associative patterns of thought also coincide. Particularism-universalism should be related to Hofstede's (1980) uncertainty avoidance dimension of cultural variability. Specifically, universalistic patterns should dominate in cultures high in uncertainty avoidance, while particularistic patterns predominate in low uncertainty avoidance cultures. Differences in universalism-particularism and abstraction-associative patterns of thought may explain differences in the approaches to the study of communication in Europe and the United States.

Triandis (1984) points out that particularism tends to be probabilistic, while universalism tends to be absolutistic. This dimension, therefore, may account for differences in probabilistic thinking discovered by Wright and his colleagues (Wright et al., 1978; Wright & Phillips, 1980). They found that the British tend to view uncertainty in terms of well-calibrated degrees of probability, while people from Hong Kong, Malaysia, and Indonesia tend to view it in a less calibrated way (i.e., either total certainty or total uncertainty). These differences also can be explained by Hofstede's (1980) theory of cultural differentiation. The four cultures have similar scores on two of Hofstede's (1983) dimensions of culture (uncertainty avoidance and masculinity) and differences on two others (power distance and individualism). The three Asian cultures, however, differ on power distance. The only dimension consistent is individualism. To account for the patterns that emerge in the relationship between individualism-collectivism, low- and high-context communication (Hall, 1976) must be taken into consideration. High-context communication (i.e., the meaning of messages is highly dependent on the context) predominates in collectivistic cultures, while low-context communication (i.e., the context has a low impact on the meaning of messages) predominates in individualistic cultures. When context provides information, certainty is dependent upon knowing the context. If the context is known, uncertainty is low; if it is not known, uncertainty is high. It, therefore, follows that members of collectivistic, high-context cultures would depend upon knowing the context in order to calibrate their uncertainty.

Persuasive Strategy Selection

Patterns of thought are related directly to styles of persuasion. Universalism and abstraction, for example, lead to an axiomatic-deductive style of persuasion, that is, a style that begins with generalities and proceeds to specifics or from fundamental principles to their implications (this style predominates in the USSR; Glenn, Witmeyer, & Stevenson, 1977). Particularism and associative thought, in contrast, are related to a factual-inductive style of persuasion, that is, beginning with the relevant facts and drawing conclusions from them (used in the United States). Both of these styles involve an affective neutrality orientation (Parsons, 1951) toward persuasion. An affective orientation toward persuasion is related to Glenn et al.'s (1977) affective-intuitive style of persuasion, that is, using affective or emotional messages to persuade (used in Arab cultures).

Burgoon, Dillard, Doran, and Miller (1982) examined differences in persuasive strategy selection between Asian-Americans and Caucasians in Hawaii. They found that culture influenced the use of 8 of the 16 strategies in Marwell and Schmitt's (1967) typology. Specifically, they found that Asian-Americans are more likely to use the strategies of promise, positive expertise, pregiving, liking, positive altercasting, negative altercasting, positive self-feeling, and positive self-esteem than Caucasians. All of these strategies tend to have high social acceptability. Miller, Reynolds, and Cambra (1982) examined specific differences between Caucasians and different Asian-American ethnic groups in Hawaii. They found that Caucasians are more likely to use strategies that are not highly socially acceptable (e.g., negative expertise, aversive stimulation, threat) than Japanese-Americans and Chinese-Americans in Hawaii. Hirokawa and Miyahara (1986) compared compliance-gaining strategies used by Japanese and North American managers. They found that North American managers tend to use reward- or punishment-based strategies, while Japanese managers tend to use altruism-based strategies. These findings appear to be consistent with Nishiyama's (1971) analysis of persuasion in Japan.

There are other cross-cultural studies of compliance-gaining strategies that yield results inconsistent with the research cited above, but they have either used international students in the United States as respondents (e.g., Lustig & Myers, 1983; Shatzer, Funkhouser, & Hesse, 1984) or studied natives in their culture with the research not conducted in their native language (e.g., Neulip & Hazleton, 1985, studied Japanese in Japan, but their research instrument was in English). They, therefore, are omitted here.

Burgoon et al.'s (1982), Miller et al.'s (1982), and Hirokawa and Miyahara's (1986) findings appear to be consistent with Hofstede's (1980) individualism-collectivism dimension of cultural variability. Specifically, members of collectivistic cultures take the context into consideration and use strategies that are socially appropriate, while members of individualistic cultures focus on the person they are trying to persuade and use strategies that may be perceived as socially inappropriate.

Conflict Management

Ting-Toomey (1985) presents a theory of culture and conflict that addresses why, when, what, and how conflict varies as a function of Hall's (1976) low- and high-context communication schema. Following Olsen (1978), she draws a distinction between "instrumental" and "expressive" reasons for conflict. Instrumental conflict is marked by "opposing practices or goals," and expressive conflict stems mainly from "desires for tension release, from hostile feelings" (Olsen, 1978, p. 308). She argues that individuals in low-context cultures are better able to separate the conflict issue from the person involved in the conflict than are individuals in high-context cultures. Low-context culture individuals can fight and scream at one another over a task-oriented point and yet are able to remain friends afterwards, whereas in the high-context culture system the instrumental issue is tied closely with the person who originated the issue. To disagree openly or confront someone in public is a severe blow and an extreme insult, causing both sides to "lose face." Especially in the case of superior-subordinate communication in the high-context culture system, individuals are supposed to engage in a normative process of "reciprocal sensitivity" toward one another, and ritualistically act out the roles of the *sempai-kohai* (senior-junior) relationship with a certain degree of respect and in accordance to the implicit, culturally written scripts.

Since low-context culture individuals view the world in analytic, linear logic terms, and view issues and persons as dichotomous, Ting-Toomey (1985) argues that persons in low-context cultures characterize conflict events as primarily instrumental-oriented. Individuals in high-context cultures, who mainly perceive the world in synthetic, spiral logic terms, punctuate the same conflict event as expressive-oriented in focus. Individuals in high-context cultures have a difficult time separating the conflict event from the affective domain. For them, the conflict issue and the conflict person are the same, hardly separable from the other.

The second question regarding conflict that Ting-Toomey (1985) addressed is concerned with the specific conditions in which conflicts are most likely to occur in the two cultural systems. Jackson's (1975) normative system model may be useful in answering this question. According to Jackson, a normative system is "any system of expectations by others for actor's conduct" (p. 237). Social actions between two actors rhyme in synchrony when "the covert, symbolic responses of others to actor's conduct coincide, i.e., the expectations are 'shared'" (p. 263).

Ting-Toomey (1985) argues that the rules are different for conflict in low-context and high-context cultures. Since the low-context cultures contain low cultural demand and low cultural constraint characteristics, a relatively high degree of uncertainty and risk prevails in each low-context culture interpersonal interaction. Conversely, given the fact that high-context cultures maintain high cultural demand and high cultural constraint characteristics, once the cultural scripts are mastered, a relatively low degree of uncertainty and risk prevails in each high-context culture interpersonal encounter. Conflict potentials are relatively higher between strangers in low-context cultures than in high-context cultures because the players in low-context cultures usually play by idiosyncratic rules and only improvise coordination on the spot. Furthermore, the probability of making an interpersonal "interaction error" is also higher in low-context cultures than in high-context cultures because there are no specific, collective (or cultural) normative rules to govern and guide the different interaction episodes.

Low-context culture misunderstandings and potential conflicts are most likely to occur when individual normative expectations of acceptable behaviors are violated. High-context culture misunderstandings and potential conflict tensions are most likely to happen when the collective or cultural normative expectations of appropriate behaviors in a situation are violated implicitly. The high-context culture interaction rituals are more stringent and rule-bound than the low-context culture interaction rituals, and it is, therefore, more noticeable when a stranger unintentionally violates high-context culture interaction routines than it is in low-context culture interaction routines. In short, interaction deviates from cultural normative expectations are more easily identified in a normative homogeneous system (as in the case of high-context cultures) than in a normative heterogeneous system (as in the case of low-context cultures).

The third question concerning the normative relation between conflict and culture Ting-Toomey (1985) addressed asks: What kinds of general attitude do the conflict players hold toward antagonisms and tensions in a low-context culture system and a high-context culture system? If an individual's interpretive scheme is grounded in a particular culture and attitude is embedded in this interpretive process, culture also frames one's attitude. Individuals who are situated in different cultural systems learn different attitudes toward conflict. In low-context cultures, which are characterized by an action- or a doing-orientation, the conflict players are likely to assume a direct, confrontational stance when differences of opinion occur. This doing-orientation approach also serves as a normative force for both conflict parties to press for resolution and early closure. In high-context cultures the predominant mode of conflict attitude can best be described as evasive and nonconfrontational. Players in high-context cultures believe in the use of implicit or restricted codes. A calculated degree of vagueness and circumlocution typically is employed when tensions and anxieties mount.

Miyahara (1984) commented on differences in communication style between North American and Japanese managers using the following vivid example: If a North American supervisor must inform his or her subordinate that she or he is not satisfied with the sales proposal, she or he would probably use a very explicit, direct response, such as, "I can't accept this proposal as submitted. You should come up with some better ideas" (p. 9). A Japanese supervisor, in contrast, would say, "While I have the highest regard for your abilities, I would not be completely honest if I did not express my disappointment at this proposal. I must ask that you reflect further on the proposal you have submitted to me" (p. 9). Hence, tactfulness and indirect speech are two modes of attitude and behavior valued in high-context cultures.

In low-context cultures, open confrontation of ideas and direct, issue-oriented discussion are valued modes of human expressiveness. Whereas revealment is vital in low-context cultures, concealment is vital in high-context systems. Although members of high-context cultures may experience tremendous inner tensions intrapersonally (culturally or individually induced), these individuals are not likely to express their emotions openly and to act on them publicly. Whereas members of low-context cultures hold a direct-active stance toward conflict, such as confronting the conflict issue or changing some aspects of the conflict situation, members of high-context cultures hold a relatively indirect-inactive stance toward conflicts, such as avoiding or ignoring the conflict situation. Barnlund (1975a) notes:

> Regardless of social circumstance [North] Americans prefer to defend themselves actively, exploring and developing the rationale for positions they have taken. When pushed, they may resort to still more aggressive forms that utilize humor, sarcasm, or denunciation. Among Japanese, the reactions are more varied, but defenses tend to be more passive, permit withdrawal, and allow greater concealment . . . the Japanese may ritualize encounters to avoid the triggering of threat, [North] Americans may find such situations an inevitable consequence of their greater expressiveness. (p. 423)

The final question on conflict and culture Ting-Toomey (1985) addressed asks: How do the players actually "play" in low-context culture conflict as compared with high-context culture conflict? Communication attitude and style are linked interdependently. Style is the overt manifestation of cognitive orientation. Style refers to the behavioral verbal and nonverbal means of expressing oneself. Style also embodies the attitudinal and affective components of one's reactions toward conflict management.

According to Glenn, Witmeyer, and Stevenson's (1977) study of cross-cultural persuasive styles, people in the United States typically engage in the factual-inductive style of argument; people in the Soviet Union typically use the axiomatic-deductive style of logic; and people in Arab cultures primarily engage in the affective-intuitive style of emotional appeal. For Glenn et al., the factual-inductive style is based on the study of pertinent facts and moves inductively toward conclusions. The axiomatic-deductive style proceeds from the general to the particular, from fundamental principles to their implications. Finally, the affective-intuitive style is based on affective, emotional messages to persuade the audience. The affective-intuitive style of communication can be divided into two levels of analysis: the use of circumlocution or flowery speech to appeal to the emotional response of the audience, and the use of ambiguity and understatement to diffuse the conflict topic.

Members of low-context cultures are more likely to bargain using the actual-inductive style or axiomatic-deductive style of handling conflicts than members of high-context cultures. People in high-context cultures, in contrast, are more likely to bargain using the affective-intuitive style of managing conflict episodes. Whereas low-context cultures value line logic, high-context cultures value point logic. Members of low-context cultures tend to approach conflicts from the mind, while members of high-context cultures tend to approach conflicts from the heart. Table 8.1 summarizes the issues regarding conflict and culture addressed in Ting-Toomey's (1985) theory.

To follow up on her theoretical work on culture and conflict, Ting-Toomey (1986a) examined conflict communication styles in Black (high-context) and White (low-context) subcultures in the United States, using Putnam and Wilson's (1982) Organizational Communication Conflict Instrument (OCCI) that measures three interpersonal conflict styles: control, nonconfrontation, and solution-orientation. Her results indicated that Blacks use more controlling styles than Whites. Conversely, Whites use more solution-orientation styles than Blacks.

Chua and Gudykunst (1987) also tested Ting-Toomey's (1985) theory of culture and conflict. Their findings support the contention that members of low-context cultures use the solution orientation more than members of high-context cultures. Chua and Gudykunst also found that nonconfrontation is used more in high- than in low-context cultures.

Ting-Toomey's (1985) theory and Chua and Gudykunst's (1987) study are consistent with Bond, Wan, Leung, and Giacalone's (1985) findings that revealed that Chinese (a collectivistic, high-context culture) respondents are likely to advise an executive to meet with an insulter and the target of the insult separately so that conflict between the two can be avoided. North Americans (an individualistic, low-

TABLE 8.1
Summary of Characteristics of Conflict in
Low- and High-Context Cultures

Key Questions	Low-Context Conflict	High-Context Conflict
Why	analytic, linear logic	synthetic, spiral logic
	instrumental-oriented	expressive-oriented
	dichtomy between conflict and conflict parties	integration of conflict and conflict parties
When	individualistic-oriented	group-oriented
	low collective normative expectations	high collective normative expectations
	violations of individual expectations create conflict potentials	violations of collective expectations create conflict potentials
What	revealment	concealment
	direct, confrontational attitude	indirect, nonconfrontational attitude
How	action and solution-oriented	"face" and relationship-oriented
	explicit communication codes	implicit communication codes
	line-logic style; rational factual rhetoric	point-logic style; intuitive affective rhetoric
	open, direct strategies	ambiguous, indirect strategies

SOURCE: From Ting-Toomey (1985).

context culture), on the other hand, are likely to advise a joint meeting so the problem between the insulter and the target could be resolved. Consistent with Bond et al.'s results are findings from research on the conflict resolution styles of Mexicans (a collectivistic, high-context culture) and Anglo-Americans (Kagan, Knight, & Martinez-Romero, 1982; Kagan & Madsen, 1971, 1972a, 1972b; Madsen, 1971; Madsen & Shapira, 1970; McGinn, Harburg, & Ginsburg, 1973). These findings revealed that Mexicans prefer to deny that conflicts exist or avoid getting into conflicts, while Anglo-Americans select direct ways to resolve conflict, such as breaking off relationships with their best friends as a result of criticism from the latter.

Ting-Toomey's (1985) theory also is consistent with discussions of conflict resolution styles in Japan (collectivistic, high-context) and the United States (individualistic, low-context). Lebra (1984), for example, argued that conflict in Japan is nonconfrontational (indirect), while Ishida (1984) suggested that it involves accommodation through indirect methods. Nomura and Barnlund (1983) also found that Japanese prefer passive forms of criticism, while North Americans prefer active forms.

More recently, Ting-Toomey (1988) extended her face-negotiation theory to explain cultural differences in resolving conflict. She argues that "face" in low-context cultures is a commodity that can be bargained and counter-bargained explicitly. "Face" in high-context cultures is a psychological-affective construct that is tied closely with other concepts such as "honor," "shame," and "obligation." In low-context cultures, "face" exists only in the immediate time-space that involves the two conflict parties, while "face" in high-context cultures involves the multiple faces of relatives, friends, and family members that are closely linked to the interactants. "Face" is a relatively "free" concept in low-context cultures, but "face" is an obligatory concept in high-context cultures that reflects one's status hierarchy, role position, and power resource. The more power one has, the more one knows how to bestow, maintain, honor, and destroy face. For members of low-context cultures, directly dealing with "face" in a conflict situation signifies an honest, up-front way of handling a problematic situation. For members of high-context cultures, the indirect, subtle dealing with "face" in a conflict situation reflects good taste and tactfulness. The ninth and tenth propositions in her theory, therefore, were proffered as follows:

> Proposition 9: Members of individualistic, low-context cultures use more dominating or controlling strategies to manage conflict than members of collectivistic, high-context cultures.

> Proposition 10: Members of collectivistic, high-context cultures use more obliging or smoothing strategies to manage conflict than members of individualistic, low-context cultures.

Dominating or controlling conflict strategies reflect the importance of self-face concern in individualistic, low-context cultures. Obliging or smoothing conflict strategies reflect the other-face concern in collectivistic, high-context cultures. In low-context cultures, "control" of one's freedom, autonomy, and choices is of paramount importance to one's sense of ego. In high-context cultures, "blending in" with others' wishes, desires, and needs is of utmost importance in upholding one's own face and at the same time not to embarrass others' face. From the high-context perspective, dominating or confrontational conflict strategies are viewed as posing a direct threat to the other person's face without leaving room for further negotiations and maneuvers in the conflict process. From the low-context perspective, the obliging or the roundabout way of handling conflict in the high-context system poses a direct insult to the face of the negotiators in the low-context culture conflict situation.

While low-context culture members view the indirect way of handling conflict as a cowardly act, members of high-context cultures view the direct way of handling conflict as lacking in good taste. On both the verbal and the nonverbal levels, members of low-context cultures tend to use more direct speech acts (such as direct demands and direct compliance-gaining strategies) and direct, personalized nonverbal style to deal with the face-negotiation process, while members of high-context cultures tend to use more indirect speech acts (such as indirect requests and indirect compliance-gaining strategies) and indirect, contextualistic nonverbal style to deal with the conflict-confrontation process. This line of reasoning suggested the eleventh and twelfth propositions of Ting-Toomey's (1988) theory:

> Proposition 11: Members of individualistic, low-context cultures use a greater degree of solution-oriented conflict style than members of collectivistic, high-context cultures.
>
> Proposition 12: Members of collectivistic, high-context cultures use a greater degree of avoidance-oriented conflict style than members of individualistic, low-context cultures.

While members of low-context cultures can separate the conflict issue from the person, members of high-context cultures typically view conflict as an integration between the issue and the problem in the person. Members of low-context cultures are able to analyze the logic of conflict from a task-oriented viewpoint, but members of high-context cultures typically combine the instrumental dimension with the affective dimension. Hence, members of low-context cultures can manage conflict face-negotiation from an instrumental, solution-oriented perspective. Members of high-context cultures, in contrast, typically take the conflict-flight approach and try to avoid the conflict person at all costs.

ATTRIBUTIONAL PROCESSES

Jones and Nisbett (1972) argue that people ("actors" is their term) performing a behavior interpret that behavior differently than people observing the behavior. Specifically, they suggest actors usually attribute their own behavior to situational factors, whereas observers attribute the behavior to qualities of the actor. Nisbett, Caputo, Legant, and Maracek (1973) offer two probable explanations for these divergent perspectives. The first is simply a perceptual one: The actors' attention at the moment of the action is focused on situational cues with which their behavior is coordinated. It therefore appears to actors that their behavior is a response to these situational cues. For observers, however, it is not the situational cues that are salient, but rather the actors' behavior. Observers are more likely to perceive the cause of the actors' behavior to be a trait or quality inherent in the actors. The second explanation suggested by Nisbett et al. for the differential bias of actors and observers stems from a difference in the nature and extent of information possessed. In general, actors know more about their own past behavior and present experiences than do observers. This difference in information may prevent actors from interpreting their behavior in terms of personal characteristics, while allowing observers to make such an interpretation. In this section, we examine cultural differences in how people make attributions about others' behavior and, in addition, cultural differences in their confidence in predicting others' behavior.

Making Attributions

Cultural variations influence the attributes on which individuals focus in making attributions. Bond (1979; Bond & Forgas, 1984), for example, found differences due to collectivism (Hong Kong) and individualism (Australia) in the attributes associated with conscientiousness, extraversion, and emotional stability. More specifically, conscientiousness was more salient to trusting others for the Chinese than Australians, while extraversion and emotional stability were more salient for trusting others for the Australians than the Chinese.

Individualism also affects the factors that people use to explain others' behavior. Miller (1984) found that people in India (collectivistic) make greater reference to contextual factors and less reference to dispositional factors than people in the United States (individualistic) when explaining others' behaviors. Similar results have been obtained in studying attributions for promotion and demotion in the United States and India (Smith & Whitehead, 1984), as well as in the use of self-serving biases in dealing with ability-related aspects of success and failure experiences in the United States and Japan (Kashima & Triandis, 1986).

In related research, Forgas and Bond (1985) examined perceptions of episodes in Hong Kong and Australia. They found that Chinese in Hong Kong differentiate among episodes based on an equal/unequal dimension (power distance) and a communal/individual dimension (individualism). Australians also used equal/unequal to differentiate among episodes, but interpretations placed on the dimension were different than the Chinese and consistent with the two cultures' scores on power distance.

Detweiler's (1975, 1978) research suggests that cultural variation (Truck Islands vs. United States) influences individuals' category width, which in turn affects their intergroup attributions. Category width refers to the tendency to classify somewhat discrepant objects in the same or different categories: Categorizing discrepant objects in the same category reflects a wide category width and placing these objects in different categories reflects a narrow category width. Detweiler (1978) found that people from the Truck Islands (collectivistic) use narrower categories than people in the United States (individualistic). His earlier work (1975) revealed that narrow categorizers make stronger and more confident attributions about members of outgroups who cause a negative outcome than do wide categorizers.

Ehrenhaus (1983) extends earlier work on culture and attribution processes by linking attributions to variations in context. He argues that "high-context culture . . . members are attributionally sensitive and predisposed toward situational features and situationally based explanations. Low-context culture . . . members are attributionally sensitive to and predisposed toward dispositional characteristics and dispositionally based explanations" (Ehrenhaus, 1983, p. 263). Given that individualistic cultures use low-context communication and collectivistic cultures use high-context communication, support for his argument can be found in Miller's (1984) study of attributions in India and the United States, as well as in Tannen's (1979) study of explanations of what occurs in films in Greece and the United States.

Bond (1983) contends there is a need for future research on cultural variability and attributional processes in three areas. First, the frequency with which attributions are made needs to be investigated. Bond suggests that there should be variation along Kluckhohn and Strodtbeck's (1961) human nature orientation, Boldt's (1978) tight versus loose social structure, and Hofstede's (1980) individualism-collectivism dimension. Second, what causal categories are used? One issue of concern in answering this question is the public or anonymous nature of the responses, since cultures vary with respect to normative structures as to what kind of statements can or should be made in public. Finally, the issue of how cultural variations affect attributions should be investigated further. Detweiler's (1978) research, for example, should be replicated with cultures selected because of their variability along specific dimensions.

Attributional Confidence

Culture appears to influence the type of information that gives individuals confidence in their ability to predict others' behavior. Specifically, the dimension of cultural variability that appears to influence attributional confidence is Hall's (1976) low-high-context schema (which corresponds to individualism-collectivism). Hall points out that

> high-context cultures make greater distinctions between insiders and outsiders than low-context cultures do. People raised in high-context systems expect more of others than do the participants in low-context systems. When talking about something that they have on their minds, a high-context individual will expect his [or her] interlocutor to know what's bothering him [or her], so that he [or she] doesn't have to be specific. The result is that he [or she] will talk round and around the point, in effect putting all the pieces in place except the crucial one. Placing it properly—this keystone—is the role of his [or her] interlocutor. (p. 98)

Okabe (1983) extends this analysis, arguing that verbal skills are more necessary and prized more highly in low-context, individualistic cultures than in high-context, collectivistic cultures. In high-context cultures, verbal skills are considered suspect and confidence is placed in nonverbal aspects of communication.

The emphasis on nonverbal aspects of communication is shared by many high-context cultures, particularly those influenced by Buddhism. Tsujimura (1987), for example, isolates four major characteristics of Japanese communication: (1) *ishin-denshin* ("traditional mental telepathy"), (2) taciturnity, (3) *kuki* (mood or atmosphere), and (4) respect for reverberation (i.e., indirect communication). Yum (1987a) points out that *i-sim jun-sim* (telepathy) is regarded as the highest form of communication in Korea. She also contends that silence and the use of indirect forms of communication are used widely in Korean cultures. Hall (1976) and Hsu (1981) make similar observations about communication in the Chinese culture.

Because of the emphasis on nonverbal communication, members of high-context cultures need to know whether others understand them when they do not verbally express their ideas and feelings and, in addition, whether they can understand others under the same circumstances in order to reduce uncertainty. While these forms of uncertainty are present in low-context cultures, they are emphasized less.

Not only is it important for members of high-context cultures to know whether others understand them when they don't express themselves, it is also necessary for them to know whether others will make allowances for them. The concept *sassi* in Japan illustrates this. Nishida (1977) defines *sassi* as a noun meaning conjecture, surmise, guess, judgment, understanding what a person means and what a sign means. In its verb form *(sassuru)* its meaning is expanded to include imagine, suppose or empathize with, feel for or make allowances for. This concept is so important in Japan that Ishii (1984) used it as the basis for his model of Japanese-Japanese interpersonal communication.

Emphasis on indirect forms of communication, silence, telepathy, and making allowances for others is related to the value of harmony in high-context cultures (Okabe, 1983). Okabe argues that the cultural values of interdependence and harmony require members of high-context cultures to use words implicitly and ambiguously. To understand verbal (or written) messages in these cultures, the context must be known.

In low-context cultures, verbal (or written) messages require less knowledge of the context in order to be correctly interpreted. Members of low-context cultures, therefore, can gather information about others' attitudes, values, emotions, and past behavior and use it to predict their future behavior (i.e., reduce uncertainty). The type of information gathered is individual specific. Members of high-context cultures, in contrast, seek out social information (e.g., where others went to school, their company). To illustrate, Alexander, Cronen, Kang, Tsou, and Banks (1986) found that Chinese college students infer more about others' intellectual and academic potential based on knowing their high school background than do college students in the United States. Nakane (1974) similarly argues that Japanese ignore an individual whose background is unknown because his or her behavior is unpredictable and it is unknown whether he or she will follow the norms/conventions appropriate in the context. In order to be able to predict others' behavior, their background and relative status must be known. Background information not only tells Japanese whether strangers' behavior is predictable, but it also tells them how to talk with strangers (i.e., it tells them how to address strangers and which form of the language to use). Without this knowledge it is impossible to communicate with strangers with any degree of comfort in the Japanese language. Yum (1987b) makes similar observations about communication in Korea.

To summarize, it appears there are social behaviors and/or types of information that are more important sources of uncertainty in high-context cultures than in low-context cultures, including (1) knowing others' social background, (2) knowing whether others will behave in a socially appropriate manner, (3) knowing that others understand individuals' feelings, (4) knowing what others mean when they communicate, and (5) knowing whether others will make allowances for individuals when they communicate. These sources of uncertainty are not incorporated in conceptualizations of attributional confidence developed and used in the United State (Alexander et al., 1986; Clatterbuck, 1979; Prisbell & Anderson, 1980). Rather, all current conceptualizations of attributional confidence focus on individual-specific information such as emotions, feelings, attitudes, responses, and behaviors.

Parks and Adelman (1983), for example, assess respondents' certainty with respect to their partner's behavior, values, preferences, attitudes, feelings, and responses. Prisbell and Anderson's (1980) measure is similar, but adds emotions, decisions, interests, and judgments Alexander and her associates' (1986) measure includes items similar to Parks and Adelman's and Prisbell and Anderson's measures, as well as questions that pertain to background similarity. Finally, Clatterbuck (1979) developed two measures of attributional confidence: (1) an uncertainty evaluation scale that assessed respondents' ability to predict specific things about another person (e.g., knowing a person's lucky number), and (2) a seven-item measure of general proactive attributions.

Gudykunst and Nishida (1986a) expanded Clatterbuck's (1979) earlier work and developed a two-factor measure of attributional confidence that is consistent with descriptions of communication in low- and high-context cultures. Each factor emphasizes sources of information that are more important in one type of culture. Members of low-context cultures focus on information specific to the individuals with whom they are communicating, which increases accuracy in direct forms of communication (Items 1-7 in Table 8.2; these items make up Clatterbuck's scale). Members of high-context cultures, in contrast, focus on information that increases accuracy in indirect, nonverbal forms of communication (Items 8-12 in Table 8.2). Both types of cultures, however, do attune to the information upon which the other culture focuses. Members of high-context cultures utilize information on individual's attitudes, values, feelings, and empathy to predict others' behavior, but this information appears to be secondary to the information used to reduce uncertainty due to the indirect forms of communication that predominates in the culture. Similarly, people in low-context cultures use information regarding whether or not the others understand their feelings, make allowances for them when they

TABLE 8.2
English Version of Attributional Confidence Items

People vary in the degree to which they can predict how other people behave and think. Please answer each of the following questions with respect to your ability to predict selected aspects of the behavior of the person you answered the previous questions about. Answer each question using a scale from zero (0) to one hundred (100). If you would have to make a total guess about the person's behavior or feelings you should answer "0"; if you have total certainty about the other person's behavior you should answer "100." Feel free to use any number between 0 and 100.

1. How confident are you in your general ability to predict how he/she will behave? _____ %

2. How confident are you that he/she likes you? _____ %

3. How accurate are you at predicting his/her attitudes? _____ %

4. How accurate are you at predicting the values he/she holds? _____ %

5. How well can you predict his/her feelings? _____ %

6. How much can you empathize with (share) the way he/she feels about him/herself? _____ %

7. How well do you know him/her? _____ %

8. How certain are you of his/her background? _____ %

9. How certain are you that he/she will behave in a socially appropriate way when this is important? _____ %

10. How certain are you that he/she can understand your feelings when you do not verbally express them? _____ %

11. How certain are you that you understand what this person means when you communicate? _____ %

12. How confident are you that this person will make allowances for you when you communicate? _____ %

SOURCE: Gudykunst and Nishida (1986a).

communicate, and the degree to which they understand the other person, but these sources of information appear to be secondary to those isolated by Clatterbuck (1979). This is consistent with Hall's (1976) contention that both low- and high-context communication are used in every culture, but one tends to predominate.

Gudykunst and Nishida (1986a) found that high-context attributional confidence was higher in the low-context culture of the United States than in the high-context culture of Japan, an unexpected finding. On the surface, this finding might suggest that the two dimensions are not conceptually distinct. This, however, does not appear to be the case. When frequency of communication, length of relationship, shared networks, interaction with others' friends, and percent of free time spent with others were correlated with the two dimensions, different patterns emerged. The only variable to have a significantly different correlation with low-context confidence was frequency of communication. Frequency correlated significantly higher with low-context attributional confidence in the U.S. sample than in the Japanese sample, suggesting that frequency of communication has less influence in high-context cultures than in low-context cultures. The correlation between frequency of communication and high-context confidence also was significantly higher in the U.S. sample than in the Japanese sample. Three other variables, in contrast, were correlated significantly higher with the high-context confidence in the Japanese sample than in the U.S. sample: overlap in social network, interaction with others' friends, and percent of free time spent with others.

Gudykunst and Nishida's (1986a) findings are consistent with previous work on communication in high-context cultures. Nakane (1974), for example, argues that Japanese differentiate others into three categories—strangers, people whose social background is known, and members of the ingroup—and that effectiveness of communication varies as a function of others' group membership. Yum (1987a) and Hsu (1981) make similar observations about Korean and Chinese cultures, respectively. Shared communication networks, interaction with others' friends, and spending free time with others—the variables correlated with high-context confidence in Japan—are characteristic of ingroup relationships, rather than relationships with members of outgroups. This suggests that high-context attributional confidence emerges from ingroup relationships, rather than from frequency of communication with the specific other person, in high-context cultures like Japan. High-context attributional confidence, in contrast, appears to be a function of individualistic interaction (i.e., frequency of communication) in low-context cultures like the United States.

CONCLUSION

We examined the influence of cultural variability on social cognitive aspects of communication in this chapter. It appears that field dependence is related to tight social structure and high power distance, while field independence is associated with loose social structures and low power distance. Particularistic patterns of thought tend to be found in low uncertainty avoidance cultures, while universalistic patterns of thought tend to predominate in high uncertainty avoidance cultures. Further, persuasive strategy selection and conflict management styles vary as a function of individualism-collectivism. Members of collectivistic cultures, for example, take the context into consideration and use strategies that are socially appropriate, while members of individualistic cultures focus on the person they are trying to persuade and use strategies that may be socially inappropriate. Finally, the attributes on which individuals focus when making attributions and their confidence in making attributions is affected by individualism-collectivism.

Given the early stages of research on cultural variability in social cognitive processes and interpersonal communication, the vast majority of the research has focused on the relationship between culture and the social cognitive processes. It is important that future research be extended to include the examination of the effect culture has on social cognitive process relationships with other aspects of interpersonal communication. Future research, for example, might examine how culture influences the relationship between field dependence-independence or universalism-particularism and communication competence. To illustrate, does field independent, particularistic information processing contribute more to competency in individualistic than collectivistic cultures? Research that examines cultural variability in relationships between social cognitive process and interpersonal outcomes is necessary to establish scope statements for interpersonal theories and to integrate culture into these theories.

9

Affective Processes

There is disagreement among researchers as to whether affect and cognition are independent (see Scherer & Ekman, 1984, for several articles dealing with this issue). Zajonc (1980), for example, argues that emotion and affective states are independent of cognitive processing. Lazarus (1982), in contrast, contends that cognition is a "necessary as well as sufficient condition for emotion" (p. 1019). The model presented in Chapter 1 conceives of communication as a function of intentions, habits, or affect, but recognizes that affect can also influence behavior through intentions, consistent with Triandis's (1977, 1980a) model of interpersonal behavior. The position taken in this chapter, therefore, is that affect can directly influence communication and that it is sometimes, but not always, mediated through the cognitive process of forming intentions (see Isen, 1984, for a more complete statement of this position).

In this chapter, we examine the influence of culture on affective communication. The discussion of emotions is developed in two sections. The first section contains a review of research on the universality of emotion expression and recognition. In the second section, we explain the cultural differences revealed in the major studies of affective communication using Hofstede's (1980, 1983) dimensions of cultural variability.

UNIVERSALITY OF EMOTION EXPRESSION
AND RECOGNITION

Before examining cultural differences in affective communication, it is necessary to review research on "universal" or pancultural aspects of emotions. There appears to be agreement on two universal aspects of affective communication: the recognition of specific emotions and the dimensions of emotions.

Emotion Recognition

Darwin's (1872) evolutionary-genetic theory predicts that the expression of emotions is innate and universal. Extensive cross-cultural research has been conducted to test this hypothesis (e.g., Ekman, 1972; Ekman & Friesen, 1971, 1975; Ekman, Friesen, & Ellsworth, 1972; Ekman, Sorenson, & Friesen, 1969; Izard, 1968, 1971; Sorenson, 1975; see Fridlund, Ekman, & Oster, 1987, for a recent review and discussion of unanswered questions in this line of research). Izard (1968; summarized in Izard, 1980), for example, had individuals classify photographs of facial expressions into one of eight categories of emotions (interest-excitement, enjoyment-joy, surprise-startle, distress-anguish, disgust-contempt, anger-rage, shame-humiliation, and fear-terror). His data revealed that there is high agreement on the category of emotion represented by the photographs in the United States (average agreement across the eight emotions = 83.4%), England (77.9%), Germany (80.6%), Sweden (83.4%), France (82.2%), Switzerland (79.6%), Greece (75.1%), and Japan (65.4%). Data obtained by Dickey and Knower (1941) in Mexico (71.7%) and Ekman and Friesen (1971) in Brazil (84.5%), Chile (84.5%), and Argentina (81.8%) yield similar results for six of the eight emotions (intent-excitement and shame-humiliation were omitted).

Izard (a study summarized in Izard, 1971) collected additional data that suggests that disgust and contempt are recognized and identified correctly in the United States, Turkey, India, and Japan. Supporting data also is presented by Vinacke and Fong (1955), Cüceloglu (1970), Boucher (1973), Niit and Valsiner (1977), Boucher and Carlson (1980), and Chan (in press). More recently, McAndrew (1986) presented data that indicates happiness and sadness are the most easily recognized facial expressions in the United States and Malaysia, while anger and fear are the most difficult to recognize. Only the ability to recognize anger, however, appeared to be influenced by culture. Winklemayer, Exline, Gottheil, and Paredes (1978) also found support for accurate identification of emotions in motion pictures of "normal" and schizophrenic individuals across cultures.

Recent research by Ekman and his associates (1987) supports the argument that there are universal facial expressions of emotions. This study in 10 cultures (Estonian S.S.R., Germany, Greece, Hong Kong, Italy, Japan, Scotland, Sumatra, Turkey, and the United States) indicated that agreement is not limited to conditions in which observers are limited to selecting one emotion for each facial expression. In this condition, there was agreement on which emotion is strongest and there was agreement on which emotion is second strongest. Ekman et al. also found agreement on the relative strength of the emotions being expressed. They point out, however, that one limit in their study is that the respondents were college students. Since college students have high exposure to the mass media, the results may be due to exposure, rather than a consequence of evolutionary process.

Ekman, Sorenson, and Friesen (1969) also collected data that suggest that six fundamental emotions (happiness, sadness, disgust, surprise, anger, and fear) are recognized correctly in preliterate cultures in New Guinea and Borneo. A follow-up study with isolated respondents (e.g., individuals who had not seen movies or magazines or lived in a government town), however, indicated that fear and surprise are confused when examined together.

Beier and Zautra (1972) extended this line of research to vocal communication. They found that Japanese and Polish students are as accurate at decoding vocal emotional expressions as students in the United States when provided with a sufficiently long sample of vocal communication. Another recent study by Bezooijen, Otto, and Heenan (1983) revealed that Dutch, Taiwanese, and Japanese adults are able to identify Dutch vocal expressions, particularly those related to the activity dimension of emotional meaning (e.g., the amount of activity involved in the expression of the emotion). Similarly, Ekman (1972) and Saha (1973) reported that intensity of emotional expression in the voice can be interpreted accurately in literate cultures.

In a related study, Rosenthal, Hall, DiMatteo, Rogers, and Archer (1979) administered the Profile of Nonverbal Sensitivity (PONS) test in 20 cultures. The PONS involves two-second segments of 20 different role-played situations that display different body parts (i.e., face only, body only, or the two combined) and different voice samples (with content removed, but paralinguistic features of speech maintained). Respondents read two verbal descriptions of the situations and select the one that represents the segment heard or seen. While the accuracy rates varied across the 20 cultures studied, respondents in all cultures are more accurate than would be expected by chance. The differences in accuracy that emerged appear to be a function of cultural dissimilarity, that is, the most accurate judgments are made by respondents in highly similar cultures (e.g., Australia) and the least accurate judgments in highly dissimilar cultures (e.g., New Guinea).

There also is preliminary evidence for increasing accuracy in judgments of emotions as a function of developmental characteristics in children across cultures. Matsumoto and Kishimoto (1983) played audio tapes for children from the United States and Japan, ranging in age from 4 to 9, and asked them to select the photograph that depicted the emotion of the person talking. They found that 4- and 5-year-old North Americans could correctly identify only surprise, while Japanese children of the same age could identify surprise and sadness. The 6-year-old and older North Americans were able to identify all four emotions (surprise, sadness, happiness, and anger), while 6-year-old Japanese could not identify anger, but 7-year-old and older Japanese could. Matsumoto and Kishimoto, however, point out that the overall rate of accurately identifying anger was low, even though it is greater than chance (e.g., a significant chi-square statistic). They argue that recognition of anger may be a cultural difference, in that Japanese are socialized from an early age to avoid the expression of emotions like anger.

Eibl-Eibesfeldt (1971, 1972) argued that there are other universal aspects of nonverbal behavior related to the expression of emotion. In the first study (1971), he contended that a greeting response consisting of raised eyebrows and wrinkles across the brow was universal. Support for this claim came from photographs of French, Warka Indians, Balinese, and Papuan people. Eibl-Eibesfeldt's (1972) study noted that movements other than facial expressions (e.g., shaking the head to indicate "no" and nodding to indicate "yes") are probably universal.

Fridlund, Ekman, and Oster (1987) draw two generalizations and raise four unanswered questions regarding universal aspects of emotion expression. Their generalizations are (1) "Observers label certain facial expressions in the same way regardless of culture" (p. 157; italics omitted here and for all following quotes); and (2) "members of different cultures show the same facial expressions when experiencing the same emotions unless culture-specific display rules interfere" (p. 158). The unanswered questions raised are (1) "How many emotions have a universal facial expression?" (p. 158); (2) "How many universal expressions are distinguishable for any emotion?" (p. 159); (3) "How great are the cultural differences in facial expression?" (p. 159); and (4) "How often do people in natural situations actually show the distinctive, universal patterns of facial expression?" (p. 160).

Dimensions of Emotion

Recent research by Lutz (1982) on Ifaluk (a small island atoll in the Western Caroline Islands in Micronesia) and by Shaver, Schwartz, Kirson, and O'Connor (1987) in the United States suggest similarities in emotion prototypes across cultures. Lutz found five clusters of emotions, four of which correspond closely to those isolated in Shaver et al.'s study in the United States. Lutz's first cluster, "emotions of good fortune," corresponds to Shaver et al.'s "love" and "joy" clusters. "Emotions of danger," Lutz's second cluster, is parallel to Shaver et al.'s "fear" cluster, while her third cluster, "emotions of connection and loss," is consistent with many of the terms in Shaver et al.'s "sadness" cluster. Lutz's fourth cluster contained words such as hate, anger, irritation, and frustration/grief, which corresponds to Shaver et al.'s "anger" cluster. Only Lutz's fifth cluster, "emotions of inability," does not correspond to the clusters obtained in the Shaver et al. study and, according to Lutz's analysis, is the least "unified." Lutz concluded that cultural differences in clusters existed. Her mistake, however, according to Shaver et al., "was to compare a cluster analysis of her Ifaluk data with conclusions drawn from multidimensional scaling studies done in Western societies. As we have shown in relation to Study 1, the two methods produce different looking results even when the same data are used" (p. 1083). Shaver et al. go on to argue that basic-level emotions should produce cross-cultural similarities (because they are biologically based), while subordinate-level emotions should produce cross-cultural differences.

Russell's (1983) study of native speakers of Guyarati, Croatian, Japanese, Chinese, and English using multidimensional scaling supports the conclusion that the conceptual organization of emotions is universal. He had individuals from each of the language groups provide similarity judgments for 28 cards with one emotion word on each card. His results revealed that the emotion-related words fell in a circular pattern that is definable by two dimensions, pleasure-displeasure and arousal-sleep, in all five language groups. Several other studies of emotion-related words in different languages support the universality of the pleasure-displeasure dimension, that is, G. Ekman's (1955) study of 23 Swedish words, Filerbaum and Rapoport's (1971) study of 15 Hebrew words, and Yoshida, Kinase, Kurokawa, and Yashiro's (1970) study of 35 Japanese words.

Based on his review of the cross-cultural research, Izard (1980) concluded:

> Robust cross-cultural data . . . lend strong support to Darwin's thesis that the expressions of the emotions are innate and universal. Some studies suggest that universality is limited to certain primary or fundamental emotions. However, even some blends (expressions representing components of two or more fundamental emotions) are correctly identified across certain cultures, though blends do not yield as high agreement as

unitary expressions when naive judges are used. Although the expressions
and inner experiences that characterize the fundamental emotions are
innate and universal, there are numerous cultural differences in attitudes
toward the emotions and their expressions. (p. 216)

CULTURAL VARIABILITY IN AFFECTIVE COMMUNICATION

There is extensive research on nonverbal communication across
cultures (see LaFrance & Mayo, 1978a, 1978b; Ramsey, 1979; for
reviews), but little of this work has focused on affective communication
per se (for reviews of research on emotion across cultures, see Boucher,
1979; Izard, 1980; Leff, 1977; Matsumoto et al., in press). There are,
nevertheless, anthropological descriptions of emotions in many different
cultures. In discussing the study of emotion in anthropology, Solomon
(1984) points out that

> the various causes of emotion are clearly cultural in their specifics. . . .
> Causes of emotion vary from culture to culture; it does not follow that
> emotions do, or do not, vary as well. The names of emotions clearly vary
> from culture to culture, along with most vocabulary entries and names for
> virtually everything else. But this obvious point hides a subtle and
> troublesome one; how do we know whether it is *only* the names (i.e.,
> phonetic sequences) that vary, rather than their reference? . . . A similar
> point can be made about the various *expressions* of emotion. Clearly
> some expressions, at least, differ from culture to culture as learned
> gestures and more or less "spontaneous" actions. Clenched fists are
> expressions of anger in one culture, not in another. Banging one's head on
> the wall is an expression of grief in one society, not in others. And the
> *verbal* expressions of emotion vary not only along with the language (of
> course) but also according to the familiar images and metaphors of the
> culture. (pp. 240-241)

The anthropological study of emotions, however, tends to be culture
specific, that is, it describes emotions in specific cultures. Such an
approach makes drawing generalizations about the influence of culture
on emotions difficult. This section, therefore, focuses on major studies
of affective communication that have reported cultural differences in
two or more cultures.

Ekman (1972) argues that the rules for emotional displays are culture
specific. These rules, learned early in life, govern the nature and type of
emotion that are acceptable to reveal in specific contexts. Throughout
the remainder of this chapter, we posit post hoc explanations for the

observed cultural differences in attitudes toward and antecedents to emotions based on Hofstede's (1980) theory of cultural variability.

Attitudes Toward Emotions

Izard (1971) reports data on attitudes toward emotions from seven cultures (the United States, England, West Germany, Sweden, France, Greece, and Japan). Respondents were asked "Which emotion do you understand best?"; "Which emotion do you understand least?"; "Which emotion do you dread the most?"; "Which negative emotion (such as distress, disgust, anger, shame, fear) do you experience most frequently?"; "Which negative emotion do you experience least frequently?"; and "Which emotion do you prefer to experience?" Izard's data revealed a culture by emotion interaction across all of the questions. No theoretical interpretation of the results, however, was presented. In order to determine if Izard's results could be interpreted theoretically using Hofstede's (1980) four dimensions of cultural variability, Spearman's rank order correlation coefficients were computed between the seven cultures' rank order on the four dimensions of cultural variability and the percentage of respondents selecting the two most frequently cited emotions for each of the questions. The results of the analysis are presented in Table 9.1.

An examination of Table 9.1 reveals that few statistically significant correlations emerged. Both uncertainty avoidance and power distance were correlated negatively with dreading fear the most. Both correlations appear consistent with Hofstede's (1980) analysis. High uncertainty avoidance cultures accept aggressive behavior more than low uncertainty avoidance cultures and, therefore, fear should be less. Similarly, high-power-distance cultures stress coercive power that is not acceptable in low-power-distance cultures.

There also was a positive correlation between masculinity and experiencing distress the most. Masculine cultures emphasize achievement, decisiveness, and excelling—all factors that can lead to distress if not met—while feminine cultures focus on service, intuition, and not trying to do better than others.

The only other significant correlations observed were with individualism: Experiencing anger the least correlated positively and preferring to experience interest correlated negatively. Since highly individualistic cultures expect individuals to be emotionally independent of each other and highly collectivistic cultures expect emotional dependence, the correlation with experiencing anger appears plausible. The negative association between individualism and the desire to experience interest may be due to filling a void. Specifically, collectivistic

TABLE 9.1

Spearman's Rank Order Correlations Between Dimensions of Cultural Variability and Percentage of Respondents Who Understood and/or Preferred Specific Emotions Best/Least Across Eight Cultures

Emotion	Dimensions of Cultural Variability			
	Individualism-Collectivism	Uncertainty Avoidance	Masculinity-Femininity	Power Distance
Understood enjoyment best	−.20	−.09	.30	−.56
Understood interest best	.42	−.29	.03	−.43
Understood shame least	−.54	.65	.40	.50
Understood disgust least	−.28	.04	−.35	−.42
Dread shame most	.68	−.25	−.17	.21
Dread fear most	.55	−.76[a]	−.33	−.78[a]
Experience distress most	.36	−.21	.75[a]	−.55
Experience disgust most	.67	−.21	−.29	.24
Experience fear least	.29	.50	.53	−.49
Experience anger least	.71[a]	−.21	.13	.10
Prefer to experience enjoyment	.43	−.07	.26	.19
Prefer to experience interest	−.78[a]	.56	.09	.02

SOURCE: From Gudykunst and Ting-Toomey (1988).
NOTE: Hofstede (1983) scores were used for the rank ordering of the dimensions of cultural variability. Rank ordering of emotions was based on percentage of respondents (with males and females averaged) reporting the response in Izard (1971). Correlations were calculated for only the two most frequent responses to each question.
a = $p < .05$.

cultures emphasize order and duty over variety and pleasure, which are the focus in individualistic cultures. It appears that members of collectivistic cultures feel a need to engage in activities that are of interest, rather than to engage in activities out of obligation. Several of the nonsignificant correlations also are compatible with Hofstede's theory of cultural differentiation. While the explanations are post hoc, the present analyses suggest that Hofstede's theory can explain some of the cross-cultural variations in attitudes toward emotions.

Antecedents to Emotions

By far the most extensive study of culture and antecedents to emotions to date was conducted by Scherer, Wallbott, and Summerfield (1986; a preliminary report appeared in Scherer, Summerfield, & Wallbott, 1983). These researchers and their collaborators studied people in Belgium (N = 77), France (N = 149), Great Britain (N = 64), Israel (N = 102), Italy (N = 100), Spain (N = 106), Switzerland (N = 91), and West Germany (N = 90). Generally, the respondents were in their early twenties, from white-collar backgrounds, and students in the social sciences (see Aebischer & Wallbott, 1986, for a complete description of the samples). Scherer and his colleagues examined the antecedents of emotional experiences, physiological patterns of reported emotional states, nonverbal reactions to emotional experiences, verbalization of emotional experiences, the effects of social factors, and the interrelatedness among these factors. Results across cultures, however, are not reported for all analyses and, therefore, the present discussion focuses on those analyses in which cross-cultural data are presented. While not fully representative of the complete range of cultural variability on Hofstede's (1980) dimensions of cultural variability (e.g., there is no highly collectivistic culture represented), the eight cultures studied allow preliminary explanations for the influence of cultural variability on antecedents to emotion to be proffered.

Wallbott and Scherer (1986) present the percentage of respondents reporting specific antecedents for four (joy, sadness, fear, anger) emotions across the eight cultures. The percentage of respondents reporting the three most frequent antecedents were correlated (using Spearman's rank order correlation coefficient) with Hofstede's (1983) scores for the eight cultures and the results are presented in Table 9.2. An examination of the table reveals significant correlations in 6 of the 12 analyses: (1) Uncertainty avoidance correlated negatively with relationships being an antecedent to joy; (2) individualism correlated negatively with temporary meetings being an antecedent to joy; (3) power distance correlated negatively with birth/death being an antecedent to sadness; (4) power distance correlated positively with traffic being an antecedent to fear; (5) uncertainty avoidance (negative), masculinity (positive), and power distance (negative) all correlated with novel situations being an antecedent to fear; and (6) power distance correlated negatively with injustice being an antecedent to anger.

The six significant relationships between Hofstede's (1983) dimensions of cultural variability and the antecedents to specific emotions appear to be consistent with Hofstede's theory of cultural differentiation. In high-power-distance cultures, for example, inequality and injustice are expected and taken for granted, while they are not expected or seen as acceptable in low-power-distance cultures. The correlation between power distance and injustice being an antecedent to anger, therefore, should be negative.

The correlations of three dimensions with novel situations being an antecedent to fear was unexpected, but all correlations are interpretable within Hofstede's theory. Cultures high on uncertainty avoidance have formal rules for interaction, while those low on this dimension do not.

TABLE 9.2

Spearman's Rank Order Correlations Between Dimensions of Cultural
Variability and Percentage of Respondents Reporting Antecedent
Categories for Specific Emotions Across Eight Cultures

	Dimensions of Cultural Variability			
Antecedent Category/Emotion	Individualism-Collectivism	Uncertainty Avoidance	Masculinity-Femininity	Power Distance
Relationships/joy	.38	−.88[b]	.29	−.38
Temporary meetings/joy	−.68[a]	.53	−.35	.14
Achievement/joy	.06	−.14	−.36	−.05
Relationships/sadness	.08	−.38	.50	−.05
Birth-death/sadness	.08	−.56	−.25	−.64[a]
Body-mind/sadness	−.21	−.05	.21	−.08
Traffic/fear	.40	.23	−.32	.73[a]
Interactions with strangers/fear	−.10	.02	−.61	−.20
Novel situations/fear	.48	−.70[a]	.69[a]	−.64[a]
Relationships/anger	.32	.20	.32	.32
Injustice/anger	−.11	−.41	−.04	−.86[b]
Interactions with strangers/ anger	−.30	−.08	−.10	−.46

SOURCE: From Gudykunst and Ting-Toomey (1988).
NOTE: Hofstede (1983) scores were used for the rank ordering of the dimensions of cultural variability.
Rank ordering of emotions was based on percentage of respondents reporting antecedent condition in
Wallbott and Scherer (1986). Correlations were calculated only for the three most frequently reported
antecedents for each question.
a = p < .05; b = p < .01.

Since novel situations have specific rules in high-uncertainty-avoidance
cultures, there is no reason for them to stimulate fear. Further, high-
power-distance cultures have the norm of "there should be an order of
inequality in this world in which everyone has his [or her] rightful place;
high and low are protected by this order" (Hofstede, 1980, p. 122). Given
this norm, novel situations should not be threatening or serve as an
antecedent to fear because individuals are "protected" by the social
order. Finally, highly masculine cultures value performance, achievement, and excelling. Novel situations serve as an antecedent to fear since
they can threaten individuals' ability to achieve these goals.

Wallbott, Ricci-Bitti, and Banninger-Huber (1986) report the nonverbal reactions to emotional experiences across the eight cultures
studied, while Cosnier, Dols, and Fernandez (1986) report results for
verbal reactions. Again, rank order correlations were computed between
the dimensions of culture and the percentage of respondents in a culture
reporting the specific type of reactions. Table 9.3 presents the results of
these analyses.

TABLE 9.3

Spearman's Rank Order Correlations Between Dimensions of Cultural
Variability and Percentage of Respondents Reporting Verbal and
Nonverbal Reactions to Emotional Experiences Across Eight Cultures

	Dimensions of Cultural Variability			
Reactions Across Emotions	Individualism-Collectivism	Uncertainty Avoidance	Masculinity-Femininity	Power Distance
Nonverbal				
vocal	.07	.10	.49	.07
nonvocal	.66[a]	−.18	.03	.11
Verbal				
verbalization	.64[a]	−.61	.49	−.30
verbal control	.26	.51	−.27	.31

SOURCE: From Gudykunst and Ting-Toomey (1988).
NOTE: Hofstede (1983) scores were used for the rank ordering of the dimensions of cultural variability.
Rank ordering of reactions was based on percentage of respondents reporting nonverbal (Wallbott et al.,
1986) and verbal (Cosnier et al., 1986) reactions. Correlations were computed for total percentages
(collapsed across specific emotions).
a = p < .05.

An examination of the table indicates that nonvocal reactions (e.g.,
reactions that include use of body) and verbalization were correlated
positively with individualism. Both correlations appear consistent with
traditional discussions of individualism. In his comparison of Japan and
the United States, Okabe (1983), for example, points out that individualistic cultures place greater emphasis on the verbal dimension of
communication, including directness of expressions, than collectivistic
cultures, where the verbal dimension often is not trusted and communication is indirect. Also, most comparisons of nonverbal communication between individualistic and collectivistic cultures (see
LaFrance & Mayo, 1978; Ramsey, 1979; for reviews of this research)
reveal that members of individualistic cultures use nonverbal displays
more than members of collectivistic cultures. (Note: Previous research
does not use the individualism-collectivism label, but when the cultures
studied are classified into these categories, the present conclusion
emerges.) This is also consistent with Hall's (1976) description of low-
and high-context cultures, which are isomorphic with individualistic
and collectivistic cultures, respectively (Gudykunst, 1987a). The present
findings also are consistent with Levine's (1985) distinction between
univocal and ambiguous forms of communication discussed in
Chapter 2.

The results of Scherer and his associates' cross-cultural study indicate
that antecedents to emotions vary across cultures. Our analysis further

suggests that many of the cultural differences are consistent with Hofstede's (1980) theory of cultural variability. There is, however, some evidence that antecedents to emotions also may be consistent across cultures. Boucher and Brandt (1981), for example, conducted an exploratory study in which individuals in the United States and Malaysia wrote narratives of situations in which they experienced six various emotions (anger, disgust, fear, happiness, sadness, and surprise). These narratives were then evaluated by another group in the United States. The evaluators were able to identify correctly the emotion about which the narratives were written for both cultures. Brandt and Boucher (1985) did a follow-up study using subjects in the United States, Korea, and Samoa. They had one group of respondents in each culture write narratives about situations in which they experienced the same six emotions, randomly sampled eight situations for each emotion (144 situations), and then had a different sample from each culture evaluate the narratives. Brandt and Boucher concluded that "the findings of the replication study suggested that different cultural groups appraise emotion antecedent events in a similar fashion. Not only did members of a cultural group agree among themselves, but they also agreed with other groups on the emotions the situations were most likely to generate" (p. 361).

In the preceding analysis, one dimension of cultural variability was used to explain cross-cultural differences in antecedents to emotions. Some differences that are not explainable by an individual dimension of cultural variability can be explained by a combination of two dimensions.

Four studies illustrate the interrelationship between the influence of individualism and uncertainty avoidance on the antecedents to emotions. Individuals in high-uncertainty-avoidance cultures, for example, tend to display emotions more than members of low-uncertainty-avoidance cultures (Hofstede, 1980). This conclusion is supported by Gudykunst and Nishida's (1984) research, which revealed that Japanese students (high uncertainty avoidance) intend to display more nonverbal affiliative expressive behaviors in initial interactions with strangers than students in the United States (low uncertainty avoidance).

If the high-uncertainty-avoidance culture is also collectivistic, the display of emotion is limited to "positive" emotions, since the display of "negative" emotions (e.g., anger) can decrease harmony in the group. This position is illustrated by Friesen's (1972) research, for example, which revealed that students in Japan and the United States display similar affect to a stressful film when viewing it alone, but when in the company of a peer, students in the United States show more negative affect than Japanese.

The relationship between individualism and uncertainty avoidance also is illustrated by Argyle and his associates' (1986) study of the display of anger and distress in 22 different relationships in Japan, Hong Kong, Italy, and England. They found that the English and Italians endorse the display of anger and distress across relationships more than the Japanese. While both cultures have lower uncertainty avoidance scores than Japan, both are individualistic and Japan is collectivistic. The Japanese, therefore, would not be expected to endorse rules regarding the display of anger and distress. Similarly, Noesjirwan (1978) found that Indonesians (collectivistic and moderate uncertainty avoidance) agreed with the rule of keeping quiet and hiding feelings when one is angry at one's boss, while Australians (individualistic and moderate uncertainty avoidance) endorsed expressing anger in the same situation. These studies clearly indicate that it is necessary to examine where cultures fall on more than one dimension of cultural variability in order to explain (or predict in a hypothesis) some patterns that are revealed in data.

RELATED RESEARCH ON CULTURE AND PSYCHOPATHOLOGY

There is extensive research on culture and psychopathology (see Triandis & Draguns, 1980, for reviews). Of particular relevance is the work on depression and anxiety as a reaction to stress. Early research by Zung (1972), for example, revealed that depression in normal populations varies across cultures. He found that the highest scores emerge in samples in Czechoslovakia, Sweden, and Germany, with respondents in Spain, England, and the United States having lower scores.

Other studies suggest there is a subjective difference in what constitutes depression. Tanaka-Matsumi and Marsella's (1976) research illustrates the findings in this line of research. They discovered that for Japanese, depression is related to words associated with the physical environment and somatic states (e.g., rain, dark, disease, weariness), while respondents in the United States associated depression with words referring to internal mood states (e.g., sadness, loneliness). These findings appear consistent with predictions that would be derived from the individualism-collectivism dimension of cultural variability.

Research on experiencing anxiety across cultures also has been conducted (see Spielberger & Diaz-Guerrero, 1976, for several studies).

Endler and Magnusson (1976) found that Swedish university students report greater anxiety vis-à-vis physical danger and ambiguous situations than do Canadian university students. Diaz-Guerrero's (1976) study also revealed that Mexican school children have higher scores on defensiveness than school children in the United States. This finding is consistent with the two cultures' scores on uncertainty avoidance, but Endler and Magnusson's data are not. Endler and Magnusson's results, however, are consistent with scores on masculinity, which also appears to be a relevant dimension for ambiguous situations (see findings from Wallbott & Scherer, 1986, discussed above). Obviously, additional research involving many cultures (e.g., more than 10) is needed to isolate which specific dimension of cultural variability is related to how anxiety is manifested in different situations.

CONCLUSION

In this chapter, we reviewed research on affective process. The research cited indicates that facial expressions representing the basic emotions are recognized universally and, in addition, dimensions of emotions appear to be similar across cultures. Attitudes toward emotions and antecedents to specific emotions, in contrast, appear to differ cross-culturally. Many of these differences can be explained by using Hofstede's theory of cultural differentiation. Some differences, however, are not consistent with the theory. Future research is needed in order to determine if this finding is due to the full range of variability on Hofstede's dimension not being represented in the research examined or whether other dimensions of cultural variability are necessary to explain the observed differences. The analyses presented herein, nevertheless, clearly suggest that culture can be theoretically linked to variability in specific responses to emotions.

ordination dimension is influenced by Hofstede's (1980) power distance dimension of cultural variability. Intimacy-formality corresponds to a dimension of cultural variability isolated by Benedict (1934) and Glenn (1981) who, among others, labeled the dimension Apollonian (which is controlled and formal) versus Dionysian (which allows emotional expressiveness and is informal).

Adamopoulos and Bontempo (1986) examined the universality of three dimensions of interpersonal relations using literary material from different historical periods. They concluded that affiliation and dominance appear to be universal, without undergoing major changes over the last 3,000 years. Intimacy, in contrast, also appears to be universal, but it has changed substantially over the same period of time.

Closely related to intimacy-formality is the issue of contact (see Chapter 6 for a more elaborate discussion of contact). Triandis (1984) argues that in contact cultures "people touch a lot, they stand much closer to each other, they orient their bodies so that they face each other, they look each other in the eye, and they employ greater amplitudes of emotional expression" (p. 324). Non-contact cultures involve the opposite pattern, for example, little touching, standing at greater distance. People in contact cultures also tend to express their emotions openly, while people in non-contact cultures tend to suppress their emotions. Finally, Triandis argues that the last dimension (overt-covert) is associated closely with the loose-tight cultural variations, that is, more overt behavior occurs in loose than in tight cultures. He also suggests that this dimension may be related to uncertainty avoidance.

Foa and Foa (1974) take a different approach to examining universal dimensions of behavior. Using an exchange framework, they argue that resources individuals exchange during interaction can be classified into six groups that are arranged in a circle: love (12 o'clock, using the face of a clock to represent the circle), services (2 o'clock), goods (4 o'clock), money (6 o'clock), information (8 o'clock), and status (10 o'clock). These resources vary along two dimensions: (1) particularism—the importance of the individual's (receiver and/or giver) identity in the exchange (runs vertically up and down the clock's face, less particularism at 6 o'clock and more at 12 o'clock); and (2) concreteness—the degree the resource has face versus symbolic value (runs horizontally across clock's face, less concreteness at 9 o'clock more at 3 o'clock).

The closer the resources are in Foa and Foa's (1974) framework, the more similar they are perceived to be and the greater satisfaction emerges when similar resources are exchanged. Data from the Foas' and their colleagues' research (summarized in Foa & Foa, 1974) indicate that the resource structure is applicable in Greece, Hawaii, India, Israel, and Senegal. Recent research also suggests that this framework is applicable in Sweden, the Philippines, Israel, and with Spanish-speaking Mexican Americans (Foa, Salcedo, Törnblom, Garner, Glaubman, & Teichman, 1987; Törnblom, Jonsson, & Foa, 1985). Also, Hwang (1983; cited in Bond & Hwang, 1986) used this theoretical perspective in explaining Chinese behavior.

Foa and Foa (1974) contend that since the basic structure is consistent across cultures, differences that emerge are a function of other cultural variations. Using Hofstede's (1980) dimensions, power distance and masculinity, for example, it would be predicted that mother and wife are treated more similarly than mother and father in a sociocultural system that is high on masculinity and low on power distance. Mother and father, in contrast, are treated more similarly than mother and wife in sociocultural systems that are high on power distance, but low on masculinity. There also may be differences in the emphasis placed on the particular dimension as a function of cultural variations (Gergen et al., 1980). These differences should be associated with universalism-particularism pattern variables (Parsons, 1951).

There is reason to believe that Triandis's (1977, 1978) dimensions and those isolated by Foa and Foa (1974) are related. Lonner (1980), for example, points out that the exchange of universalistic resources is associated with formal behavior, while exchange of particularistic resources is associated with intimate behavior. Formal attempts to integrate the two perspectives, however, are just beginning (see Adamopoulos, 1984, for a test of his proposed integration in the United States). Also, as Bond (1979) points out, the dimensions of personality structure isolated in Chapter 7 are related to Triandis's dimensions of behavior.

Given the preceding overview of the universal dimensions of interpersonal relations, we now turn our attention to cross-cultural variations in interpersonal relationships. Our focus is on cross-cultural variations in social penetration and uncertainty reduction processes, the two theoretical perspectives we use in our research. By focusing on research using these two perspectives, we do not mean to imply that no other research examining interpersonal relationships across cultures exists. There are, for example, several studies (e.g., Alexander et al., 1986; Nakanishi, 1986; Wolfson & Pearce, 1983) and at least two theoretical analyses (Cronen, Chen, & Pearce, 1988; Cronen & Shuter, 1983) using a coordinated management of meaning perspective (e.g., Pearce & Cronen, 1980). These studies, however, tend to treat culture atheoretically and, therefore, are omitted here (for other approaches, see Kim & Gudykunst, 1988).

SOCIAL PENETRATION PROCESSES

Social penetration theory (Altman & Taylor, 1973) posits four stages of relationship development: orientation, exploratory affective exchange, affective exchange, and stable exchange. The orientation stage is characterized by responses that are stereotypical and reflect superficial aspects of the personalities of the individuals involved in a relationship. Exploratory affective exchange involves interaction at the periphery of the personalities of the partners. This stage includes relationships that are friendly and relaxed, but commitments are limited or temporary. The third stage, full affective exchange, involves "loose" and "free-wheeling" interaction and an increase of self-disclosure in central areas of the partner's personalities. Stable exchange, the final stage, emerges when partners have described themselves fully to each other and communication is efficient. This stage, however, is achieved in very few relationships.

Research on Social Penetration

Eight broad dimensions of communication behavior are hypothesized to vary with the stage of a relationship (Altman & Taylor, 1973; Knapp, 1978). As relationships become more intimate, (1) communication takes on a more personalistic focus, (2) depth of interaction increases, (3) breadth of interaction increases, (4) difficulty of interaction decreases, (5) flexibility of interaction increases, (6) spontaneity of interaction increases, (7) smoothness of interaction increases, and (8) evaluation of interaction increases. Changes along these dimensions, however, do not necessarily involve "linear progressions" such that increases on one dimension involve corresponding increases on another dimension (Knapp, Ellis, & Williams, 1980; see Altman, Vinsel, & Brown, 1981, for a discussion of social penetration as a "dialectical" process). The changes along each dimension also do not go on forever. Rather, changes occur until both partners feel comfortable with the interaction. While the theory focuses on actual changes that occur in relationships, perceptions of change should covary with actual changes that occur.

Knapp, Ellis, and Williams (1980) examined perceptions of communication along the eight dimensions as a function of type of relationship, sex of respondent, sex of partner, and selected demographic variables in the United States. Their data revealed three factors: (1) "personalized communication," which includes items that relate to the intimacy of communication (e.g., "We tell each other personal things about ourselves—things we don't tell most people"); (2) "synchronized communication" involves items that relate to the coordination of communication between partners (e.g., "Due to mutual cooperation, our conversations are generally effortless and smooth flowing"); and (3) "difficult communication" encompasses items that relate to "barriers" to communication (e.g., "It is difficult for us to know when the other person is being serious or sarcastic"). Knapp, Ellis, and Williams (1980) concluded that personalized communication is aligned most closely with Altman and Taylor's (1973) depth dimension, but some aspects of other dimensions (i.e., uniqueness, flexibility, and evaluation) are included. Synchrony, in contrast, was associated most closely with smoothness, but it also includes some statements from spontaneity. Difficulty was aligned most closely with Altman and Taylor's difficulty dimension, but it includes some statements that are the opposite of smoothness (i.e., awkwardness). At least seven of the eight dimensions isolated by Altman and Taylor, therefore, were included in the three factors. According to Knapp et al. (1980), "the dimensions of communication which predicted changes in the depth, smoothness and difficulty of interaction with perceived changes in intimacy seem to have centrality around which the other dimensions cluster" (pp. 273-274).

Results of Knapp, Ellis, and Williams's (1980) research revealed main effects for relationship type, respondents' sex, as well as an interaction between respondents' sex and partners' sex. Relationships were perceived as more personal as intimacy increased, with intimate relationships being less discrepant from each other than nonintimate. Males also perceived their relationships as less personal and synchronized than females. Two-way interactions indicated that males perceived relationships with females as more personal than relationships with other males; females also rated relationships with males as more personal than relationships with other females. These results suggest that both types of relationship and dyadic composition (same/opposite sex relationships) influence perceptions of communication.

Cross-Cultural Variations in Social Penetration

Variability along Hofstede's (1980) dimensions influences social penetration processes across cultures. Differences in the uncertainty avoidance dimension, for example, are related to the expression of emotion in relationships, that is, members of cultures high on uncertainty avoidance express more emotion in relationships than members of cultures low on the dimension. Translating this line of argument to Knapp, Ellis, and Williams's (1980) dimensions, members of high uncertainty avoidance cultures perceive their relationships to be more personal than members of low uncertainty avoidance cultures. The rationale for the influence of masculinity-femininity on communication behavior in relationships is straightforward; it influences how same-sex and opposite-sex relationships are perceived. Specifically, because of differentiated sex roles, members of cultures high on masculinity perceive less personalization and synchronization, but more difficulty in opposite-sex relationships than members of cultures low on masculinity. Further, members of high masculinity cultures perceive opposite-sex relationships as less intimate than members of low masculinity cultures.

Triandis (1986) suggests that members of collectivistic cultures draw sharper distinctions between members of ingroups (e.g., those with whom they go to school or work) and outgroups and perceive ingroup relationships to be more intimate than members of individualistic cultures. Ingroup relationships include coworker and colleague (company ingroup) or classmate (university ingroup), to name only a few. Because of the perceived intimacy of these relationships, members of collectivistic cultures also perceive these same ingroup relationships to involve more personalization and synchronization and less difficulty than members of individualistic cultures.

Power distance also has a direct influence on selected aspects of relationship development and organizational communication. Cultural variability along this dimension affects the way interpersonal relationships form and develop when differences in "power" are perceived. In high power distance cultures, for example, differences in power are assumed to be natural. "Superiors" and "subordinates" are considered as being of a different kind and this difference simply reflects an "existential inequality" (Hofstede, 1980). In low power distance cultures, in contrast, people are seen as equal; inequalities in roles are viewed as being established for convenience's sake. While the impact of this dimension of communication between superiors and subordinates in an organization is straight-forward, other types of relationships also are affected, for instance, teacher-student, old person-young person, and parent-child, to name only a few. Also, some cultures (e.g., Chinese) reconstruct or explain interpersonal relationships in power distance terminology (Forgas & Bond, 1985).

Gudykunst and Nishida (1983, 1986b) cross-culturally compared social penetration in Japan and the United States. The first study (1983) examined perceptions of social penetration across 10 topics of conversations isolated by Taylor and Altman (1966). Only 3 of the 10 analyses (own marriage and family, love/dating and sex, emotions and feelings), revealed differences by culture in same-sex close friendships, with North American means being higher than Japanese means on each topic (i.e., North Americans perceived more social penetration on these topics than did Japanese). Overall, the patterns of social penetration in close friendships in Japan and the United Stated were very similar. The differences that emerged in Gudykunst and Nishida's (1983) study appear to be related to Hofstede's (1980) masculinity dimension. The Japanese have the highest masculinity score of all cultures studied, while the United States falls in the middle. It, therefore, would be expected that the Japanese place less emphasis on opposite-sex relationships than people in the United States.

Gudykunst and Nishida's (1986b) research extended Knapp, Ellis, and Williams's (1980) work in the United States. Specifically, they examined the influence of culture (Japan vs. the United States) on perceptions of the intimacy of relationship terms (Study I), and the effect of culture, relationship type (stranger, acquaintance, classmate, friend, best friend, and lover), and dyadic composition (same vs. opposite sex relationships) on perceptions of personalization, synchronization, and difficulty in communication with specific partners (Study II). The results of the comparison of Japanese and North Americans' ratings of relationship terms are presented in Table 10.1. Consistent with Triandis's (1986) description of the focus on ingroup relationships in collectivistic cultures, the Japanese respondents rated relationship terms associated with two of their major ingroups, people from their university and people with whom they work, as more intimate than respondents from the United States. The same individuals are members of ingroups for people in the highly individualistic culture of the United States, but relationships with the ingroup are not emphasized or perceived as important in individualistic cultures, unless individuals are engaging in intergroup behavior.

While the score on Hofstede's (1980) masculinity dimension for the United States falls in the middle and Japan's score is high, six of the seven opposite-sex relationships in Gudykunst and Nishida's (1986b) Study I revealed significant differences in the posited direction. Consistent with Hofstede's description, sex roles in high masculinity cultures are differentiated clearly, while sex roles in low masculinity cultures are fluid and a unisex or androgyny ideal predominates. When sex roles are differentiated clearly, relatively little informal interaction occurs between males and females, and when interaction takes place, the

TABLE 10.1

Means and Standard Deviations of Intimacy Ratings
of Relationship Terms by Culture

Relationship Terms	United States		Japan		F	p	eta^2
	M	SD	M	SD			
Cohort (*Nakama*)	5.40	1.95	2.85	1.45	157.63	.001	.36
Brother (*Kyodai*)	3.12	1.90	3.51	2.61	< 1	ns	.00
Mother (*Hahaoya*)	2.35	1.62	2.06	1.37	< 1	ns	.00
Acquaintance (*Chijin*)	6.79	1.72	4.95	1.86	74.44	.001	.21
Coworker (*Shigato-makama*)	5.76	1.68	5.27	2.16	4.74	.05	.14
Aunt (*Oba*)	4.53	1.70	4.99	1.93	4.32	.05	.01
Employer (*Koyosha*)	6.39	1.89	6.86	2.02	3.96	.05	.01
Colleague (*Doryo*)	5.33	1.77	4.76	2.18	5.79	.05	.02
Lover (*Koibito*)	1.25	.80	2.81	2.44	61.62	.001	.16
Sister (*Shimai*)	2.88	1.94	3.78	2.82	9.28	.01	.04
Roommate (*Doshukusha*)	3.85	1.80	4.88	2.60	18.20	.001	.05
Cousin (*Itoko*)	4.67	1.78	4.66	1.82	< 1	ns	.00
Grandparent (*Sofubo*)	3.75	2.00	4.15	2.21	3.78	.05	.01
Fiance (*Konyakusha*)	1.29	.84	4.32	2.49	107.43	.001	.25
Classmate (*Dokyusei*)	5.72	1.66	3.84	1.74	74.65	.001	.24
Best Friend							
(*Ichiban no shinyu*)	2.51	1.56	1.73	1.32	12.84	.001	.06
Father (*Chichioya*)	2.75	2.01	2.57	1.88	< 1	ns	.00
Son (*Musuko*)	2.59	2.05	4.76	3.37	48.28	.001	.15
Uncle (*Oji*)	4.55	1.78	5.21	1.95	11.47	.001	.03
Neighbor (*Kinjo no hito*)	5.72	1.71	5.92	1.92	92.80	.001	.25
Mate (*Tsureai*)	1.75	1.40	4.45	2.55	138.90	.001	.31
Companion (*Tomodachi*)	3.08	1.32	3.05	1.47	< 1	ns	.00
Spouse (*Haigusha*)	1.33	1.01	4.32	3.38	111.34	.001	.25
Boy/Girlfriend							
(*Otoko/onna tomodachi*)	1.70	1.02	3.32	1.55	116.78	.001	.26
Daughter (*Musume*)	2.55	1.93	4.87	3.28	57.51	.001	.16
Date (*Detonoaite*)	4.02	1.51	3.48	2.10	4.94	.05	.03
Close Friend (*Shinyu*)	2.85	1.28	1.83	.99	48.27	.001	.16
Stranger (*Shiranai hito*)	8.35	1.23	7.99	1.72	4.50	.05	.03
Friend (*Tomo*)	3.67	1.34	3.42	1.49	< 1	ns	.00
Steady (*Kosai shiteiru hito*)	2.27	1.24	2.92	2.23 ·	8.18	.01	.04

SOURCE: From Gudykunst and Nishida (1986b).
NOTE: Items were rated on a nine-point scale with 1 = intimate and 9 = nonintimate. Japanese translations for each term are given in parentheses following the term in English.

content of communication tends to be superficial. These relationships, therefore, are perceived as less intimate in highly masculine cultures than in cultures low on the dimension.

The Japanese sample perceived six of the nine family relationship terms as less intimate than the U.S. sample in Gudykunst and Nishida's

(1986b) first study. Nakane (1970) argues that the company for which a Japanese works is the ingroup with the most influence on individuals' behavior. In cultures where the company is the most influential, other ingroups (e.g., family) appear to be less important and relationships with these ingroups are perceived as less intimate. The clear pattern that emerged in the data is consistent with Triandis's (1986) conceptualization of individualism-collectivism, that is, collectivistic cultures that do not rank family as the number one ingroup do not perceive family relationships to be highly intimate (e.g., less intimate than an individualistic culture). The ingroup that is perceived as most important may be related to other dimensions of culture, that is, it is plausible that cultures high in masculinity attribute a larger social role to the organizations for which they work, while cultures low in masculinity attribute larger social roles to other institutions, such as the family.

Results of Gudykunst and Nishida's (1986b) Study II revealed culture by relationship type and culture by dyadic composition interactions. The interaction between culture and relationship term was due to differences in perceptions of classmate and acquaintance relationships. The Japanese perceived acquaintance relationships as more personalized and synchronized than classmate relationships, while the opposite pattern emerged for North American respondents. The culture by dyadic composition interaction revealed that North American female-male relationships were perceived as the most personalized, followed by male-male, male-female, and female-female dyads. The Japanese, in contrast, perceived the most personalization in male-female dyads, followed by female-female, female-male, and male-male dyads.

Gudykunst and Nishida's (1986b) data displayed patterns predictable from three of Hofstede's (1980) four dimensions: individualism-collectivism, uncertainty avoidance, and masculinity-femininity. Specifically, the masculinity-femininity dimension influences perceptions of communication behavior associated with opposite- versus same-sex relationships and has direct bearing on generalizing theory and research regarding interpersonal relationship development in general and the development of romantic relationships in particular. It would be predicted, for example, that opposite-sex relationships are formed and develop more easily in feminine cultures than in masculine cultures. The uncertainty avoidance dimension influences the expression of emotion in relationships, with more emotion being expressed in high uncertainty avoidance cultures than in low uncertainty avoidance cultures. This dimension also affects the amount of consensus present in a relationship.

To illustrate, it would be hypothesized that there is greater consensus within dyads on the nature of their communication in high uncertainty avoidance cultures than in low uncertainty avoidance cultures.

UNCERTAINTY REDUCTION PROCESSES

As indicated in Chapter 1, uncertainty reduction involves the creation of proactive predictions and retroactive explanations about others' behavior. Uncertainty reduction theory appears to be generalizable across cultures (Gudykunst, Yang, & Nishida, 1985). It also has been used as the basis for several cross-cultural comparisons of communication (e.g., Gudykunst & Nishida, 1984, 1986a). Prior to examining the differences in uncertainty reduction processes across cultures, a brief overview of the theory is necessary.

Uncertainty Reduction Theory

Berger and Calabrese's (1975) theory of initial interactions is presented in 7 axioms and 21 theorems that specify the interrelationships among uncertainty, amount of communication, nonverbal affiliative expressiveness, information seeking, intimacy level of communication content, reciprocity, similarity, and liking. The first axiom of the theory posits a reciprocal relationship between amount of communication and uncertainty. This axiom is based on Lalljee and Cook's (1973) research, which revealed that speech acts increase and filled pause rates decrease as interaction between strangers progresses. Axiom 1 also is consistent with research on the desire to obtain information under conditions of uncertainty (Berlyne, 1960, 1965; Weick, 1979). Not only does the amount of communication reduce uncertainty, but information seeking (Axiom 3) and similarity between communicators (Axiom 6) reduces it too. Axiom 3 is derived from Frankfurt's (1965) research, which revealed that the number of questions strangers ask each other declines as a function of time. The posited relationship between similarity and uncertainty reduction is supported by extensive research (Clatterbuck, 1979; Parks & Adelman, 1983; Prisbell & Anderson, 1980).

Under high levels of uncertainty, responses to questions seeking information involve low levels of intimacy (Axiom 4); and high levels of uncertainty tend to decrease interpersonal attraction, while liking tends to increase attributional confidence (Axiom 7). Axiom 4 is consistent with studies on relationship development (Altman & Taylor, 1973). Support for Axiom 7 can be found in Clatterbuck's (1979) research, which indicated that there is a positive correlation between several standard measures of attraction and attributional confidence and that people are more confident about their predictions for those they like than those they do not like.

Berger and Calabrese (1975) also argue that uncertainty produces high rates of reciprocity (Axiom 5). This axiom was generated in part from Jourard's (1960) research, which found evidence for a "dyadic effect" with respect to the intimacy of self-disclosure. Specifically, he discovered that there is an association between what people disclose and what others disclose to them. The notion of self-disclosure reciprocity is consistent with some research (e.g., Feigenbaum, 1977), but other research suggests there is a difference depending upon the sex composition of the dyad (Cline, 1983).

Cross-Cultural Variations in Uncertainty Reduction

Cross-cultural differences in uncertainty reduction processes in interpersonal relationships appear to be related to Hall's (1976) low-high-context distinction and Hofstede's (1980) individualism-collectivism dimension. The conceptual link is clearest to low-high-context, but, as indicated in Chapter 2, this dimension appears to be isomorphic with individualism-collectivism; specifically, low-context communication predominates in individualistic cultures, while high-context communication is prevalent in collectivistic cultures. While there are no empirical data to support this claim, Hall's description of high-context cultures is consistent with Triandis's (1986) description of collectivistic cultures, and virtually all of the low-context cultures Hall discusses are individualistic and all high-context cultures are collectivistic.

Exploratory research by Gudykunst (1983c) revealed that members of high-context cultures are more cautious in initial interactions with strangers, make more assumptions about strangers based upon their background, and ask more questions about strangers' backgrounds than do members of low-context cultures. His research also suggested members of low-context cultures engage in more nonverbal affiliative expressiveness than do members of high-context cultures.

Gudykunst and Nishida (1984) found that culture influences self-disclosure, interrogation, nonverbal affiliative expressiveness, and attributional confidence. As would be predicted from Hall's (1976) theory, the Japanese sample displayed a higher level of attributional confidence about strangers' behavior than the United States sample. Moreover, higher levels of interrogation and self-disclosure were reported in the United States sample than in the Japanese sample. These results are consistent with Nakane (1974), Johnson and Johnson (1975), and Okabe (1983), who point out that people in the United States engage in more verbal communication, including interrogation and self-disclosure, than do Japanese. This finding, however, is inconsistent with Gudykunst (1983c), who reported members of high-context cultures asked more questions about a stranger's background than did members of low-context cultures. The difference in results of the two studies may be due to the high-context subjects in Gudykunst's study being international students from Japan, Korea, Hong Kong, and Taiwan studying in the United States, while the high-context subjects in Gudykunst and Nishida's study were Japanese living in Japan. Japanese also reported displaying more nonverbal affiliative expressiveness than the respondents from the United States. This finding is consistent with Johnson and Johnson's (1975) position that there is "a conspicuous focus on the interpretation of nonverbal communication" in Japan (p. 455). Similarly, Okabe (1983) points out that Japanese "use *haragei,* or the 'art of the belly' for the meeting of minds or at least the viscera, without clear verbal interaction" (p. 39).

As reported in Chapter 8, Gudykunst and Nishida (1986a) found that two types of attributional confidence can be isolated across cultures. These correspond to patterns of communication in low- and high-context cultures and were labeled low- and high-context attributional confidence, accordingly. Significant differences in low- and high-context attributional confidence scores emerged by culture and stage of relationship. As would be expected from research on interpersonal relationship development (Altman & Taylor, 1973), both low- and high-context attributional confidence increased as relationships increased in intimacy. The interaction effect between culture and stage of relationship that emerged suggests there may be differences in the perceived intimacy of relationships across cultures. At least one of the findings is consistent with previous research. Members of high-context cultures, for example, establish relationships with classmates early in their school careers. These relationships are part of the in-group and last for life (Nakane, 1974; Yum, 1987b). It, therefore, would be expected that members of high-context cultures have more low- and high-context attributional confidence regarding classmates than acquaintances. Members of low-context cultures, however, do not establish the same type of relationships with classmates. Rather, acquaintance relationships tend to be perceived as more intimate and members of low-context cultures are more confident in predicting acquaintances' than classmates' behavior.

Gudykunst, Nishida, and Schmidt (1988) examined the influence of masculinity-femininity in uncertainty reduction processes in same- and opposite-sex relationships. They argued that members of masculine cultures draw sharp distinctions between same- and opposite-sex relationships and predicted that there are differences in uncertainty reduction processes with members of the same- and opposite-sex in masculine cultures, but not in feminine cultures. More specifically, they expected that there is more self-disclosure, attraction, perceived similarity, display of nonverbal affiliative expressiveness, shared networks, low-context and high-context attributional confidence in opposite-sex than in same-sex relationships in masculine cultures.

Gudykunst, Nishida, and Schmidt's (1988) multivariate findings for culture and dyadic composition generally supported the predictions from Hofstede's (1980) theory of cultural differentiation. Specifically, there was a main effect for dyadic composition in the Japanese sample, but not in the U.S. sample. The pattern in the mean scores that emerged was consistent with Gudykunst and Nishida's (1986b) study of social penetration in Japan and the United States, that is, mean scores were highest in male-female relationships. On the surface, this finding may appear inconsistent with Hofstede's conceptualization. Given Hofstede's conceptualization, it might be expected that same-sex relationships would involve more self-disclosure, shared networks, and attributional confidence than opposite sex relationships. If all other things (e.g., interpersonal salience, ingroup-outgroup status) were equal, this would probably be the case. In a study like this, however, all other things are not equal. When asked to select a member of the same sex, members of masculine cultures do not have a wide variety of target persons from whom to choose because there is generally little contact between members of the opposite sex. The most likely target person to be selected is a member of the opposite sex with whom respondents have a lot of contact, that is, the person they "date." Since date is the only opposite-sex relationship term Japanese perceived as more intimate than North Americans (Gudykunst & Nishida, 1986b), these findings are to be expected.

Gudykunst, Nishida, and Schmidt (1988) also examined the influence of self-monitoring (Snyder, 1974) on uncertainty reduction processes. Given the results of previous studies (Gudykunst & Nishida, 1984; Gudykunst, Yang, & Nishida, 1985), they expected that self-monitoring influences uncertainty reduction processes. More specifically, they predicted that self-monitoring is associated positively with self-disclosure, interrogation, display of nonverbal affiliative expressiveness, and low-context and high-context attributional confidence. Their results indicated that self-monitoring influences three variables (inter-rogation, display of nonverbal affiliative expressiveness, and low-context attributional confidence) in their overall analysis. These results are consistent with Snyder's (1987) contention that self-monitoring influences the way relationships are formed and are compatible with previous cross-cultural research on self-monitoring and uncertainty reduction processes (Gudykunst, Yang, & Nishida, 1985). When controlling for culture, self-monitoring had a significant effect on three dependent variables (interrogation, nonverbal, and low-context at-tributional confidence) in the United States sample and one variable (nonverbal) in the Japanese sample. These findings appear to be consistent with the cultural differences in self-monitoring observed in Gudykunst, Yang, and Nishida's (1987) study. Specifically, since self-monitoring (as measured by Snyder & Gangestad's, 1986, version of the scale) does not incorporate the status or ingroup-outgroup relation-ships among the individuals, it has less of an influence on communi-cation in collectivistic cultures than it does in individualistic cultures.

Finally, Gudykunst, Nishida, and Schmidt (1988) looked at the effect of predicted outcome value on uncertainty reduction processes. Sunnafrank (1986) argues that uncertainty reduction is not the primary concern in initial interactions with strangers. Rather, he suggests that increasing positive relational outcomes is the primary concern. Predicted outcome value in a relationship, therefore, must be taken into con-sideration. Sunnafrank contends:

> First, individuals should be more attracted to partners and relationships when greater predicted outcome values are expected in the relational future. Second, increasingly positive predicted outcomes will produce more communicative attempts to extend initial interactions and establish future contact. Conversely, increasingly negative predicted outcomes will result in communicative attempts to terminate or curtail the conversation and future contacts. Finally, individuals will attempt to guide con-versations toward topics expected to result in the most positive predicted outcomes. (pp. 10-11)

Sunnafrank's modifications of Berger and Calabrese's (1975) original axioms of uncertainty reduction theory posit a positive relationship between predicted outcome value and amount of communication, the display of nonverbal affiliative expressiveness, information seeking, intimacy of communication, and attraction, as well as uncertainty reduction.

Gudykunst, Nishida, and Schmidt (1988) found several differences in the effect of predicted outcome value on the dependent variables that emerged when controlling for culture. Predicted outcome value had a significant positive effect on all but one dependent variable (perceived similarity) in the United States sample and on all dependent measures in the Japanese sample. Based on the B-values, the effect for predicted outcome value was stronger in the Japanese sample than in the U.S. sample for self-disclosure, attraction, networks, low-context attributional confidence, and high-context attributional confidence. Only similarity had a higher B weight in the United States sample than in the Japanese sample.

In related research, Ting-Toomey (1987) examined the communicative dimensions of love, self-disclosure maintenance, ambivalence, and conflict in interpersonal relationships in France, Japan, and the United States using Braiker and Kelley's (1979) Relational Dimension Scale. She found that the Japanese report the lowest level of feelings of attachment, belongingness, and commitment (love) toward the relational partner, while the respondents from the United States report the highest and the French fell in the middle. This pattern is consistent with the three cultures' position on Hofstede's (1980) individualism dimension of cultural variability. Given that individualism and Hall's (1976) low-high-context schema are related, this pattern was expected. Specifically, it would be predicted that members of individualistic, low-context cultures feel more attached to other individuals than members of collectivistic cultures. There are at least two reasons for this. First, members of collectivistic cultures tend to have feelings of attachment for groups, particularly their ingroups, rather than individuals. Second, members of low-context (individualistic) cultures use more direct forms of communication than do members of high-context (collectivistic) cultures where indirect communication predominates. Less expression of commitment, therefore, would be expected to take place in interpersonal relationships in collectivistic cultures than in individualistic cultures.

Results of Ting-Toomey's (1987) study also revealed that the lowest level of the quality and quantity of self-disclosure occurred in Japan, the most in the United States, and France fell in the middle. These results are consistent with other research on self-disclosure in Japan and the United States (e.g., Barnlund, 1975a). As with the love dimension, these results appear to be consistent with scores on Hofstede's (1980) individualism dimension. Given that low-context, individualistic cultures tend to use direct forms of communication and high-context, collectivistic cultures tend to use indirect forms of communication, it would be expected that greater self-disclosure occurs in individualistic cultures than in collectivistic cultures, since self-disclosure is a direct form of communication.

Ting-Toomey's (1987) findings vis-à-vis the feelings of confusion and uncertainties about the partner and the relationship (ambiguity) indicated that the least ambiguity occurred in Japanese relationships and the most in U.S. relationships, with French relationships falling in the middle. The pattern of results is consistent with the preceding two dimensions and, therefore, may be due to individualism. It is more likely, however, that the findings are related to Hofstede's (1980) uncertainty avoidance dimension. Japan has the highest uncertainty avoidance score, the United States the lowest, and France falls in the middle. Since uncertainty avoidance is related to the desire for certainty, it appears reasonable to argue that the degree of uncertainty avoidance influences the ambiguity individuals perceive in interpersonal relationships. The greater the desire to avoid uncertainty in the culture, the less ambiguity will be perceived in interpersonal relationships.

The final dimension examined in Ting-Toomey's (1987) study was conflict (i.e., the frequency of overt arguments and the seriousness of the problems in the relationship). Her data revealed that the lowest score is reported in France, the highest in Japan, and the United States falls in the middle. This pattern is consistent with the three cultures' scores on Hofstede's (1980) masculinity dimension: Japan has the highest score, France the lowest, and the United States falls in the middle. Given that high masculinity involves a focus on things and a focus on performance while low masculinity involves a focus on people and quality of life, it appears reasonable to argue that the greater the masculinity in a culture, the more conflict would be seen as problematic in interpersonal relationships.

CONCLUSION

We examined universal aspects of interpersonal relationships and cross-cultural variations in interpersonal relationship development in this chapter. At least four dimensions of interpersonal relationships appear to exist in all cultures: association-dissociation, super-ordination-subordination, intimacy-formality, and overt-covert. How individuals within specific cultures perceive interpersonal relationships, however, differs as a function of selected dimensions of cultural variability. Association-dissociation, for example, is a function of Kluckhohn and Strodtbeck's (1961) human nature value orientation. Hofstede's (1980) individualism-collectivism and Hall's (1976) low-high-context dimensions appear to be the major influences on social penetration and uncertainty reduction processes.

Future research and theorizing in this area must link cultural variability in interpersonal relationship development to other interpersonal communication processes. Given Cushman and Cahn's (1985) perspective, for example, self-conceptions influence how interpersonal relationships form and change over time. Research, therefore, is necessary to establish how the association between self-conceptions and interpersonal relationship development is affected by cultural variability. Or from an uncertainty reduction perspective, how does cultural variability influence the relationship between self-disclosure, shared networks, frequency of communication, and so forth, and attributional confidence?

11

Intergroup Relationships

In Chapter 1, we indicated that both interpersonal and intergroup factors are relevant in any encounter with another person. Chapters 3 through 10 focused on the interpersonal factors. This chapter focuses on the intergroup factors. Lewin (1948) illustrates the importance of intergroup factors when he points out:

> During most of his [or her] life the adult acts not purely as an individual but as a member of a social group. However, the different groups a person belongs to are not all equally important at a given moment. Sometimes his [or her] belonging to one group is dominant, sometimes his [or her] belonging to another.... Generally, in every situation the person seems to know what group he [or she] belongs to and to what group he [or she] does not belong. He [or she] knows more or less clearly where he [or she] stands, and this position largely determines his [or her] behavior. (p. 46)

Brewer and Kramer (1985) draw a distinction between "process" and "outcome" intergroup research. Process-oriented research includes the "intraindividual and interpersonal *processes* underlying the formation and maintenance of intergroup orientations," while outcome-oriented research refers to studies "that are concerned with the perceptual and behavioral consequences or outcomes of such processes" (p. 220). The emphasis in this chapter is on process-oriented research on the ingroup bias and outcome-oriented intergroup research on intergroup contact, and on the development of relationships between members of different groups (for reviews of research not included here, see Brewer & Kramer, 1985; Gudykunst, 1986c; Stephan, 1985; Tajfel, 1982; Wilder, 1986). To begin, we examine cultural variability in the ingroup bias.

INGROUP BIAS

Social categorization of individuals into distinct social groups results in the assignment of positive traits and rewards to the ingroup (Doise & Sinclair, 1973), as well as differential attitudes toward the groups involved (Doise et al., 1972). Ingroup bias occurs when negative interpersonal attraction is associated with category membership (Turner, Shaver, & Hogg, 1983) and occurs even when category membership is arbitrary and a member of the outgroup is a close personal friend (Vaughan, Tajfel, & Williams, 1981). Ingroup bias is reduced when membership in social groups is "crossed," that is, situations in which others are members of an outgroup on one criterion and members of ingroup on another criterion (Deschamps & Doise, 1978).

Wetherell (1982) found that both Europeans (individualistic) and Polynesians (collectivistic) in New Zealand display bias in the minimal group situation, but Polynesians moderate their discrimination and show greater generosity to outgroup members (i.e., maximize joint profit) compared to Europeans. One interpretation of this study is that members of collectivistic cultures moderate their discrimination toward outgroups more than members of individualistic cultures. Triandis (1987) disagrees with this conclusion. He suggests, in contrast, that there is no difference between individualistic and collectivistic cultures in the way they deal with outgroups. Rather, the strength of the distinction between ingroup and outgroup is different. The distinction between family and neighbors, for example, in collectivistic cultures is large, but it is small in individualistic cultures. He therefore suggests an alternative hypothesis, "there is more trust toward neighbors in individualistic than in collectivistic cultures" (p. 2).

The Wetherell (1982) findings, however, are compatible with Bond and Hewstone's (1986) research, which revealed that British high school students in Hong Kong endorse more intergroup differentiation than do Chinese students. Wetherell's results likewise appear to be consistent with Triandis, Vassiliou, and Nassiakou's (1968) study of role perception in ingroups and outgroups in Greece and the United States, as well as Feldman's (1968) field study in Paris, Boston, and Athens. Feldman found that outgroup members were "treated better" in Athens (the most collectivistic) than in Boston and Paris (both individualistic). Feldman's results, however, may be unique to Greece, where foreigners and guests are perceived as potential members of the ingroup. Strangers in other collectivistic cultures generally are not viewed as potential members of the ingroup (Triandis, 1986). Bond, Hewstone, Wan, and Chiu's (1985) study further suggests that group-serving attributions are maintained in the presence of an audience in individualistic cultures, but not in collectivistic cultures. They argue that this is due to collectivistic socialization for maintaining harmony by suppressing open conflict compared to individualistic socialization for developing harmony by resolving conflict openly in public.

Several studies reveal that Chinese, Japanese, and Columbians (all collectivistic) use the equity norm with members of outgroups more than people in the United States (Leung & Bond, 1984; Mahler et al., 1981; Marin, 1981). Congruous findings emerge when decision rules for ingroup and outgroup members are compared in Japan and Australia (Mann et al., 1985), as well as when the use of the equality norm in ingroups is examined in Hong Kong and the United States (Bond et al., 1982; Leung & Bond, 1982), that is, Chinese use the equality norm more with members of the ingroup than do people in the United States. The results of these studies appear to be consistent with Triandis's (1986) conceptualization of ingroup-outgroup behavior in individualistic and collectivistic cultures. Sinha (cited in Triandis et al., 1986), however, argues that allocentrics in individualistic cultures yield to the ingroup more than idiocentrics in collectivistic cultures.

Research further suggests that some ingroup-outgroup behavior is a function of combinations of dimensions of cultural variability. Bond, Wan, Leung, and Giacalone (1985), for example, found that Chinese are less critical of insulters from an outgroup if they are higher in status than are people in the United States. No specific effect emerged for status or group membership in the United States. They argue that this pattern emerges because Hong Kong Chinese are collectivistic and high in power distance, while people in the United States are individualistic *and* moderate in power distance.

Cross-cultural differences that emerge with respect to the ingroup bias may be moderated when members of one culture are sojourning in another culture. To illustrate, Bond (1986a, 1986b) found that both exchange students from the United States and Hong Kong Chinese students perceived members of the other group to be more beneficient than members of their ingroup.

INTERGROUP CONTACT

The majority of research on outcomes of intergroup behavior has focused on the "contact hypothesis." Based on the work of Williams (1947) and Allport (1954), this hypothesis suggests that it is not the amount of contact that increases favorable attitudes (e.g., decreases prejudice) between members of different groups, rather it is the "nature of the contact" that occurs. For intergroup contact to reduce prejudice, Cook (1978) argues that it is necessary for five conditions to exist: (1) individuals should have equal status, (2) negative outgroup stereotypes should be disconfirmed, (3) cooperation should exist (e.g., participants work on a joint goal), (4) the situation should have high "acquaintance potential," and (5) there should be a supportive social climate. The majority of models developed to explain how different types of intergroup contact influence intergroup attitudes are based on an interpersonal, not an intergroup, perspective. Miller and Brewer (1986), for example, focus almost exclusively on similarity at the interpersonal level in their models of intergroup contact, even though they begin from Tajfel's (1978) social identity theory. Hewstone and Brown (1986) also build on social identity theory, but in addition emphasize Tajfel's distinction between interpersonal and intergroup behavior. They argue that interpersonal interactions between members of different groups will produce changes in stereotypes only when categorization occurs (e.g., the other individual is viewed as a representative of the outgroup).

Affective reactions are one of the major by-products of intergroup contact (Pettigrew, 1986). Bobad and Wallbott's (1986) cross-cultural research in eight cultures, for example, reveals that there is greater fear associated with interactions with people who are unfamiliar (e.g., members of outgroups) than with people who are familiar (e.g., members of ingroups). Their research also demonstrates that there is less verbalization of, and less control over, expressing anger with people who are unfamiliar than with people who are familiar. There were cultural differences across the emotions experienced with strangers and whether emotions are experienced with familiar or unfamiliar people (see Appendix D, Scherer, Wallbott, & Summerfield, 1986), but the researchers did not examine culture by familiarity interaction effects so cultural hypotheses cannot be generated from the data. A comparison of the eight cultures across Hofstede's (1980) dimensions of cultural variability, however, allows for a potential theoretical explanation to be derived. The eight cultures are all moderate to high in individualism, moderate in masculinity, and low to moderate in power distance, while five of the eight are high in uncertainty avoidance and the remaining three are low to moderate. Given that uncertainty avoidance is the dimension Hofstede relates to the express of emotion, it appears that this dimension may explain the differences that exist.

Contact also appears to influence specific aspects of social identity. Jaspars and Warnaen (1982), for example, found greater intergroup differentiation (e.g., more negative attitudes) in Jakarta, where the groups have a large amount of contact, than in provincial samples in Indonesia, where the groups have relatively low contact. Compatible findings emerge from Hamilton, Carpenter, and Bishop's (1984) study of residential desegregation in the United States. They discovered that White residents who have Black neighbors but have little contact with them have positive changes in their social attitudes. Given that one study was conducted in a collectivistic culture and one in an individualistic, it appears reasonable to assume that contact is not a necessary condition for positive attitude change or a decrease in intergroup differentiation across cultures.

Research (e.g., Trew's, 1986, work in Northern Ireland, and Taylor, Dubé, & Bellerose's, 1986, study in Quebec) indicates that harmonious interpersonal contact can take place between members of different groups even in the presence of a long history of intergroup tension in the society. This does not always occur, however, as Foster and Finchilescu's (1986) research in South Africa demonstrates. As Pettigrew (1986) points out, these studies document that "the use of intergroup contact as a means of alleviating conflict is largely dependent on the social structure that patterns relations between the groups" (p. 191, italics omitted). Are there, however, specific dimensions of cultural variability that are related to the aspects of the social structure that influence intergroup relations? There is no research to date directly bearing on this question. The three cultures cited are relatively individualistic and are similar (e.g., have moderate Hofstede, 1980, scores) on power distance, uncertainty avoidance, and masculinity. One plausible dimension of variability that might influence this process is the degree of structural tightness, the "degree of hierarchical structure among sociocultural elements in a society" (Witkin & Berry, 1975, p. 11). Boldt and Roberts (1979) argue that "role relatedness" (e.g., the degree to which roles are interrelated) defines a culture as "tight" or "loose." Ireland and Canada appear to have a high degree of role relatedness with respect to the roles that members of different ethnic groups fill, while South Africa appears to have little Black-White role relatedness.

COMMUNICATION IN INGROUP AND OUTGROUP RELATIONSHIPS

The specific relationship between members of an ingroup and an outgroup depends, at least in part, on the ingroup's attitude toward outgroups and the outgroup's perceived intention toward the ingroup.

Gudykunst (1985) and Levine (1985) utilize these two dimensions to develop typologies of stranger-ingroup relationships (nine and six types, respectively). Gudykunst specifies how the normative power and conflict potential of ingroup-outgroup relationships vary depending upon the two dimensions (e.g., when the ingroup has a positive attitude toward the outgroup and the outgroup seeks to assimilate with the ingroup, normative power is moderate and conflict potential is high). Levine argues that there is cultural variability in the way ingroups deal with strangers. Wood (1934) suggests that the differences are related to the degree of homogeneity and heterogeneity and the composition of the group in terms of percentage of "natives" and "foreigners." While neither Wood nor Levine uses the term, their discussions focus on individualism and appear to be consistent with the research cited above. It, therefore, appears reasonable to argue that strangers establish relationships with members of the ingroup more easily in individualistic than in collectivistic cultures.

There are also cross-cultural studies that have examined communication in ingroup and outgroup relationships. Noesjirwan (1978), for example, found that the rule-guided behavior with respect to the ingroup in Indonesia (collectivistic) is that members of the group should adapt to the group so that the group can present a united front. In Australia (individualistic), on the other hand, members are expected to do their own thing even if they must go against the group. Similarly, Argyle, Henderson, Bond, Iizuka, and Contarello (1986) found that rules regarding ingroups, such as maintaining harmonious relations, are highly endorsed in collectivist cultures (Japan and Hong Kong), but not in individualistic cultures (Britain and Italy). These findings are consistent with Levine's (1985) discussions of the functions of direct and indirect forms of communication. Direct communication, which predominates in individualistic cultures, allows for open conflict. Indirect communication, which is used extensively in collectivistic cultures, in contrast, does not allow for open conflict, but allows individuals to allude to shared experiences and, at the same time, conceal what is on their mind. The impact of individualism on social penetration processes in ingroup and outgroup relationships in Japan, Korea, and the United States was examined in Gudykunst, Yoon, and Nishida's (1987) study. This study revealed that the greater the degree of collectivism present in a culture, the greater the amount of personalization and synchronization, but the less the difficulty perceived in communication with classmates (ingroup). These results for communication in ingroup relationships clearly support predictions derived from Triandis's (1986) conceptualization of individualism-collectivism. Members of collectivistic cultures perceive greater social penetration (more personalization and synchronization, but less difficulty) in ingroup relationships than do members of individualistic cultures.

Gudykunst, Yoon, and Nishida's (1987) results for communication with outgroup members were not as clear-cut. The data indicated that there is an inverse linear relationship between perceived personalization of communication with members of outgroups and individualism, that is, the greater the individualism, the less the perceived personalization. This finding is consistent with the prediction derived from previous research in collectivistic cultures (Leung & Bond, 1984; Wetherell, 1982). Specifically, since there are strong situational demands on behavior in collectivistic cultures, the amount of personalization in communication with members of outgroups is specified by the situation, while in individualistic cultures, where situational demands are relatively weak, the amount of personalized communication is determined by the specific individuals involved.

Perceptions of synchronization in communication with outgroup members did not fit the same pattern in Gudykunst, Yoon, and Nishida's (1987) study. Rather, the least synchronization occurred in Japan, while approximately the same amount was perceived in the U.S. and Korean samples. One potential explanation for this pattern is that Japan and Korea emphasize different forms of collectivism. Japan emphasizes what Triandis (1986) labels "contextual collectivism," where the ingroup's influence is specific. Korea, in contrast, emphasizes what Triandis calls "simple collectivism," where if more than one ingroup influences a person's behavior, the person can balance the views of the various groups and decide how to behave him- or herself without feeling norm or role conflict. The relevant ingroups that Korean students use to deal with strangers, therefore, appear to prescribe that relatively the same degree of personalization takes place, but do not all prescribe the same degree of synchronization between their behavior and that of strangers. The contextual collectivism of Japanese student ingroups, on the other hand, appears to require relatively low levels of both personalization and synchronization in communication with members of outgroups.

Finally, Gudykunst, Yoon, and Nishida's (1987) results for perceived difficulty in communicating with strangers were consistent with the predicted pattern: The least difficulty was perceived in the United States, while the most was perceived in Japan and Korea, with mean scores being approximately the same. This finding is consistent with Triandis's (1986) conceptualization of individualism-collectivism.

Given Triandis's (1986) conceptualization and the results of Gudykunst, Yoon, and Nishida's (1987) research, Gudykunst, Nishida, and Schmidt (1988) predicted that there are differences in uncertainty reduction processes with members of ingroups and outgroups in collectivistic cultures, but not in individualistic cultures. More specifically, they hypothesized that there is more self-disclosure, attraction, perceived similarity, display of nonverbal affiliative expressiveness, shared networks, and low-context and high-context attributional confidence in ingroup relationships than in outgroups in collectivistic cultures, but not in individualistic cultures.

Gudykunst, Nishida, and Schmidt's (1988) results for ingroup-outgroup communication generally support the predictions. There was a significant multivariate effect for the Japanese sample, but there was no significant effect in the U.S. sample. The specific patterns that emerged in the mean scores for the eight dependent measures, however, are not all consistent. As expected, there were significantly more shared networks with members of ingroups than with members of outgroups. This finding is compatible with Triandis's (1986) conceptualization of ingroups and outgroups in collectivistic cultures and with Nakane's (1970, 1974) discussion of ingroups in Japan. There also was a tendency for more interrogation and display of nonverbal affiliative expressiveness with members of ingroups than with members of outgroups. The finding for nonverbal affiliative expressiveness is consistent with Gudykunst and Nishida's (1986a) discussion of uncertainty reduction processes in low- and high-context cultures. No apparent differences between ingroup and outgroup communication occurred with respect to attraction, similarity, or low-context or high-context attributional confidence. The one unexpected result was for self-disclosure, that is, there was more self-disclosure with members of outgroups than with members of ingroups. The most plausible explanation for this finding is methodological, that is, respondents were asked to think of a person whom they did not know well. Greater self-disclosure would be expected with members of the ingroup who are known well than with members of the outgroup who are known well.

INTERPERSONAL RELATIONSHIPS
BETWEEN MEMBERS OF DIFFERENT CULTURES

The preceding sections of this chapter have looked at cross-cultural variations in communication in intergroup relationships. This section focuses on a different line of research regarding culture and interpersonal communication, namely, interpersonal relationships between members of different cultures (i.e., intercultural relationships). Group memberships (including culture) have a differential impact on relationships at different levels of intimacy. Altman and Taylor (1973) argue that in the affective exchange stage (i.e., close friendships) "the dyad has moved to the point where interaction is relatively free both in peripheral and in more central areas of personality. Cultural stereotypy is broken down in these more intimate areas and there is willingness to move freely in and out of such exchanges" (pp. 139-140). If cultural and group stereotypy is broken down, the group from which a person comes should not be a major factor influencing interaction. This line of reasoning is consistent with Bell's (1981) conceptualization of friendship: "The development of friendship is based on private negotiations and is not imposed through cultural values or norms" (p. 10).

The position outlined above also is compatible with Miller and Steinberg's (1975) "developmental" theory of interpersonal relationships. Specifically, it can be inferred that when communicators move from using cultural and sociological data (both based on group membership) to the use of psychological data in making predictions about their partners, the group from which a person comes is no longer a major relevant variable in making predictions about his or her communication behavior. Given this position, it would be expected that when relationships reach the point of close friendship, and the individuals are basing their predictions about their partner on psychological data, that the degree of social penetration in which people engage should not differ in intragroup and intergroup relationships as a function of group membership.

Both Altman and Taylor's (1973) and Miller and Steinberg's (1975) theories support the argument that the influence of group membership on interpersonal relationships varies as relationships become more intimate. Initially, group memberships have an effect on the relationship and how it develops. As relationships between people from different groups move through the stages of relationship development, however, the effect of group membership begins to disappear. Once interpersonal relationships between people from different groups reach the friendship stage (i.e., Altman & Taylor's, 1973, full affective exchange stage), group memberships appear to have little effect on the relationship because the majority of interaction in friendships has a personalistic focus. As Wright (1978) observes, "in friendship, each person reacts to the other as a person-qua-person or, more specifically, with respect to his/her genuineness, uniqueness, and irreplaceability in the relationship" (p. 199).

Research further suggests that when members of one culture travel to another culture, they experience difficulties in adjusting to the host culture. One of the major factors that explains the degree of difficulty is the similarity of the host culture and the sojourner's native culture. Babiker, Cox, and Miller (1980), for example, found a positive correlation between cultural dissimilarity and the anxiety sojourners experience. Stephan and Stephan (1985) discovered a similar relationship for intergroup contact in the United States. Similarly, Furnham and Bochner (1982) observed a positive relationship between cultural dissimilarity and the social difficulties sojourners have in a foreign culture. Cultural dissimilarity also interacts with the type of relationship to influence the communication sojourners have with host nationals. Research on social penetration theory and uncertainty reduction theory further supports the claims made here.

Social Penetration Processes

One study has compared social penetration processes in intracultural and intercultural relationships. Gudykunst (1985b) found a high correlation between perceptions of social penetration across 13 typical areas in close intra- and intercultural relationships. The canonical coefficients and canonical component loadings had very similar patterns in the intra- and intercultural relationships. Gudykunst's data also revealed a moderate correlation ($r = .51$) between the amount of perceived similarity in the two types of relationships.

Given results of Gudykunst's (1985b) and Gudykunst and Nishida's (1983, 1986b) research, Gudykunst, Nishida, and Chua (1987) predicted that as relationships increase in intimacy, communication is perceived as more personalized and synchronized, but less difficult. Knapp, Ellis, and Williams's (1980) research and Gudykunst and Nishida's (1986b) study also suggest that the social penetration process is influenced by dyadic composition. Extending their findings, Gudykunst, Nishida, and Chua (1987) argued that opposite-sex relationships are perceived as more personal than same-sex relationships. Data were collected from both partners in Japanese-North American dyads and were examined using both summation and dispersion scores. Results of this study were consistent with predictions derived from Altman and Taylor's (1973) social penetration theory, as well as with Knapp, Ellis, and Williams's (1980) intracultural research in the United States. Summation scores for high intimacy dyads revealed that partners perceive more personalized and synchronized communication, but less difficulty in communication than partners in low intimacy dyads. These results are clearly consistent with social penetration theory. Mixed dyads, however, were between the low and high intimacy dyads with respect to personalized communication and higher than both groups for synchronized communication and difficulty of communication. Relationship type explained 62% of the variance in personalized communication, 20% of synchronized communication, and 15% of difficulty in communication.

The results from the analysis of the dispersion scores in Gudykunst, Nishida, and Chua's (1987) study revealed that mixed dyads have significantly less agreement than low intimacy dyads on the amount of personalized communication and less, but not significantly less, agreement than low intimacy dyads. On the remaining two factors, high intimacy dyads had lower dispersion scores than low intimacy dyads, but the low intimacy dyads' scores were higher than the mixed dyads' scores. These findings suggest that there is greater agreement in high intimacy dyads than in low intimacy dyads, but mixed dyads do not fit a specific pattern.

Several noteworthy patterns also emerged in Gudykunst, Nishida, and Chua's (1987) correlational analysis. Perceived synchrony and perceived difficulty of communication, for example, had a high negative correlation, suggesting that as difficulty is reduced synchronization occurs, or vice versa. Further, while perceived personalization and perceived synchronization had a moderate correlation, perceived personalization and perceived difficulty were uncorrelated. These patterns imply that perceived personalization and perceived synchrony covary in intercultural dyads, but perceived personalization and perceived difficulty do not, a finding consistent with Knapp, Ellis, and Williams's (1980) intracultural research. The length of relationship and frequency of communication also were correlated moderately with perceived personalization, but neither correlated with perceived synchronization or perceived difficulty of communication. These findings, in combination with the analysis by relationship type, suggest that relationship type, not length or frequency, influences perceived synchronization and perceived difficulty, consistent with Altman and Taylor (1973). Only the perceived synchronization findings, however, were consistent with Knapp, Ellis, and Williams (1980). This may suggest that relationship type has more of an influence on perceived difficulty of communication in intercultural relationships than in intracultural relationships.

Perceived second language competence was correlated moderately (in a positive direction) with each of the three social penetration variables in Gudykunst, Nishida, and Chua's (1987) study. It, therefore, appears that the ability to use the partners' native language influences perceptions of social penetration in intercultural dyads, or vice versa. It should be noted, however, that these results may be due primarily to the Japanese partners' ability to use English rather than the North American partners' ability to use Japanese or a combination of the two, because the ethnolinguistic vitality (see Giles, Bourhis, & Taylor, 1977) of Japanese probably was low. Closely related to second language competence, clear patterns emerged for perceived intercultural effectiveness. Specifically, perceived effectiveness was related moderately to highly to each of the three social penetration dimensions. The results appear to be consistent with Hammer, Gudykunst, and Wiseman's (1978) conceptualization of intercultural effectiveness. Their research suggests that a large part of intercultural effectiveness is the ability to establish interpersonal relationships with people from other cultures.

Finally, communication satisfaction was correlated positively with each of the dimensions of social penetration in Gudykunst, Nishida, and Chua's (1987) study, with the weakest correlation occurring with perceived personalization. These findings appear to be consistent with Hecht (1984), but his research also suggests that the correlations may vary across type of relationship. He found, for example, that personalness and synchrony are related more strongly to satisfaction in relationships at lower levels of intimacy than in relationships at higher levels of intimacy. The data further revealed a high correlation between satisfaction and perceived effectiveness. This is consistent with Hecht's (1978) argument that "communication satisfaction is one of the outcomes commonly associated with competent communication" (p. 253). Gudykunst, Nishida, and Chua's results, therefore, suggest that this conclusion may be generalizable to some intercultural relationships.

Uncertainty Reduction Processes

Simard's (1981) research with Francophones and Anglophones in Canada revealed that both groups "perceive it as more difficult to know how to initiate a conversation, to know what to talk about during the interaction, to be interested in the other person, and to guess in which language they should talk" when communicating with someone culturally different than when communicating with someone culturally similar (p. 179). Her research also indicated that subjects who form an acquaintance relationship with a culturally different person perceive this person to be as similar to them as do subjects who form an acquaintance with a person who is culturally similar.

Other research is consistent with Simard's (1981) findings. Gudykunst (1983a), for example, found that people make more assumptions about strangers, prefer to talk less, ask more questions about strangers' backgrounds, and have less attributional confidence about predicting strangers' behavior in initial intercultural encounters than in initial intracultural encounters. Similarly, in a study of Japanese and North Americans, Gudykunst and Nishida (1984) discovered that cultural similarity/dissimilarity has a multivariate effect on intent to self-disclose, interrogate, display nonverbal affiliative expressiveness, attraction, and attributional confidence.

Gudykunst (1985c) found a significant interaction effect between cultural similarity and type of relationship. The univariate analyses revealed significant independent effects on two variables—attributional confidence and shared communication networks—while interrogation and self-disclosure approached significance. With respect to self-disclosure and attributional confidence, the mean scores were higher for dissimilar acquaintances than for similar ones, but higher for culturally similar friends than for dissimilar ones. Results for shared communication networks indicated that the mean scores were approximately the same for culturally similar and dissimilar acquaintances, but culturally similar friends shared twice as many networks as culturally dissimilar friends. Culturally dissimilar friends, however, shared significantly more communication networks than culturally similar acquaintances. This difference can be explained by Blau and Schwartz's (1984) theory of intergroup relations. Drawing upon Simmel's (1950) analysis of "cross-cutting social circles," they point out that close relations between people who do not share similar ethnic or cultural backgrounds "tend to be the result of their having other social relations in common" (Blau & Schwartz, 1984, p. 88).

Findings from Gudykunst's (1985c) study with respect to the cultural similarity by type of relationship interaction did not display the patterns that might be predicted from Altman and Taylor's (1973) social penetration theory. Using this perspective it would be predicted that there are differences between culturally similar and dissimilar acquaintances, but no significant differences between culturally similar and dissimilar friends because cultural stereotypy is broken down. Gudykunst's data revealed only one significant difference between the two types of acquaintances, a higher level of attraction in the cultural dissimilarity condition than in the cultural similarity condition. This might suggest that a higher level of attraction is necessary to call someone from another culture an acquaintance than is necessary if the person comes from the same culture. The only differences to emerge between culturally similar and dissimilar friends were on attributional confidence and the percent of shared networks. The difference in shared communication networks is to be expected since a large percent of the culturally dissimilar friends' networks of international students in the United States are in their home culture. The level of attributional confidence in culturally dissimilar friendships was significantly lower than for culturally similar ones, but at the same time it is significantly higher than culturally dissimilar and culturally similar acquaintances. The difference between the two types of friendships may be due to the differences in the shared communication networks, since the correlations between the two variables are approximately equal in the two conditions. This explanation appears to be consistent with Parks and Adelman's (1983) research on romantic relationships.

The lack of predicted interactions may be due to the nature of the relationships studied in Gudykunst's (1985c) study. Specifically, the acquaintance relationships may have been in the later phases of Altman and Taylor's (1973) exploratory affective exchange stage of relationship development (i.e., close to the affective exchange stage), rather than in earlier phases (i.e., nearer the orientation stage). If this is the case, then the predicted interactions would not be observed. These results, therefore, appear to extend Ting-Toomey's (1981) and Gudykunst's (1985a) conclusions that once intercultural relationships become established (i.e., acquaintances or friendships are formed) there are few significant differences attributable to culturally dissimilar backgrounds.

Gudykunst, Chua, and Gray's (1987) research revealed significant interaction effects between dissimilarities on all of Hofstede's (1980) dimensions of cultural variability and stage of relationship development. Specifically, they found that power distance interacted with stage of relationship to influence self-disclosure, attraction, similarity, shared networks, low- and high-context attributional confidence; uncertainty avoidance interacted with stage of relationship to influence self-disclosure, similarity, low- and high-context attributional confidence; individualism interacted with stage of relationship to influence self-disclosure, interrogation, shared networks, low- and high-context attributional confidence; and masculinity interacted with stage of relationship to influence self-disclosure, similarity, shared networks, and low- and high-context attributional confidence. The data suggest that as relationships become more intimate, cultural dissimilarities have less effect on uncertainty reduction processes.

Gudykunst, Sodetani, and Sonoda's (1987) research supports extensions of ethnolinguistic identity theory (Beebe & Giles, 1984) to interethnic uncertainty reduction processes. Overall, their data indicated that ethnolinguistic identity influences the set of uncertainty reduction processes examined. Specifically, the data revealed that the stronger the interethnic comparisons, the weaker other group identification, and the less the perceived vitality, the greater the perceived similarity. Gudykunst, Sodetani, and Sonoda's (1987) study also suggested that the greater the perceived vitality, the less the self-disclosure, interrogation, and low-context attributional confidence. Similarly, they found that the stronger the interethnic comparisons, the less the high-context attributional confidence. Finally, their study indicated that the more positive the interethnic comparisons, the more interethnic networks overlap. Findings from Gudykunst, Sodetani, and Sonoda's (1987) research are generally consistent with extensions of Giles and Johnson (1981) and Giles and Byrne (1982), who hypothesize that the lower the perceived vitality, the higher second language competence.

Gudykunst, Sodetani, and Sonoda (1987) also found that type of relationship influences uncertainty reduction processes. Not only was there a significant multivariate effect by stage of relationship, there was a significant univariate effect for all dependent variables (e.g., self-disclosure, interrogation, attributional confidence, attraction). These findings are consistent with Altman and Taylor's (1973) social penetration theory, as well as Gudykunst's (1985b) research comparing intracultural and intercultural relationships. Uncertainty reduction processes, therefore, appear to vary systematically as stage of relationships changes, intraculturally, interculturally, and interethnicly.

Gudykunst, Nishida, and Chua's (1986) research revealed that high intimacy dyads involved significantly greater self-disclosure, interrogation, shared networks, amount of communication, and low-context attributional confidence than did low intimacy dyads, based on the analysis of summation scores. These findings are consistent with Gudykunst's (1985c) research on intercultural relationships and Gudykunst, Sodetani, and Sonoda's (1987) study of Japanese-Caucasian interethnic communication in Hawaii. The results from the analysis of the dispersion scores revealed that high intimacy dyads are more consistent than low intimacy dyads in the amount they self-disclose and the degree of high-context attributional confidence they have about each other.

Several noteworthy patterns also emerged in Gudykunst, Nishida, and Chua's (1986) post hoc correlational analysis. The data indicated that self-disclosure, interrogation, amount of communication, length of relationship, and shared networks are correlated with low-context, but not high-context, attributional confidence. The associations for amount and self-disclosure supported Axioms 1 and 4 of Berger and Calabrese's (1975) original theory, but the data indicated the axioms cannot be extended to high-context attributional confidence in intercultural dyads. Gudykunst, Sodetani, and Sonoda's (1987) findings suggest that this may be due to differences between the North American and Japanese partners. In their study, amount and high-context confidence were correlated for Caucasians, but not for Japanese-Americans. Similarly, Gudykunst and Nishida's (1986a) research revealed that amount and length of relationship are correlated with both low-context and high-context confidence for North Americans, but only related to low-context confidence for Japanese.

Perceived second language competence was correlated with self-disclosure, interrogation, low-context attributional confidence, and length of relationship in Gudykunst, Nishida, and Chua's (1986) study. These results are consistent with Gudykunst's (1988) theory of inter-group uncertainty reduction, which predicts that second language competence influences the use of interactive uncertainty reduction strategies (i.e., self-disclosure and interrogation), as well as attributional confidence. Closely related to second language competence, clear patterns emerged for perceived intercultural effectiveness. Specifically, perceived effectiveness was related to self-disclosure, interrogation, attraction, and similarity, as well as both low- and high-context attributional confidence. These results appear to be consistent with Hammer, Gudykunst, and Wiseman's (1978) conceptualization of intercultural effectiveness. Finally, communication satisfaction was correlated with self-disclosure, interrogation, attraction, similarity, effectiveness, and low- and high-context attributional confidence. These findings appear to be consistent with Hecht's (1978) conceptualization of communication satisfaction and Hecht's (1984) research.

CONCLUSION

Predictions regarding the influence of culture on intergroup processes have been posited. Some predictions were based on data from several studies, others were generated logically. Taken together, the predictions emphasize the necessity of taking cultural variability into consideration when examining intergroup processes. Research conducted in highly individualistic cultures like the United States and England suggests that group memberships are less important than they are in influencing behavior and that when group membership is salient, the outgroup is discriminated against. Studies in collectivistic cultures, however, demonstrate that group memberships play a large role in affecting behavior and that outgroups are not necessarily discriminated against simply because they are outgroups. Given that Triandis and his associates'

(1985) work on idiocentrism-allocentrism indicates that this personality dimension varies within cultures, future work must consider variability along this cultural/personality factor to explain intergroup behavior fully. The predictions proffered also suggest that both cognitive and affective factors must be incorporated in any explanation of intergroup behavior. More importantly, the predictions clearly indicate that the various levels of analysis (e.g., cultural, intergroup, interpersonal) must be articulated if processes occurring at any of the levels are to be explained adequately (Doise, 1986).

12

Concluding Remarks

Our purpose in writing this book was to link culture to interpersonal communication theoretically. In Chapter 1, we presented a theoretical framework that linked cultural variability to situational factors in interpersonal communication (i.e., norms, rules, roles, networks, language, the environment, use of space, nonverbal signals, difficulties, and skills), as well as social cognitive and affective processes in interpersonal communication. In Chapter 2, we presented the major conceptualizations of cultural variability. Throughout the remainder of the book, we examined cross-cultural research on interpersonal communication, linking previous findings to variations on dimensions of cultural variability whenever possible. Many of the explanations proffered are post hoc and, therefore, must be considered hypotheses for future research.

The purpose of this chapter is threefold. The first section contains a discussion of the generalizability of the model presented in Chapter 1. Next, we overview the issues that must be taken into consideration when conducting cross-cultural research on interpersonal communication. We conclude with some final remarks on the current state of the research and broad suggestions for future work.

GENERALITY OF THE FRAMEWORK

The framework proffered in Chapter 1 is applicable across the areas of inquiry in the study of cultural systems and communication (i.e., intercultural, cross-cultural, international, and comparative mass communication). The applicability to cross-cultural communication is most direct, as indicated throughout the book. To understand similarities and differences across cultures, researchers cannot simply compare different systems; rather, the cultures studied must be selected because of specific cultural variations. These variations, in turn, should be linked theoretically to the dependent variables being examined. Communication between members of ingroups and outgroups, for example, might be hypothesized to vary systematically as a function of the individualism-collectivism dimension (e.g., Leung & Bond, 1984).

The applicability of the framework to intercultural communication is also relatively straightforward. The study of communication between members of different cultures also needs to be based on cultural similarity/dissimilarity on specific dimensions and these dimensions must be linked to the other variables in the theory. Communication between members of collectivistic and individualistic cultures, for example, might be hypothesized to be different than communication between members of two different collectivistic or two different individualistic cultures.

The framework also is applicable to comparative mass communication and international communication. Williams (1975) argues that television or any other medium of communication cannot be understood in isolation, that it must be seen as an "intrinsic outcome" of a particular sociocultural system. Similarly, Nordenstreng (1984) contends that both a theory of "society" and a theory of knowledge are needed to understand the role of the media. The present framework begins to specify how cultural variabilities affect intrapersonal processes that, in turn, influence individuals' communication and understanding. The role of the media in the "cultivation of reality" also can be incorporated into the model. Comparative mass communication research has utilized selected cultural variations as independent variables in previous research; for example, "socialist" versus "capitalist" systems (e.g., Gerbner, 1966), systems of control or ownership (e.g., Wells, 1974), national development (e.g., Farace, 1966), and the traditional-modernity continuum (e.g., Lerner, 1958). These approaches, however, have been criticized because of their ideological biases (e.g., Mowlana, 1976). The sociocultural variations used also have not been incorporated into theory and, in addition, they ignore "other socioeconomic and cultural factors that influence the structure and operations of media systems" (Hur, 1982, p. 539). Smith (1979) argues that cultural variability can explain differences in media systems, and while Hur (1982) concurs, he concludes that "cultural" data generally are omitted from comparative media studies.

The cultural variations elaborated here can be incorporated in comparative mass communication research and should be useful in explaining similarities and differences in content of and responses to media across sociocultural systems (see Murray & Kippax, 1979, for a review of research on television's effect across 16 cultures). Cultures displaying different scores on Hofstede's (1980) masculinity index, for example, would be predicted to depict different images of male and female relations in the media, particularly with regard to work. Cultures low on this dimension (e.g., Sweden, Norway) should display less sex role differentiation in advertisements than systems high on this dimension (e.g., Japan). Similar predictions could be made for the other dimensions of cultural variability. Comparisons of "cultural indicators" in the mass media across cultures (e.g., Melischek, Rosengren, & Stappers, 1984), therefore, should incorporate cultural variations as independent variables that influence the patterns of indicators across cultures.

The framework proposed herein is consistent with current models of mass communication. Palmgreen (1984), for example, proposes an integrative gratification model of mass media consumption. The major exogenous variable in his model is "society-culture," which includes media structure and media technology. Society-culture influences social circumstances (including availability of specific behaviors), beliefs (e.g., expectations about the media), psychological variables, needs, and values. The framework proffered specifies potential dimensions of cultural variability that influence the other factors in Palmgreen's model and, in addition, the social factors and social cognitive processes that are influenced by cultural variability.

The current model also is applicable to the study of international communication, particularly in assessing the effects of mediated messages transmitted from one culture to another. Hur's (1982) review of the effects of television and/or film from the United States on members of other systems suggests that "the effects of U.S. television and film content, if any, are at best cognitive, rather than attitudinal or behavioral" (p. 547). While some effects have been isolated, no theoretical explanation has been offered (see DeSousa, 1982, for a review). An initial application of Kluckhohn and Strodtbeck's (1961) value orientations to implementing new communication technologies, however, has been suggested (Contractor, Fulk, Monge, & Singhal, 1986). The model proffered here can be extended to suggest other potential lines of inquiry and theoretical development.

As the model suggests, cultural variability influences social cognitive processes, social factors, affect, and habits. Humans are active information processors, but the way they process the incoming information is influenced by their sociocultural environment. Cultural variations influence the information to which people attune (i.e., perceptual selectivity), the way information is "chunked" or "framed" for encoding and storage (i.e., cognitive unitizing; Newtson, 1973), the attributions they make about what they observe, the implicit theories they hold regarding what is expected from the various media, and the scripts individuals have for dealing with mass media. Each of these factors, in turn, affect the way mediated messages from other cultures are interpreted and the effects they have (see Kellerman, 1985, for a review of the role of cognitive processes in media effects).

Several questions for future research in comparative mass communication and international communication are suggested by the framework: (1) Do individuals attune to the same content of mediated messages from other cultures than they attune to in messages from their own culture? (2) Do individuals "chunk" messages from other cultures in the same manner as they "chunk" messages from within their own culture? (3) Do individuals make similar attributions about content originating in other cultures than they do about messages originating in their own culture? (4) Do individuals have different scripts for dealing with mediated messages from other cultures than they do for dealing with messages from within their own? (5) Do individuals employ different implicit theories in understanding the content of mediated messages from other cultures than they use for messages from within their own culture? These five questions all deal with differences and/or similarities in the processing of intranational and international mediated messages. Each, however, may be influenced by the degree of similarities/differences in the cultures under consideration. If both systems are high on Hofstede's masculinity dimension, for example, content of intranational and international mediated messages regarding sex role differentiation may be processed similarly. If the originating system is high on masculinity and the receiving system is low, the processing of messages dealing with sex role differentiation may be different. Cultural variations related to the content of the messages, therefore, must be taken into consideration. Individual differences also must be taken into account. To illustrate, Detweiler's (1975, 1978) research suggests that category width may mediate the impact of cultural variations on the way individuals categorize incoming messages from other cultures and the attributions they make about these messages.

UNIQUE METHODOLOGICAL ISSUES

Doing research across cultures involves some unique methodological issues that are not major problems in other areas of communication. Triandis (1980b) points to many of the problems inherent in this area of research:

> Since methods change their meaning across cultures, reliance on a single method to establish a cultural difference is methodologically unsound. What *appears* to be a cultural difference may be a result of different response sets, differences in familiarity with the stimuli, differences in the definition of the testing situation, differential reactions to the experimenter, differences in the motivation to respond to that test, differences in the social desirability of the responses, problems of interpretation, differential reactions to anonymity and a myriad of other factors. . . . Obviously, any *one* difference cannot be interpreted. However, if multimethod measurement of a variable leads to consistencies in results . . . , one is more justified in assuming that a difference is really there. If the difference is observed in *both* behavioral and pencil-and-paper measures, *and* it fits theoretical expectations, *and* is observed at both the individual and group level, one may begin believing that the difference is really there. Furthermore, it is crucial to establish a broad set of similarities in the way variables are interrelated before small differences are interpreted. Above all, one needs to have a good theory that expects cultural differences, if one is to believe that the observed differences are real. (p. 8)

Obviously all of the issues involved in doing research in different cultures cannot be addressed here (see Gudykunst & Kim, 1984b; Lonner & Berry, 1986; Triandis & Berry, 1980, for recent coverages). There are, however, three major areas that need to be addressed: level of analysis, emic versus etic research, and the issue of equivalence across cultures.

Level of Analysis

In examining cultural variations and communication, researchers must constantly be aware of their level of analysis: Are they studying individuals, organizations, or cultures? Shweder (1973) argued that "valid indicators of a theoretical variable may be discovered across a representative sample of cultures without being discoverable within any of them, or may be discovered within each of the cultures without being discoverable across them" (p. 543). If responses to a set of items are considered, culture can, therefore, have two different effects (Leung & Bond, 1987).

First, culture can affect the relationships among the items. Two items, for example, may be uncorrelated in one culture, positively correlated in a second, and negatively correlated in a third. This is the patterning effect of culture. If the correlations are similar across cultures, the relationship has cross-cultural generalizability. If the correlations are different (e.g., correlations are culture specific), explanations that account for the differences must be generated.

Second, culture can affect how "average" individuals respond from different cultures to a set of items, that is, a location effect. This is the effect examined in most of the research discussed throughout the book. The same correlations may exist between two items, but average individuals in the two cultures may respond to the items differently. Similarly, different correlations may exist between two items in two cultures, while average individuals in the two cultures respond the same way to the items.

To establish dimensions of variation at the cultural- (ecological-) level, mean scores on a series of items from individuals from a large number of cultures are either factor analyzed (e.g., Smith & Crano, 1977) or clustered using nonmetric multidimensional scaling (e.g., Ronen & Shenkar, 1985). These procedures isolate the location effect for culture, and only the location effect. Alternatively, a pancultural analysis can be conducted. This type of analysis yields both a location and a pattern effect for culture. Neither procedure (ecological or pancultural analyses) allows for dimensions at the individual level to be isolated.

In order to isolate dimensions at the individual level, Leung and Bond (1987) suggest that an "iso-region" analysis be conducted. This procedure begins with within subject standardization across a series of items (e.g., self-reports of communication behavior). Within-culture standardization is then performed to eliminate the location effect for culture (i.e., the mean will be zero [0] on each item and each item will have a standard deviation of 1.0). If these data are factor analyzed, the factors that emerge are "pure" in that there is no location effect for culture. There is, however, still a patterning effect for culture in the data. This procedure allows investigators to examine cultural differences at the individual level of response or to ignore culture and look for universals at the individual level.

Given this introduction to the issue of levels of analysis, we will look at specific issues that affect interpretation of data across cultures and levels of analysis. If data are collected from individuals in several organizations across cultures, it is possible to (1) compare data for individuals globally across organizations and cultures, (2) compare within-organization data, (3) compare within-cultures data, (4) compare between-organization data, and (5) compare between-cultures data. If correlational data are being analyzed, the five different correlations are, in all likelihood, not equal. One concern is whether the within-organization (2) correlations are equal across organizations or whether the within cultures (3) correlations are equal across cultures. If these correlations are not equal, useful information is obtained about the organizational and cultural system levels. Also, if these correlations are significantly different, global correlations (1) will be misleading. Ecological correlations (i.e., correlations calculated from mean values for each organization or culture, 4 and 5 above), tend to be higher than the individual (1), within-organization (2), and within-cultures (3) correlations.

When correlations at the individual (1), within-organization (2), or within-cultures (3) levels are confused with ecological correlations (4 and 5), the ecological fallacy occurs. The ecological fallacy was isolated originally by Thorndike (1939), but the most widely cited analysis is Robinson (1950). Robinson illustrated the fallacy with data on skin color and illiteracy in the United States. When ecological data from states were used, Robinson found a correlation of .77 between skin color and illiteracy; however, at the individual level the correlation was only .20. Both correlations are useful, but the ecological fallacy occurs if the ecological correlation is interpreted as though it applies to individuals. The correlations between dimensions of cultural variability and emotional responses to situations (see Chapter 9) are ecological correlations and, therefore, should not be applied at the individual level. Ecological data can be used to draw conclusions at the organizational or systems level (e.g., Blau & Schwartz's, 1984, use of ecological data to test their macrostructural theory of intergroup relations), but care must be taken when drawing conclusions at the individual level.

Hofstede (1980) points out that cross-cultural researchers also must be careful not to commit the reverse ecological fallacy. That is, create dimensions within cultural systems and then use these dimensions to correlate ecological data. If dimensions are to be used, mean scores for each item for each system (or organization depending on level of analysis) must be used and dimensions formed across cultures. To illustrate, Hofstede's four dimensions of cultures were obtained by using mean scores for each of the 40 countries on each of the variables. Using the mean scores for the items, dimensions were obtained using ecological data (i.e., the number of cases was 40, not the over 100,000 individuals from whom data were collected).

The Emic-Etic Distinction

The distinction between the emic and etic approaches to cross-cultural research can be traced to Pike's (1966) discussion of phonetics (vocal utterances that are universal) and phonemics (culturally specific vocal utterances). The implications of the distinction for cross-cultural research have been discussed widely in past literature (e.g., Berry, 1969, 1980; Hall, 1985; Jahoda, 1983; Lonner, 1979). Brislin (1983) argues that in current usage the distinction is employed basically as a metaphor for differences between the culture specific (emic, single culture) and culture general (etic, universal) approaches to research. Berry (1980, pp. 11-12) presented a succinct summary of the distinction:

Emic approach	*Etic approach*
studies behavior from within the system	studies behavior from a position outside the system
examines only one culture	examines many cultures, comparing them
structure discovered by the analyst	structure created by the analyst
criteria are relative to internal characteristics	criteria are considered absolute or universal (pp. 11-12)

Given the distinction between the two approaches, most research in psychology and sociology across cultures is etic, while most anthropological research is emic.

When the concepts tested using the etic method are assumed to exist they are referred to as imposed etics (Berry, 1969) or pseudo etics (Triandis, Malpass, & Davidson, 1973). Derived etics (Berry, 1969), in contrast, emerge from empirical data—the common features of the concept under examination in the cultures studied (e.g., Hofstede's, 1980, dimensions of cultural variability). While the emic and etic approaches generally are viewed as opposite ends of a continuum, attempts have been made to integrate the two approaches. Triandis (1972), for example, recommends that when studying subjective culture researchers should utilize combined emic and etic measures. Specifically, attributes of concepts under study should be elicited in all cultures studied and both unique (emic) and common (etic) attributes should be included in the final instrument.

Constructing a derived etic measure is a time-consuming process.

Aspects of the concept under study must be generated in each culture (e.g., through intensive interviews). The culture specific aspects of the concept must then be integrated into one measure, translated (and back translated), and pretested in each culture. Based on the pretest, items not appropriate in each of the cultures are discarded and a final measure developed (for examples of studies following these procedures, see Araki & Barnlund, 1985; Nomura & Barnlund, 1983). Ideally, this process also includes a complete assessment of the reliability and validity of the final measure before it is used in hypothesis-testing research.

Davidson, Jaccard, Triandis, Morales, and Diaz-Guerrero (1976) argue that etic models can be tested using emic operationalizations of variables. More recently, Triandis and Marin (1983) found that appropriate etic scales provide cultural differences similar to those obtained using emic scales.

The distinction between emic and etic approaches has not been emphasized throughout the book. The reason for this is that we have focused upon studies using an etic approach (the exception is in Chapter 5, in which the focus was on emic characteristics). Most of the studies have used imposed etic measures. While we believe the measures used are reasonable, future research should attempt to develop derived etic measures of the variables studied (e.g., Gudykunst & Nishida's, 1986a, measure of attributional confidence in low- and high-context cultures). To illustrate, Snyder's (1974) conceptualization and measure of self-monitoring does not take into consideration the context in which the self-monitoring occurs or the status relationships among the participants, factors important in self-monitoring in collectivistic cultures. Using Snyder's measure in collectivistic cultures, therefore, requires a counter-intuitive prediction, that is, members of individualistic cultures engage in greater self-monitoring than members of collectivistic cultures (see the discussion of Gudykunst, Yang, & Nishida's, 1987, study in Chapter 7). If self-monitoring was conceptualized and measured more con-textually (e.g., more than Snyder's conceptualization and measurement) so that it took into consideration context and status relationships, members of collectivistic cultures would be expected to self-monitor more than members of individualistic cultures (this is the argument Snyder, 1987, makes). The cultural specificity of Snyder's (1974, 1979) conceptualization and measurement (i.e., based on the United States context), therefore, is critical to the predictions that are made regarding cultural differences.

The emic-etic issue is not considered important by all cross-cultural researchers. Jahoda (1983), for example, argues that most discussions of this issue are unclear in differentiating between the objectives of the two approaches because they tend to be entirely abstract. Jahoda believes that concentrating on the emic-etic issue obscures the starting point and goals of cross-cultural research and, therefore, the focus should be on the critical and theoretical and epistemological problems facing social science. A complete discussion of the emic-etic issue and its relevance in communication research can be found in Hall (1985).

Equivalence

"If comparisons are to be legitimately made across cultural boundaries, it is first necessary to establish equivalent bases upon which to make comparisons" (Lonner, 1979, p. 27). Equivalence here refers to equality in quantity, value, meaning, and so forth. Without establishing equivalence, cross-cultural researchers may compare apples in one culture with oranges in another. Five types of equivalence are involved in cross-cultural research: functional, conceptual, linguistic, metric, and sample equivalence.

Functional equivalence involves the relationship between specific observations and the inferences that are made from the observations. This form of equivalence can be traced to Goldschmidt's (1966) discussion of comparative functionalism. He argued that activities must have similar functions if they are to be used for purposes of comparison. Berry (1969) elaborated:

> Functional equivalence of behavior exists when the behavior in question has developed in response to a problem shared by two or more societal/cultural groups, even though the behavior in one society does not appear to be related to its counterpart in another society. These functional equivalences must pre-exist as naturally occurring phenomena; they are discovered and cannot be created or manipulated . . . without this equivalence, it is suggested, no valid cross-cultural behavioral comparison can be made. (p. 122)

To illustrate, one area of research in communication in which functional equivalence is of concern is research on communication apprehension (e.g., Klopf & Cambra, 1979; Klopf, 1984). While communication apprehension is viewed as undesirable in North America, where the concept originated, this view is not shared in other cultures where the concept has been examined (i.e., Japan and Korea) .

Functional equivalence involves equivalence at the macro or cultural level. Conceptual equivalence, in contrast, "focuses upon the presence (or absence) of meanings that individuals attach to specific stimuli" (Lonner, 1979, p. 27). Sears (1961) argues that researchers must discover the meaning of concepts to individuals within the cognitive systems of the members of the culture being examined.

Linguistic (or translation) equivalence is related very closely to conceptual equivalence, but the focus is on the language used in questionnaires, interviews, or instructions used in research. Administration of research instruments in a language of one culture to people in another culture for whom this language is not the native language or who are not bilingual in the language yields data that lacks equivalence. Research instruments should be administered in the respondents' native language and the forms used in different cultures for comparison must be linguistically equivalent. The most widely used method to establish translation equivalence is back-translation. This procedure generally involves one bilingual translating the instrument from the original language to the second language and another bilingual back-translating the instrument from the second language to the original. Variations in the original instrument and the back-translated instrument may suggest areas in which conceptual equivalence has not been achieved (see Brislin, 1976, for a complete discussion of translation; see Candell & Hulin, 1986; Hulin, 1987; Hui & Triandis, 1985, for discussions of psychometric methods for evaluating item and scale translations).

The fourth type of equivalence, metric, involves establishing that the score levels obtained on an instrument in one culture are equivalent to score levels obtained in another culture. Poortinga (1975a) argues that there are at least three alternative interpretations of differences in scores between two cultures: (1) the differences exist and are real, (2) the test measures qualitatively different aspects of the concept; and (3) the test measures quantitatively different aspects of the concept. Without established metric equivalence, the second and third explanations cannot be ruled out and are, therefore, rival hypotheses to explain differences between two samples. Minimally, both raw and standardized scores should be examined in all cross-cultural studies.

The final equivalence is sample equivalence. Berry (1976) points out that choice of cultures represents a "quasi-manipulation by selection" of the independent variable. He argues that the cultures selected do not have to be representative of all systems, but they should represent values of the dimension of cultural variability under consideration if covariation is to be examined. Stated differently, samples should represent theoretically interesting dimensions of cultural variability.

In cross-cultural research the same ideals apply as in intracultural research, that is, random samples are desirable, but this is an ideal often not met. Brislin and Baumgardner (1971) contend that most cross-cultural research uses "samples of convenience," rather than randomly selected samples. They go on to argue that since random sampling is "almost impossible" in cross-cultural research, steps should be taken to ensure that nonrandom samples lead to "good research." Specifically, they suggest that researchers describe their samples in great detail. This description serves three purposes: (1) later researchers can select their samples with certainty of results; (2) other researchers can incorporate findings into their own work; and (3) it allows researchers to rule out plausible rival hypotheses that could be attributed to sampling. Given that samples of convenience are the norm, it is necessary for researchers to demonstrate that samples from different cultures are equivalent and, thereby, rule out other factors (i.e., different sample compositions by sex, age, social class, etc.) that may be rival hypotheses to explain significant differences between cultures. Throughout the book, we used only studies that we believe rule out rival hypotheses. That is, we have tried not to draw conclusions from studies in which sex or social class differences, to name only two, could also explain the differences observed.

FINAL REMARKS

In the preceding sections, we examined the generalizability of the model presented in Chapter 1 and overviewed the methodological issues that are unique to cross-cultural research. In this section, we conclude by proffering suggestions for future research and specifying ways in which culture can be systematically incorporated into theories of interpersonal communication.

One caveat that must be kept in mind in interpreting the results of the studies presented herein is that the vast majority involved self-reports of communication behavior, not observations of actual behavior. The same problem obviously exists in other areas of communication. We have omitted studies that, in our opinion, did not have conceptual and linguistic equivalence, but virtually all studies were based on self-reports.

The use of self-reports is understandable given the additional problems that arise when cross-cultural observational, interview, and conversational analysis studies are conducted. Coding behavior, and obtaining equivalent categories with high intercoder reliability, is not only extremely time-consuming, but also is highly problematic when the behavior or conversations are being coded in two different languages and the researchers are not in the same location. Ideally, coders from each culture should code the respondents' behavior or conversations in each language in each culture. This requires bilingual coders. If bilingual coders are not available, some form of derived etic coding scheme must be developed. In order to accomplish this, several iterations of coding are necessary just to develop a viable coding scheme.

The difficulty associated with cross-cultural observational studies should not deter scholars from conducting this type of research. Research that observes "talk" between respondents is necessary to draw firm conclusions regarding the influence of cultural variability on interpersonal communication. It will require, however, that researchers from one culture develop close working relationships with researchers from other cultures and for multicultural research teams to work together over extended periods of time.

The research teams *ultimately* must be *multi*cultural, not *bi*cultural. To draw firm conclusions regarding the influence of cultural variability on interpersonal communication, at least three comparison points are necessary. When only two cultures are compared, there is always the possibility that specific cultural difference findings are due to a dimension of cultural variability other than the one hypothesized. If Japan and the United States, for example, are used to test a hypothesis regarding individualism-collectivism (the United States is individualistic, Japan is collectivistic), uncertainty avoidance is a plausible rival explanation for findings supporting the original hypothesis, that is, Japan is high on uncertainty avoidance, the United States is low. With only two cultures, researchers are limited to making a logical argument as to why the effect is due to individualism-collectivism and not uncertainty avoidance. If, however, a third culture that has a moderate individualism score but a high or low uncertainty avoidance score were included in the study, the effect of the two dimensions can be differentiated clearly.

In addition to improving the "quantitative" research on communication across cultures, there is a need for solid "qualitative" research across cultures. Cross-cultural qualitative inquiry, however, is still in its infancy. The few qualitative studies that have followed the premises of the interpretive paradigm are nested mainly in the coordinated management of meaning approach (e.g., Cronen et al., 1988) or the cultural communication (e.g., Katriel, 1986) perspective. The studies conducted are primarily intracultural studies, rather than cross-cultural. They also have employed mainly textual analysis methods (that is, the analysis of monologue forms such as narrative texts, speeches, retrospective accounts), rather than an interpretive study of face-to-face interaction. Further, although most researchers have been interested in eliciting the conversants' interpretations of the discourse or situation, the concept of "cultural situatedness" (or the conjoint concept of "expectational principle" and "contextual principle") is still a neglected area of investigation. Symbolic discourse is only meaningful in a normative-expectational context and in a socially situated context. Beyond eliciting the key actors' and actresses' responses in the situation, attention should be paid to the supporting casts who constitute the cultural and social contexts.

There are several reasons qualitative cross-cultural communication studies are still in the infancy stage. First, conducting a good, solid piece of qualitative study is a time-consuming enterprise. In order to collect reliable and valid data in the field, the researcher's participation in a setting for a lengthy period under a variety of conditions is vital. Second, qualitative research usually is confined to the intracultural setting because the ethnographer usually is confronted with linguistic barriers. There is a lack of well-trained bilingual or multilingual scholars to conduct cross-cultural comparative observational studies. Third, the participant-observer often is confronted with situational barriers—it is difficult to record and capture symbolic discourse in naturalistic settings without some form of intrusion. Hence, in many instances, it is easier to base qualitative data on triangulated methods such as retrospective interviews, unobtrusive measures, and life histories. This then leads to the last point. Even after the painstaking process of methodological triangulation, data triangulation, or investigator triangulation, one can never be absolutely certain about the issue of validity because the data may appear different but compatible. The conflicting pieces of information may all be valid; they may also represent highly subjective accounts from specific situations being observed. Hence, the question of validity is still a central knot that needs to be untied by qualitative cross-cultural researchers. Especially in qualitative cross-cultural inquiry (since one can never measure and control all the emergent concepts in the naturalistic setting), qualitative cross-cultural differences can be attributed to a host of factors such as language difference, situational difference, personality difference, or competence difference. Finally, the analysis of qualitative cross-cultural data ideally should involve multicultural team efforts, multicultural interpretation processes, and multicultural analytical processes.

Three directions for qualitative cross-cultural research can be suggested. One of the most pressing tasks is the study of "contextual principles." Do conversants in different cultures draw on different aspects of situational cues to interpret each other's meanings? Do participants in different cultures vary in their reliance of "contextual rules" over "interpretive rules," or "interpretive rules" over "expectational rules" in the encountering process? How do we triangulate the participant's symbols and definitions of the social situation with the social groups that provide those conceptions?

Another important task is to continue the work on the interpretive cognitive processing of discourse (as versus cognitive psychology perspective) across cultures. What, for example, are the implicit taken-for-granted rules operating in conversational settings across cultures? What kinds of discourse repair mechanisms are needed to realign the "misaligned talks" in different cultures? How do conversants "code-switch" from one form of discourse to another in order to adjust to the situations that vary across cultures?

It also is vital to pursue the qualitative work in *intra*cultural setting. How, for example, do symbolic activities reflect, transmit, and create the values, assumptions, and ideologies of a culture? How does a cultural community supply a multiplicity of meanings to its different communication forms such as speech acts, rituals, and myths? How can we account for the relationship between "contextual principles" and "interpretive principles" in the "sense-making" expectational processes of culture? The results of qualitative studies must, of course, ultimately be linked to dimensions of cultural variability in order to generate theoretical explanations for the differences and similarities observed.

Given the discussion of issues in conducting research, we now turn our attention to theoretical issues. There are two ways culture can be integrated into theories of interpersonal communication: Culture can be used as scope statements of the theory or dimensions of cultural variability can be included as variables in the theory. The simplest way to integrate culture is to make it part of scope statements in theories. Following Lakatos (1970), Walker and Cohen (1985) argue that theories should be made conditional through explicit statements of their scope. A theory's scope "is a set of conditions such that, if the conditions are satisfied the theory will not be found false" (p. 291). Scope statements, therefore, restrict the class of individuals to which theories apply and allow theories to be falsified. A statement in a theory could be limited to members of a specific cultures (e.g., the United States), a particular ethnic group within a culture (e.g., Blacks in the United States), or a group of cultures (e.g., individualistic cultures), and so forth. Unless explicitly stated otherwise, we believe all theoretical statements should be assumed to be limited in scope to the culture in which they originated.

While including culture as a scope statement in theories is a viable technique, we contend that it is not as theoretically rich as incorporating cultural variability directly into theories of interpersonal communication. Gudykunst (1988), for example, includes two axioms dealing with cultural variability in his theory of intergroup communication:

> Axiom 12: An increase in collectivism will produce an increase in the differences in attributional confidence between ingroup and outgroup communication.
>
> Axiom 13: An increase in uncertainty avoidance will produce an increase in the anxiety strangers experience when interacting with members of other groups.

More statements such as these could have been included in the theory, but an overt decision was made to limit statements involving cultural variability to those related to the major dependent variables in the theory (uncertainty reduction or its reverse, attributional confidence, and anxiety) in the initial formulation.

There is an alternative way to develop a theory that includes culture and interpersonal communication, namely, to construct a theory that specifically focuses on how culture influences a particular aspect of interpersonal communication. Ting-Toomey's (1985, 1988) theories of face-negotiation and culture and conflict are examples of this approach (see our discussion of these theories in Chapters 6 and 8).

Incorporating cultural variability into interpersonal theories overcomes at least two of the major problems with theories in communication and social psychology isolated by Pettigrew (1986):

> (1) They are more often loose frameworks than testable theories.
> (2) They have centered on cold cognition to the relative exclusion of affective considerations.
> (3) They stress similarities (mechanical solidarity) to the virtual exclusion of differences (organic solidarity) as social bonds.
> (4) They focus largely on isolated, noncumulative effects.
> (5) They too glibly assume universality across time, situations and cultures.
> (6) They are narrow- to middle-range in scope with bold generic theory that links various levels of analysis conspicuous by its absence. (p. 179)

By including statements about how cultural variability affects other variables in the theories, the fifth and sixth problems Pettigrew isolates are at least partially overcome, namely, universality across cultures is not assumed and levels of analysis are linked or "articulated" to use Doise's (1986) term. Articulating the intrapersonal, interpersonal, intergroup, and cultural levels of analysis is ultimately necessary to develop a comprehensive theory of interpersonal communication that cuts across ethnic and cultural boundaries.

REFERENCES

Abe, H., & Wiseman, R. (1983). A cross-cultural confirmation of the dimensions of intercultural effectiveness. *International Journal of Intercultural Relations, 7,* 53-68.

Abelson, R. (1976). Script processing in attitude formation and decision-making. In J. Carroll & T. Payne (Eds.), *Cognition and social behavior.* Hillsdale, NJ: Lawrence Erlbaum.

Adamopoulos, J. (1984). The differentiation of social behavior: Toward an explanation of universal interpersonal structures. *Journal of Cross-Cultural Psychology, 15,* 487-508.

Adamopoulos, J., & Bontempo, R. (1986). Diachronic universals in interpersonal structures: Evidence from literary sources. *Journal of Cross-Cultural Psychology, 17,* 169-189.

Adelman, M., & Lustig, M. (1981). Intercultural communication problems as perceived by Saudi Arabian and American managers. *International Journal of Intercultural Relations, 5,* 349-364.

Aebischer, V., & Wallbott, H. (1986). Measuring emotional experiences: Questionnaire design and procedure, and the nature of the sample. In K. Scherer, H. Wallbott, & A. Summerfield (Eds.), *Experiencing emotions.* Cambridge: Cambridge University Press.

Ajiferuke, M., & Boddewyn, J. (1970). Culture and other explanatory variables in comparative management studies. *Academy of Management Journal, 13,* 153-178.

Alba, R. (1978). Ethnic networks and tolerant attitudes. *Public Opinion Quarterly, 42,* 1-16.

Albert, E. (1972). Culture patterning in Burundi. In J. Gumperz & D. Hymes (Eds.), *Directions in sociolingustics.* New York: Holt, Rinehart & Winston.

Albrecht, L., & Adelman, M. (1984). Social support and life stress: New directions for communication research. *Human Communication Research, 11,* 3-32.

Alexander, A., Cronen, V., Kang, K., Tsou, B., & Banks, J. (1986). Patterns of topic sequencing and information gain: A comparative study of relationship development in Chinese and American cultures. *Communication Quarterly, 34,* 66-78.

Allard, R., & Landry, R. (1986). Subjective ethnolinguistic vitality viewed as a belief system. *Journal of Multilingual and Multicultural Development, 7,* 1-12.

Allen, V., & Wilder, D. (1975). Categorization, belief similarity, and group discrimination. *Journal of Personality and Social Psychology, 32,* 971-977.

Allport, G. (1954). *The nature of prejudice.* Reading, MA: Addison-Wesley.

Almaney, A., & Alwan, A. (1982). *Communicating with the Arabs.* Prospect Heights, IL: Waveland Press, Inc.

Altman, I. (1973). Reciprocity of interpersonal exchange. *Journal of the Theory of Social Behavior, 3,* 246-261.

Altman, I. (1975). *The environment and social behavior.* Monterey, CA: Brooks/Cole.

Altman, I. (1977). Privacy: Culturally universal or culturally specific? *Journal of Social Issues, 33,* 66-84.

Altman, I., & Chemers, M. (1980a). *Culture and environment.* Monterey, CA: Brooks/Cole.

Altman, I., & Chemers, M. (1980b). Cultural aspects of environment-behavior relationships. In H. Triandis & R. Brislin (Eds.), *Handbook of cross-cultural psychology* (Vol. 5). Boston, MA: Allyn & Bacon.

Altman, I., & Gauvain, M. (1981). A cross-cultural dialectic analysis of homes. In L. Liben, A. Patterson, & N. Newcombe (Eds.), *Spatial representation and behavior across the life span.* New York: Academic Press.

Altman, I., & Haythorn, W. (1965). Interpersonal exchange in isolation. *Sociometry, 28,* 411-426.

Altman, I., & Rogoff, B. (1987). World views on psychology. In D. Stokols & I. Altman (Eds.), *Handbook of environmental psychology.* New York: John Wiley.

Altman, I., & Taylor, D. (1973). *Social penetration: The development of interpersonal relationships.* New York: Holt, Rinehart, & Winston.

Altman, I., Vinsel, A., & Brown, B. (1981). Dialectical conceptions in social psychology: An application to social penetration and privacy regulation. In L. Berkowitz (Ed.), *Advances in experimental social psychology* (Vol. 14). New York: Academic Press.

Amir, Y. (1969). The contact hypothesis in ethnic relations. *Psychological Bulletin, 71,* 319-342.

Andersen, P. (1987, November). *Explaining intercultural differences in nonverbal communication.* Paper presented at the Speech Communication Association Convention, Boston.

Andersen, P., & Leibowitz, K. (1978). The development and nature of the construct touch avoidance. *Environmental Psychology and Nonverbal Behavior, 3,* 89-106.

Andrews, F. (1984). Construct validity and error components of survey measures. *Public Opinion Quarterly, 48,* 409-422.

Applegate, J., & Sypher, H. (1983). A constructionist outline. In W. Gudykunst (Ed.), *Intercultural communication theory.* Beverly Hills, CA: Sage.

Araki, S., & Barnlund, D. (1985). Intercultural encounters: The management of compliments by Japanese and Americans. *Journal of Cross-Cultural Psychology, 16,* 9-27.

Argyle, M. (1979). New developments in the analysis of social skills. In A. Wolfgang (Ed.), *Nonverbal behavior: Applications and cultural implications.* New York: Academic Press.

Argyle, M., Furnham, A., & Graham, J. (1981). *Social situations.* Cambridge: Cambridge University Press.

Argyle, M., & Hendersen, M. (1985). The rules of relationships. In S. Duck & D. Perlman (Eds.), *Understanding personal relationships: An interdisciplinary approach.* Beverly Hills, CA: Sage.

Argyle, M., Henderson, M., Bond, M., Iizuka, Y., & Contarelo, A. (1986). Cross-cultural variations in relationship rules. *International Journal of Psychology, 21,* 287-315.

Asante, M., & Gudykunst, W. (Eds.). (in press). *Handbook of intercultural and development communication.* Newbury Park, CA: Sage.

Asch, S. (1956). Studies of independence and conformity. *Psychological Monographs, 70*(9), Whole No. 46.

Babiker, I., Cox, J., & Miller, P. (1980). The measurement of cultural distance and its relationship to medical consultation, symptomatology, and examination performance of overseas students at Edinburgh University. *Social Psychiatry, 15,* 109-116.

Ball-Rokeach, S. (1973). From pervasive ambiguity to a definition of the situation. *Sociometry, 36,* 378-389.

Bargh, J. (1984). Automatic and conscious processing of social information. In R. Wyler & T. Srull (Eds.), *Handbook of social cognition* (Vol. 3). Hillsdale, NJ: Lawrence Erlbaum.

Barnett, G., & Kincaid, D. (1983). Cultural convergence. In W. Gudykunst (Ed.), *Intercultural communication theory.* Beverly Hills, CA: Sage.

Barnlund, D. (1975a). *Public and private self in Japan and the United States.* Tokyo: Simul Press.

Barnlund, D. (1975b). Communicative styles in two cultures: Japan and the United States. In T. Williams (Ed.), *Socialization and communication in primary groups.* The Hague: Mouton.

Barrett, G., & Bass, B. (1970). *Comparative surveys of managerial attitudes and behavior* (Technical Report No. 36). Rochester, NY: University of Rochester, Management Research Center.

Barrett, P., & Eysenck, S. (1984). The assessment of personality factors across 25 countries. *Personality and Individual Differences, 5,* 615-632.

Basso, K. (1970). To give up on words: Silence in Western Apache culture. *Southern Journal of Anthropology, 26,* 213-230.

Baumeister, R. (Ed.). (1986). *Public self and private self.* New York: Springer-Verlag.

Baxter, L. (1982). Conflict management: An episodic approach. *Small Group Behavior, 13,* 23-42.

Baxter, L. (1984). An investigation of compliance-gaining as politeness. *Human Communication Research, 10,* 427-456.

Beebe, L., & Giles, H. (1984). Speech accommodation theories: A discussion in terms of second-language acquisition. *International Journal of the Sociology of Language, 46,* 5-32.

Befu, H. (1977). Power in the great white tower. In R. Fogelson & R. Adams (Eds.), *The anthropology of power.* New York: Academic Press.

Befu, H. (1980a). A critique of the group model of Japanese society. *Social Analysis, 5/6,* 29-43.

Befu, H. (1980b). The group model of Japanese society and an alternative. *Rice University Studies, 66,* 169-187.

Beier, E., & Zautra, A. (1972). Identification of vocal communication of emotions across cultures. *Journal of Consulting and Clinical Psychology, 34,* 166.

Bell, R. (1981). *World of friendship.* Beverly Hills, CA: Sage.

Bellah, R., Madsen, R., Sullivan, W., Swidler, A., & Tipton, S. (1985). *Habits of the heart: Individualism and commitment in American life.* New York: Harper & Row.

Benedict, R. (1934). *Patterns of culture.* Boston: Houghton Mifflin.

Berger, C. (1979). Beyond initial interactions: Uncertainty, understanding, and the development of interpersonal relationships. In H. Giles & R. St. Clair (Eds.), *Language and social psychology.* Oxford: Basil Blackwell.

Berger, C. (1986). Social cognition and intergroup communication. In W. Gudykunst (Ed.), *Intergroup communication.* London: Edward Arnold.

Berger, C. (1987). Communicating under uncertainty. In M. Roloff & G. Miller (Eds.), *Interpersonal processes.* Newbury Park, CA: Sage.

Berger, C., & Bradac, J. (1982). *Language and social knowledge: Uncertainty in interpersonal relations.* London: Edward Arnold.

Berger, C., & Calabrese, R. (1975). Some explorations in initial interactions and beyond: Toward a developmental theory of interpersonal communication. *Human Communication Research, 1,* 99-112.

Berger, C., & Douglas, W. (1981). Studies in interpersonal epistemology: III. Anticipated interaction, self-monitoring, and observational context selection. *Communication Monographs, 48,* 183-196.

Berger, C., Gardner, R., Parks, M., Schulman, L., & Miller G. (1976). Interpersonal epistemology and interpersonal understanding. In G. Miller (Ed.), *Explorations in interpersonal communication.* Beverly Hills, CA: Sage.

Berger, C., & Perkins, J. (1978). Studies in interpersonal epistemology: I. Situational attributes in observational context selection. In B. Ruben (Ed.), *Communication yearbook 2.* New Brunswick, NJ: Transaction Books.

Berger, J., & Zelditch, M. (1985). *Status, rewards, and influence.* San Francisco: Jossey-Bass.

Berlo, D. K. (1960). *The process of communication.* New York: Holt, Rinehart & Winston.

Berlyne, D. (1960). *Conflict, arousal, and curiosity.* New York: McGraw-Hill.

Berlyne, D. (1965). *Structure and direction in thinking.* New York: John Wiley.

Bernstein, B. (1971). *Class, codes and control.* Boston: Routledge & Kegan Paul.

Berry, J. (1969). On cross-cultural comparability. *International Journal of Psychology, 4,* 119-128.

Berry, J. (1976). *Human ecology and cognitive style: Comparative studies in cultural and psychological adaptation.* New York: John Wiley.

Berry, J. (1980). Introduction to methodology. In H. Triandis & J. Berry (Eds.), *Handbook of cross-cultural psychology* (Vol. 2). Boston: Allyn & Bacon.

Berscheid, E., Graziano, W., Monson, T., & Dermer, M. (1976). Outcome dependency: Attention, attribution, and attraction. *Journal of Personality and Social Psychology, 34,* 978-989.

Best, D., & Williams, J. (1984). A cross-cultural examination of self and ideal self description using transactional analysis ego states. In I. Lagunes & Y. Poortinga (Eds.), *From a different perspective: Studies of behavior across cultures.* Lisse, The Netherlands: Swets & Zeitlinger.

Best, D., Williams, J., Edwards, J., & Giles, H. (1985). Masculinity-femininity in self and ideal self descriptions in Canada, England, and the United States. In R. Diaz-Guerrero (Ed.), *Cross-cultural and national studies in social psychology.* North-Holland: Elsevier.

Bezooijen, R., Otto, S., & Heenan, T. (1983). Recognition of vocal expressions of emotion: A three-nation study to identify universal characteristics. *Journal of Cross-Cultural Psychology, 14,* 387-406.

Bharati, A. (1985). The self in Hindu thought and action. In A. Marsella, G. DeVos, & F. Hsu (Eds.), *Culture and self: Asian and Western perspectives.* New York: Tavistock.

Bijnen, E., Van Der Net, T., & Poortinga, Y. (1986). On cross-cultural comparative studies with the Eysenck personality questionnaire. *Journal of Cross-Cultural Psychology, 17,* 3-16.

Billig, M. (1987). *Arguing and thinking: A rhetorical approach to social psychology.* Cambridge: Cambridge University Press.

Birdwhistell, R. (1970). *Kinesics and context.* New York: Ballantine.

Bishop, G. (1979). Perceived similarity in interracial attitudes and behavior. *Journal of Applied Social Psychology, 9,* 446-465.

Blake, R., & Mouton, J. (1964). *The managerial grid.* Houston: Gulf.

Blau, P., & Schwartz, J. (1984). *Cross-cutting social circles: Testing a macro theory of intergroup relations.* New York: Academic Press.

Bobad, E., & Wallbott, H. (1986). The effects of social factors on emotional reactions. In K. Sherer, H. Wallbott, & A. Summerfield (Eds.), *Experiencing emotions: A cross-cultural study.* Cambridge: Cambridge University Press.

Bochner, S., McCleod, B., & Lin, A. (1977). Friendship patterns of overseas students: A functional model. *International Journal of Psychology, 12,* 277-294.

Bochner, S. & Orr, F. (1979). Race and academic status as determinants of friendship formation. *International Journal of Psychology, 14,* 37-46.

Boldt, E. (1978). Structural tightness and cross-cultural research. *Journal of Cross-Cultural Psychology, 9,* 151-165.

Boldt, E., & Roberts, L. (1979). Structural tightness and social conformity. *Journal of Cross-Cultural Psychology, 10,* 221-230.

Bond, M. (1979). Dimensions of personality used in perceiving peers: Cross-cultural comparisons of Hong Kong, Japanese, American, and Filipino university students. *International Journal of Psychology, 14,* 47-56.

Bond, M. (1983). A proposal for cross-cultural studies of attribution. In M. Hewstone (Ed.), *Attribution theory: Social and functional extensions.* Oxford: Basil Blackwell.

Bond, M. (Ed.). (1986a). *The psychology of the Chinese people.* Hong Kong: Oxford University Press.

Bond, M. (1986b). Mutual stereotypes and the facilitation of interaction across cultural lines. *International Journal of Intercultural Relations, 10,* 259-276.

Bond, M. (1987). Intergroup relations in Hong Kong: The tao of stability. In J. Boucher, D. Landis, & K. Arnold Clark (Eds.), *Ethnic conflict: International perspectives.* Newbury Park, CA: Sage.

Bond, M., & Cheung, T. (1983). College students' spontaneous self-concept: The effects of culture among respondents in Hong Kong, Japan, and the United States. *Journal of Cross-Cultural Psychology, 14,* 153-171.

Bond, M., & Forgas, J. (1984). Linking person perception to behavior intention across cultures: The role of cultural collectivism. *Journal of Cross-Cultural Psychology, 15,* 337-353.

Bond, M., & Hewstone, M. (1986). *Social identity theory and the perception of intergroup relations in Hong Kong.* Unpublished manuscript, Chinese University of Hong Kong.

Bond, M., Hewstone, M., Wan, K., & Chiu, C. (1985). Group-serving attributions across intergroup contexts: Cultural differences in the explanation of sex-typed behaviours. *European Journal of Social Psychology, 15,* 435-451.

Bond, M., & Hwang, K. (1986). The social psychology of the Chinese people. In M. Bond (Ed.), *The psychology of the Chinese people.* Hong Kong: Oxford University Press.

Bond, M., & Iwata, Y. (1976). Proxemics and observation anxiety in Japan: Nonverbal and cognitive responses. *Psychologia, 19,* 119-126.

Bond, M., & Komai, H. (1976). Targets of gazing and eye contact during interviews: Effect of Japanese nonverbal behavior. *Journal of Personality and Social Psychology, 34,* 1276-1284.

Bond, M., Leung, K., & Wan, K. (1982). How does cultural collectivism operate? The impact of task and maintenance contributions on reward allocation. *Journal of Cross-Cultural Psychology, 13,* 186-200.

Bond, M., Nakazato, H., & Shiraishi, D. (1975). Universality and distinctiveness in dimensions of Japanese person perception. *Journal of Cross-Cultural Psychology, 6,* 346-357.

Bond, M., & Shiraishi, D. (1974). The effect of body lean and status of an interviewer on the non-verbal behavior of Japanese interviewees. *International Journal of Psychology, 9,* 117-128.

Bond, M., & Tornatzky, L. (1973). Locus of control in students from Japan and the United States: Dimensions and levels of response. *Psychologia, 16,* 209-213.

Bond, M., Wan, K., Leung, K., & Giacalone, R. (1985). How are responses to verbal insults related to cultural collectivism and power distance? *Journal of Cross-Cultural Psychology, 16,* 111-127.

Boucher, J. (1973). *Facial behavior and the perception of emotion: Studies of Malays and Temuan Orang Asli.* Paper presented at the Conference on Psychology and Related Disciplines, Kuala Lumpur.

Boucher, J. (1979). Culture and emotion. In A. Marsella, R. Tharp, & T. Ciborowski (Eds.), *Perspectives on cross-cultural psychology.* New York: Academic Press.

Boucher, J., & Brandt, M. (1981). Judgment of emotion from American and Malay antecedents. *Journal of Cross-Cultural Psychology, 12,* 272-283.

Boucher, J., & Carlson, G. (1980). Recognition of facial expression in three cultures. *Journal of Cross-Cultural Psychology, 11,* 263-280.

Boucher, J., Landis, D., & Clark, K. (Eds.). (1987). *Ethnic conflict: International perspectives.* Newbury Park, CA: Sage.

Bourhis, R. (1979). Language in ethnic interaction. In H. Giles & R. Saint-Jacques (Eds.), *Language and ethnic relations.* Elmsford, NY: Pergamon.

Bourhis, R., Giles, H., & Rosenthal, D. (1981). Notes on the construction of a subjective vitality questionnaire for ethnolinguistic groups. *Journal of Multilingual and Multicultural Development, 2,* 145-155.

Bourhis, R., & Sachdev, I. (1984). Subjective vitality perceptions and language attitudes: Some Canadian data. *Journal of Language and Social Psychology, 3,* 97-126.

Bowerman, M. (1981). Language development. In H. Triandis & A. Heron (Eds.), *Handbook of cross-cultural psychology* (Vol. 4). Boston, MA: Allyn & Bacon.

Boyanowsky, E., & Allen, V. (1973). In-group norms and self-identity as determinants of discriminatory behavior. *Journal of Personality and Social Psychology, 25,* 408-418.

Braiker, H., & Kelley, H. (1979). Conflict in the development of close relationships. In R. Burgess & T. Huston (Eds.), *Social exchange in developing relationships.* New York: Academic Press.

Brandt, D., Miller, G., & Hocking, J. (1980a). Effects of self-monitoring and familiarity on deception detection. *Communication Quarterly, 28,* 3-10.

Brandt, D., Miller, G., & Hocking, J. (1980b). The truth-deception attribution: Effects of familiarity on the ability of observers to detect deception. *Human Communication Research, 6,* 99-110.

Brandt, M., & Boucher, J. (1985). Judgement of emotions from antecedent situations in three cultures. In I. Lagunes & Y. Poortinga (Eds.), *From a different perspective: Studies of behavior across cultures.* Lisse, The Netherlands: Swets & Zeitlinger.

Brandt, M., & Boucher, J. (1986). Concepts of depression in emotion lexicons of eight cultures. *International Journal of Intercultural Relations, 10,* 321-346.

Brewer, M. (1969). Determinants of social distance among East African tribal groups. *Journal of Personality and Social Psychology, 10,* 279-289.

Brewer, M. (1979a). Ingroup bias in the minimal group situation. *Psychological Bulletin, 56,* 307-324.

Brewer, M. (1979b). The role of ethnocentrism in intergroup conflict. In W. Austin & S. Worchel (Eds.), *The social psychology of intergroup relations.* Monterey, CA: Brooks/Cole.

Brewer, M. (1981). Ethnocentrism and its role in interpersonal trust. In M. Brewer & B. Collins (Eds.), *Scientific inquiry and the social sciences.* San Francisco: Jossey-Bass.

Brewer, M., & Campbell, D. (1976). *Ethnocentrism and intergroup attitudes.* New York: John Wiley.

Brewer, M., Ho, H., Lee, J., & Miller, N. (1987). Social identity and social distance among Hong Kong school children. *Personality and Social Psychology Bulletin, 13,* 156-165.

Brewer, M., & Kramer, R. (1985). The psychology of intergroup attitudes and behavior. *Annual Review of Psychology, 36,* 219-243.

Briggs, S., & Cheek, J. (1986). The role of factor analysis in the development and evaluation of personality scales. *Journal of Personality, 54,* 106-148.

Briggs, S., Cheek, J., & Buss, A. (1980). An analysis of the self-monitoring scale. *Journal of Personality and Social Psychology, 38,* 679-686.

Brislin, R. (1970). Back-translation for cross-cultural research. *Journal of Cross-Cultural Psychology, 1,* 185-216.

Brislin, R. (1976). *Translation: Application and research.* New York: Garner.

Brislin, R. (1983). Cross-cultural research in psychology. *Annual Review of Psychology, 34,* 363-400.

Brislin, R., & Baumgardner, S. (1971). Non-random sampling of individuals in cross-cultural research. *Journal of Cross-Cultural Psychology, 2,* 397-400.

Brislin, R., Cushner, K., Cherrie, C., & Yong, M. (1986). *Intercultural interactions: A practical guide.* Beverly Hills, CA: Sage.

Brockner, J. (1979). Self-esteem, self-consciousness, and task performance: Replications, extensions, and possible explanations. *Journal of Personality and Social Psychology, 37,* 447-461.

Brown, C., Yelsma, P., & Keller, P. (1981). Communication-conflict predisposition: Development of a theory and an instrument. *Human Relations, 34,* 1103-1117.

Brown, P., & Levinson, S. (1978). Universals in language usage: Politeness phenomenon. In E. Goody (Ed.), *Questions and politeness: Strategies in social interaction.* Cambridge: Cambridge University Press.

Buck, E., Newton, B., & Muramatsu, Y. (1984). Independence and obedience in the United States and Japan. *International Journal of Intercultural Relations, 8,* 279-300.

Burgoon, J. (1978). A communication model of personal space violations: Explication and an initial test. *Human Communication Research, 4,* 129-142.

Burgoon, J. (1983). Nonverbal violations of expectations. In J. Wiemann & R. Harrison (Eds.), *Nonverbal interaction.* Beverly Hills, CA: Sage.

Burgoon, J. (1985). Nonverbal signals. In M. Knapp & G. Miller (Eds.), *Handbook of interpersonal communication.* Beverly Hills, CA: Sage.

Burgoon, M., Dillard, J., Doran, N., & Miller, M. (1982). Cultural and situational influences on the process of persuasive strategy selection. *International Journal of Intercultural Relations, 6,* 85-100.

Burk, J. (1976). The effects of ethnocentrism on intercultural communication. In F. Casmir (Ed.), *International and intercultural communication annual* (Vol. 3). Annandale, VA: Speech Communication Association.

Buss, A. (1980). *Self-consciousness and social anxiety.* San Francisco: Jossey-Bass.

Butcher, J., & Pancheri, P. (1976). *A handbook of cross-national MMPI research.* Minneapolis: University of Minnesota Press.

Butcher, J., & Spielberger, C. (1985). *Advances in personality assessment* (Vol. 4). Hillsdale, NJ: Lawrence Erlbaum.

Byrne, D. (1971). *The attraction paradigm.* New York: Academic Press.

Caddick, B. (1980). Equity theory, social identity, and intergroup relations. *Review of Personality and Social Psychology, 1,* 219-245.

Candell, G., & Hulin, C. (1986). Cross-language and cross-cultural comparisons in scale translations. *Journal of Cross-Cultural Psychology, 17,* 417-440.

Carver, C., & Glass, O. (1976). The self-consciousness scale: A discriminant validity study. *Journal of Personality Assessment, 40,* 169-172.

Carver, C., & Scheier, M. (1981). Self-consciousness and reactance. *Journal of Research in Personality, 15,* 16-29.

Casson, R. (1983). Schemata in cognitive anthropology. *Annual Review of Psychology, 12,* 429-462.

Cattell, R., & Brennan, J. (1984). The cultural types of modern nations by two quantitative classification methods. *Sociology and Social Research, 86,* 208-235.

Chan, D. (in press). Perceptions and judgement of facial expressions among the Chinese. *International Journal of Psychology.*

Chinese Culture Connection. (1987). Chinese values and the search for culture-free dimensions of culture. *Journal of Cross-Cultural Psychology, 18,* 143-164.

Chu, G. (1985). The changing concept of self in contemporary China. In A. Marsella, G. DeVos, & F. Hsu (Eds.), *Culture and self: Asian and Western perspectives.* New York: Tavistock.

Chua, E., & Gudykunst, W. (1987). Conflict resolution styles in low- and high-context cultures. *Communication Research Reports, 4,* 32-37.

Church, A. (1982). Sojourner adjustment. *Psychological Bulletin, 91,* 540-572.

Cioffi-Revilla, C. (1979). Diplomatic communication theory. *International Interactions, 6,* 209-265.

Clancy, P. (1986). The acquisition of communicative style in Japanese. In B. Schieffelin & E. Ochs (Eds.), *Language socialization across cultures.* Cambridge: Cambridge University Press.

Clatterbuck, G. (1979). Attributional confidence and uncertainty in initial interactions. *Human Communication Research, 5,* 147-157.

Clément, R., & Kruidenier, B. (1985). Aptitude, attitude and motivation in second language competency: A test of Clément's model. *Journal of Language and Social Psychology, 4,* 21-37.

Cleveland, H., Mangone, G., & Adams, J. (1960). *The overseas Americans.* New York: McGraw-Hill.

Cline, R. (1983). The acquaintance process as relational communication. In R. Bostrom (Ed.), *Communication yearbook 7.* Beverly Hills, CA: Sage.

Cohen, E. (1984). The sociology of tourism. *Annual Review of Sociology, 10,* 373-392.

Cohen, J. (1977). *Statistical power analysis for the behavioral sciences* (rev. ed.). New York: Academic Press.

Cohen, R. (1969). Conceptual styles, culture conflict and nonverbal tests of intelligence. *American Anthropologist, 71,* 828-856.

Cohen, R. (1987). Problems of intercultural communication in Egyptian-American diplomatic relations. *International Journal of Intercultural Relations, 11,* 29-47.

Cole, M., & Means, B. (1981). *Comparative studies of how people think.* Cambridge: Harvard University Press.

Cole, M., & Scribner, S. (1974). *Culture and thought.* New York: John Wiley.

Collier, M. (1986). Culture and gender: Effects on assertive behavior and communication competence. In M. McLaughlin (Ed.), *Communication yearbook 9.* Beverly Hills, CA: Sage.

Collier, M., Ribeau, S., & Hecht, M. (1986). Intracultural communication rules and outcomes within three domestic cultures. *International Journal of Intercultural Relations, 10,* 439-457.

Condon, J., & Yousef, F. (1975). *An introduction to intercultural communication.* Indianapolis, IN: Bobbs-Merrill.

Contractor, N., Fulk, J., Monge, P., & Singhal, A. (1986). Cultural assumptions that influence the implementation of communication technologies. *Vikalpa, 11,* 287-299.

Cook, S. (1978). Interpersonal and attitudinal outcomes in cooperating interracial groups. *Journal of Research and Development in Education, 12,* 97-113.

Cosnier, J., Dols, J., & Fernandez, A. (1986). The verbalization of emotional experiences. In K. Scherer, H. Wallbott, & A. Summerfield (Eds.), *Experiencing emotions.* Cambridge: Cambridge University Press.

Craig, R., Tracy, K., & Spisak, F. (1986). The discourse of requests: Assessment of a politeness approach. *Human Communication Research, 12,* 437-468.

Crocker, W., Klopf, D., & Cambra, R. (1978). Communication apprehension and its educational implication: Some initial Australian data. *Australian Journal of Education, 23-33,* 262-270.

Cronen, V., Chen, V., & Pearce, W. (1988). The coordinated management of meaning. In Y. Y. Kim & W. B. Gudykunst (Eds.), *Theory in intercultural communication.* Newbury Park, CA: Sage.

Cronen, V., & Shuter, R. (1983). Forming intercultural bonds. In W.Gudykunst (Ed.), *Intercultural communication theory.* Beverly Hills, CA: Sage.

Cüceloglu, D. (1970). Perception of facial expressions in three cultures. *Ergonomics, 13,* 93-100.

Cushman, D., & Cahn, D. (1985). *Interpersonal communication.* Albany: State University of New York Press.

Cushman, D., & King, S. (1985). National and organizational cultures in conflict resolution: Japan, the United States, and Yugoslavia. In W. Gudykunst, L. Stewart, & S. Ting-Toomey (Eds.), *Communication, culture, and organizational processes.* Beverly Hills, CA: Sage.

Cushman, D., & King, S. (1986). The role of communication rules in explaining intergroup interaction. In W. Gudykunst (Ed.), *Intergroup communication.* London: Edward Arnold.

Cushman, D., & Nishida, T. (1984). *Mate selection in the United States and Japan.* Unpublished manuscript, State University of New York, Albany.

Cushman, D., & Whiting, G. (1972). An approach to communication theory: Toward a consensus on rules. *Journal of Communication, 22,* 217-233.

D'Andrade, R. (1981). The cultural part of cognition. *Cognitive Science, 5,* 179-195.

D'Andrade, R. (1984). Cultural meaning systems. In R. Shweder & R. LeVine (Eds.), *Culture theory: Essays on mind, self, and emotion.* Cambridge: Cambridge University Press.

Daly, J. (1987). Personality and interpersonal communication. In J. McCroskey & J. Daly (Eds.), *Personality and interpersonal communication.* Newbury Park, CA: Sage.

Daly, J., & Stafford, L. (1984). Correlates and consequences of social-communicative anxiety. In J. Daly & J. McCroskey (Eds.), *Avoiding communication: Shyness, reticence, and communication apprehension.* Beverly Hills, CA: Sage.

Dance, F. (1970). The concept of communication. *Journal of Communication, 20,* 201-210.

Darwin, C. (1872). *The expression of the emotions in man and animals.* London: John Murray.

Davey, W. (1982). The bilingual education movement: Critical issues for language planning. In N. Jain (Ed.), *International and intercultural communication annual* (Vol. 6). Annandale, VA: Speech Communication Association.

Davidson, A., Jaccard, J., Triandis, H., Morales, M., & Diaz-Guerrero, R. (1976). Cross-cultural model testing. *International Journal of Psychology, 11*, 1-13.

Davidson, A., & Thomson, E. (1980). Cross-cultural studies of attitudes and beliefs. In H. Triandis & R. Brislin (Eds.), *Handbook of cross-cultural psychology* (Vol. 5). Boston, MA: Allyn & Bacon.

Deregowski, J. (1980). Perception. In H. Triandis & W. Lonner (Eds.), *Handbook of cross-cultural psychology* (Vol. 3). Boston, MA: Allyn & Bacon.

Derlega, V., & Chaikin, A. (1977). Privacy and self-disclosure in social relationships. *Journal of Social Issues, 3*, 102-115.

Deschamps, J., & Doise, W. (1978). Crossed category memberships in intergroup relations. In H. Tajfel (Ed.), *Differentiation between social groups*. London: Academic Press.

DeSousa, M. (1982). The cultural impact of American television abroad. In N. Jain (Ed.), *International and intercultural communication annual* (Vol. 6). Annandale, VA: Speech Communication Association.

Detweiler, R. (1975). On inferring the intentions of a person from another culture. *Journal of Personality, 43*, 591-611.

Detweiler, R. (1978). Culture, category width, and attributions. *Journal of Cross-Cultural Psychology, 9*, 259-284.

DeVos, G. (1980). Ethnic adaptation and minority status. *Journal of Cross-Cultural Psychology, 11*, 101-124.

DeVos, G. (1985). Dimensions of the self in Japanese culture. In A. Marsella, G. DeVos, & F. Hsu (Eds.), *Culture and self: Asian and Western perspectives*. New York: Tavistock.

Diaz-Guerrero, R. (1976). Test anxiety in Mexican and American school children. In C. Spielberger & R. Diaz-Guerrero (Eds.), *Cross-cultural anxiety*. Washington, DC: Hemisphere.

Dickey, E., & Knower, F. (1941). A note on some ethnological differences in recognition of simulated expressions of the emotions. *American Journal of Sociology, 47*, 190-193.

Dillard, J., Hunter, J., & Burgoon, M. (1984, May). *Questions about the construct validity of the emotional empathy scale, the self-consciousness scale, and the self-monitoring scale*. Paper presented at the International Communication Association convention, San Francisco, CA.

diSciullo, A., Van Amerigen, A., Cedergren, H., & Pupier, P. (1976). Étude d'interaction verbale chez des Montrealis d'origine Italienne. *Cashier de Linguistique: La Sociolinguistique arc Quebec, 6*, 127-153.

Doelger, J., Hewes, D., & Graham, M. (1986). Knowing when to "second-guess": The mindful analysis of messages. *Human Communication Research, 12*, 301-338.

Doi, T. (1973). *The anatomy of dependence* (J. Bester, Trans.). Tokyo: Kodansha.

Doi, T. (1986). *The anatomy of self: The individual versus society* (M. Harlison, Trans.). Tokyo: Kodansha.

Doise, W. (1986). *Levels of explanation in social psychology*. Cambridge: Cambridge University Press.

Doise, W., Csepeli, G., Dann, H., Gouge, C., Larsen, K., & Ostell, A. (1972). An experimental investigation into the formation of intergroup representations. *European Journal of Social Psychology, 2*, 202-204.

Doise, W., & Sinclair, A. (1973). The categorization process in intergroup relations. *European Journal of Social Psychology, 3*, 145-157.

Donohue, W., & Diez, M. (1985). Directive use in negotiation interaction. *Communication Monographs, 52,* 305-318.

Drenth, P., Kooperman, P., Rus, V., Odar, M., Heller, F., & Brown, A. (1979). Participative decision-making: A comparative study. *Industrial Relations, 18,* 295-309.

Driver, E., & Driver, A. (1983). Gender, society, and self-conceptions. *International Journal of Comparative Sociology, 24,* 200-217.

Ehrenhaus, P. (1983). Culture and the attribution process. In W. Gudykunst (Ed.), *Intercultural communication theory.* Beverly Hills, CA: Sage.

Eibl-Eibesfeldt, I. (1971). *Love and hate.* New York: Holt, Rinehart & Winston.

Eibl-Eibesfeldt, I. (1972). Similarities and differences between cultures in expressive movements. In R. Hinde (Ed.), *Nonverbal communication.* Cambridge: Cambridge University Press.

Eisenberg, E. (1984). Ambiguity as a strategy in organizational communication. *Communication Monographs, 51,* 227-242.

Ekman, G. (1955). Dimensions of emotions. *Acta Psychologia, 11,* 279-288.

Ekman, P. (1972). Universals and cultural differences in facial expression of emotion. In J. Cole (Ed.), *Nebraska symposium on motivation* (Vol. 19). Lincoln: University of Nebraska Press.

Ekman, P., & Friesen, W. (1971). Constants across cultures in the face and emotion. *Journal of Personality and Social Psychology, 17,* 124-129.

Ekman, P., & Friesen, W. (1975). *Unmasking the face.* Englewood Cliffs, NJ: Prentice-Hall.

Ekman, P., Friesen, W., & Ellsworth, P. (1972). *Emotion in the human face.* New York: Pergamon.

Ekman, P., Friesen, W. V., O'Sullivan, M., Diacoyanni-Tarlatzis, I., Krause, R., Pitcairn, T., Scherer, K., Chan, A., Heider, K., LeCompte, W. A., Ricci-Bitti, P. E., Tomita, M., & Tzavaras, A. (1987). Personality processes and individual differences: Universals and cultural differences in the judgments of facial expressions of emotion. *Journal of Personality and Social Psychology, 53,*712-717.

Ekman, P., Sorenson, E., & Friesen, W. (1969). Pan-cultural elements in facial displays of emotion. *Science, 164,* 86-88.

Ellingsworth, H. (1983). Adaptive intercultural communication. In W. Gudykunst (Ed.), *Intercultural communication theory.* Beverly Hills, CA: Sage.

Elliot, S., Scott, M., Jensen, A., & McDonald, M. (1982). Perceptions of reticence: A cross-cultural investigation. In M. Burgoon (Ed.), *Communication yearbook 5.* New Brunswick, NJ: Transaction.

Elliott, G. (1979). Some effects of deception and level of self-monitoring on planning and reacting to a self-presentation. *Journal of Personality and Social Psychology, 37,* 1282-1292.

Enber, C. (1977). Cross-cultural cognitive studies. *Annual Review of Anthropology, 6,* 33-56.

Endler, N., & Magnusson, D. (1976). Multidimensional aspects of state and trait anxiety: A cross-cultural study of Canadian and Swedish college students. In C. Spielberger & R. Diaz-Guerrero (Eds.), *Cross-cultural anxiety.* Washington, DC: Hemisphere.

Engebretson, D., & Fullmer, D. (1970). Cross-cultural differences in territoriality: Interaction distances of native Japanese, Hawaii Japanese, and American Caucasians. *Journal of Cross-Cultural Psychology, 1,* 261-269.

England, G., Negandhi, A., & Wilpert, B. (Eds.). (1979). *Organizational functioning in a cross-cultural perspective.* Kent, OH: Kent State University Press.

Evans-Pritchard, E. (1940). *The Nuer.* Oxford: Carledon.

Eysenck, H. (1986). Cross-cultural comparisons: The validity of assessment by indices of factor comparison. *Journal of Cross-Cultural Psychology, 17,* 493-505.

Farace, V. (1966). Mass communication and national development. *Journalism Quarterly, 43,* 305-313.

Fayer, J., McCroskey, J., & Richmond, V. (1982). *Communication apprehension in Puerto Rico and the United States: A preliminary report.* Paper presented at the Speech Communication Association of Puerto Rico convention, San Juan.

Feig, J., & Blair, J. (1975). *There is a difference.* Washington, DC: Meriden International House.

Feigenbaum, W. (1977). Reciprocity in self-disclosure within the psychological interview. *Psychological Reports, 40,* 15-26.

Feldman, R. (1968). Response to compatriot and foreigner who seek assistance. *Journal of Personality and Social Psychology, 10,* 202-214.

Fenigstein, A. (1979). Self-consciousness, self-attention, and social interaction. *Journal of Personality and Social Psychology, 37,* 75-86.

Fenigstein, A., Scheier, M., & Buss, A. (1975). Public and private self-consciousness: Assessment and theory. *Journal of Consulting and Clinical Psychology, 43,* 522-527.

Filerbaum, S., & Rapoport, A. (1971). *Structures in the subjective lexicon.* New York: Academic Press.

Fisher, G. (1979). *American communication in a global society.* Norwood, NJ: Ablex.

Fisher, G. (1983). *International negotiation.* Chicago, IL: Intercultural Press.

Foa, U., & Foa, E. (1974). *Societal structures of the mind.* Springfield, IL: Charles C Thomas.

Foa, U., Salcedo, L., Tornblom, K., Gardner, M., Glaubman, H., & Teichman, M. (1987). Interrelation of social resources: Evidence of pancultural invariance. *Journal of Cross-Cultural Psychology, 18,* 221-233.

Folger, J., & Poole, M. (1984). *Working through conflict: A communication perspective.* Glenview, IL: Scott, Foresman & Company.

Forgas, J. (1982). Episode cognition. In L. Berkowitz (Ed.), *Advances in experimental social psychology* (Vol. 15). New York: Academic Press.

Forgas, J. (Ed.). (1985). *Language and social situations.* New York: Springer-Verlag.

Forgas, J., & Bond, M. (1985). Cultural influences on the perception of interaction episodes. *Personality and Social Psychology Bulletin, 11,* 75-88.

Foschi, M. (1980). Theory, experimentation, and cross-cultural comparisons in social psychology. *Canadian Journal of Sociology, 5,* 91-102.

Foschi, M., & Hales, W. (1979). The theoretical role of cross-cultural comparisons in experimental social psychology. In L. Eckensberger, W. Lonner, & Y. Poortinga (Eds.), *Cross-cultural contributions to psychology.* Lisse, The Netherlands: Swets & Zeitlinger.

Foster, B. (1979). Formal network studies and the anthropological perspective. *Social Networks, 1,* 241-255.

Foster, D., & Finchilescu, G. (1986). Contact in a "non-contact" society: The case of South Africa. In M. Hewstone & R. Brown (Eds.), *Contact and conflict in intergroup encounters.* Oxford: Basil Blackwell.

Frager, R. (1970). Conformity and anti-conformity in Japan. *Journal of Personality and Social Psychology, 15,* 203-210.

Frankfurt, L. (1965). *The role of some individual and interpersonal factors in the acquaintance process.* Unpublished Ph.D. thesis, American University.

Fridlund, A., Ekman, P., & Oster, H. (1987). Facial expression of emotion: Review of the literature, 1970-1983. In A. Siegman & S. Feldstein (Eds.), *Nonverbal behavior and communication* (2nd ed.). Hillsdale, NJ: Lawrence Erlbaum.

Friesen, W. (1972). *Cultural differences in facial expression in a social situation: An experimental test of the concept of display rules.* Unpublished Ph.D. thesis, University of California at San Francisco.

Fromming, W., & Carver, C. (1981). Divergent influences of private and public self-consciousness in a compliance paradigm. *Journal of Research in Personality, 15,* 159-171.

Furnham, A., & Bochner, S. (1982). Social difficulty in a foreign culture. In S. Bochner (Ed.), *Cultures in contact.* New York: Pergamon.

Furnham, A., & Bochner, S. (1986). *Culture shock: Psychological reactions to unfamiliar environments.* London: Meuthen.

Gabrenya, W., & Arkin, R. (1980). Self-monitoring scale: Factor structure and correlates. *Personality and Social Psychology Bulletin, 6,* 13-22.

Gabrenya, W., & Wang, Y. (1983, March). *Cultural differences in self schemata.* Paper presented at the Southeast Psychological Association convention, Atlanta, GA.

Gangestad, S., & Snyder, M. (1985a). On the nature of self-monitoring: An examination of latent causal structure. In P. Shaver (Ed.), *Review of personality and social psychology* (Vol. 6). Beverly Hills, CA: Sage.

Gangestad, S., & Snyder, M. (1985b). To cause nature at its joints: On the existence of discrete classes in personality. *Psychological Review, 93,* 65-85.

Gardner, H. (1984). The development of competence in culturally defined domains: A preliminary framework. In R. Shweder & R. LeVine (Eds.), *Culture theory: Essays on mind, self, and emotion.* Cambridge: Cambridge University Press.

Gardner, R., LaLonde, R., & Pierson, R. (1983). The socio-emotional model of second language acquisition. *Journal of Language and Social Psychology, 2,* 1-15.

Garrison, V. (1978). Support systems of schizophrenic and nonschizophrenic Puerto Rican migrant women in New York City. *Schizophrenia Bulletin, 4,* 591-596.

Geertz, C. (1966). *Person, time and conduct in Bali: An essay in cultural analysis.* Yale Southeast Asia Program, Cult. Rep., Ser. No. 14.

Geertz, C. (1973). *The interpretation of culture.* New York: Basic Books.

Geertz, C. (1975). On the nature of anthropological understanding. *American Scientist, 63,* 47-53.

Geertz, C. (1984). "From the native's point of view": On the nature of anthropological understanding. In R. Shweder & R. LeVine (Eds.), *Culture theory: Essays on mind, self, and emotion.* Cambridge: Cambridge University Press.

Genesee, F., & Bourhis, R. (1982). The social psychological significance of code switching in cross-cultural communication. *Journal of Language and Social Psychology, 1,* 1-27.

Gerbner, G. (1966). Images across cultures: Teachers in mass media fiction and drama. *School Review, 74,* 12-30.

Gergen, K., Morse, S., & Gergen, M. (1980). Behavior exchange in cross-cultural perspective. In H. Triandis & R. Brislin (Eds.), *Handbook of cross-cultural psychology* (Vol. 5). Boston, MA: Allyn & Bacon.

Ghosh, E., & Huq, M. (1985). A study of social identity in two ethnic groups in India and Bangladesh. *Journal of Multilingual and Multicultural Development, 6,* 239-251.

Gibbs, J. (1965). Norms: The problem of definition and classification. *American Journal of Sociology, 70,* 586-594.

Gibson, W. (1966). *Tough, sweet and stuffy: An essay on modern American prose styles.* Bloomington: Indiana University Press.

Giles, H., Bourhis, R., & Taylor, D. (1977). Towards a theory of language in ethnic group relations. In H. Giles (Ed.), *Language, ethnicity, and intergroup relations*. London: Academic Press.

Giles, H., & Byrne, J. (1982). An intergroup approach to second language acquisition. *Journal of Multilingual and Multicultural Development, 3*, 17-40.

Giles, H., & Hewstone, M. (1982). Cognitive structures, speech, and social situations. *Language Sciences, 4*, 187-219.

Giles, H., & Johnson, P. (1981). The role of language in ethnic group relations. In J. Turner & H. Giles (Eds.), *Intergroup behavior*. Chicago, IL: University of Chicago Press.

Giles, H., & Johnson, P. (1987). Ethnolinguistic identity theory: A social psychological approach to language maintenance. *International Journal of the Sociology of Language, 68*, 69-70.

Giles, H., Rosenthal, D., & Young, L. (1985). Perceived ethnolinguistic vitality: The Anglo- and Greek-Australian setting. *Journal of Multilingual and Multicultural Development, 6*, 253-269.

Giles, H., & Ryan, E. (1982). Prolegomena for developing a social psychological theory of language attitudes. In E. Ryan & H. Giles (Eds.), *Attitudes toward language variation*. London: Edward Arnold.

Glenn, E. (1981). *Man and mankind*. Norwood, NJ: Ablex.

Glenn, E., Johnson, R., Kimmel, P., & Wedge, B. (1970). A cognitive model to analyze culture conflict in international relations. *Journal of Conflict Resolution, 14*, 35-48.

Glenn, E., Witmeyer, D., & Stevenson, K. (1977). Cultural styles of persuasion. *International Journal of Intercultural Relations, 1*, 52-66.

Goffman, E. (1955). On face-work: An analysis of ritual elements in social interaction. *Psychiatry: Journal for the Study of International Processes, 18*, 213-231.

Goffman, E. (1959). *The presentation of self in everyday life*. Garden City, NY: Doubleday.

Goffman, E. (1961). *Asylums*. Garden City, NY: Doubleday.

Goffman, E. (1967). *Interaction ritual: Essays on face-to-face interaction*. Garden City, NY: Doubleday.

Goffman, E. (1971). *Relations in public*. New York: Harper & Row.

Goldschmidt, W. (1966). *Comparative functionalism*. Berkeley: University of California Press.

Goodenough, W. (1961). Comment on cultural evolution. *Daedalus, 90*, 521-528.

Gouldner, A. (1960). The norm of reciprocity: A preliminary statement. *American Sociological Review, 25*, 161-179.

Greenberg, B., Burgoon, M., Burgoon, J., & Korzenny, F. (1983). *Mexican Americans and the mass media*. Norwood, NJ: Ablex.

Greenberg, B., & Reeves, B. (1976). Children and the perceived reality of television. *Journal of Social Issues, 32*(4), 86-97.

Grice, H. (1975). Logic and conversation. In P. Cole & J. Morgan (Eds.), *Syntax and semantics: Vol. 3. Speech acts*. New York: Academic Press.

Griswold, W. (1987). A methodological framework for the sociology of culture. In C. Clogg (Ed.), *Sociological methodology 1987*. Washington, DC: American Sociological Association.

Gross, J., & Rayner, S. (1985). *Measuring culture*. New York: Columbia University Press.

Gudykunst, W. (1977). Intercultural contact and attitude change. In N. Jain (Ed.), *International and intercultural communication annual* (Vol. IV). Annandale, VA: Speech Communication Association.

Gudykunst, W. (1983a). Similarities and differences in perceptions of initial intracultural and intercultural encounters. *Southern Speech Communication Journal, XLIX,* 49-65.

Gudykunst, W. (1983b). Uncertainty reduction and predictability of behavior in low- and high-context cultures. *Communication Quarterly, 31,* 49-55.

Gudykunst, W. (Ed.). (1983c). *Intercultural communication theory.* Beverly Hills, CA: Sage.

Gudykunst, W. (1983d). Theorizing in intercultural communication. In W. Gudykunst (Ed.), *Intercultural communication theory.* Beverly Hills, CA: Sage.

Gudykunst, W. (1985a). A model of uncertainty reduction in intercultural encounters. *Journal of Language and Social Psychology, 4, 79-98.*

Gudykunst, W. (1985b). An exploratory comparison of close intracultural and intercultural friendships. *Communication Quarterly, 33,* 270-273.

Gudykunst, W. (1985c). The influence of cultural similarity, type of relationship, and self-monitoring on uncertainty reduction processes. *Communication Monographs, 52,* 203-217.

Gudykunst, W. (1985d). Normative power and conflict potential in intergroup relationships. In W. Gudykunst, L. Stewart, & S. Ting-Toomey (Eds.), *Communication, culture and organizational processes.* Beverly Hills, CA: Sage.

Gudykunst, W. (1985e). Uncertainty reduction during intercultural encounters. *Journal of Language and Social Psychology, 4,* 79-98.

Gudykunst, W. (1986a). Ethnicity, type of relationship, and intraethnic and interethnic uncertainty reduction. In Y. Kim (Ed.), *Interethnic communication.* Beverly Hills, CA: Sage.

Gudykunst, W. (1986b). *Intergroup communication.* London: Edward Arnold.

Gudykunst, W. (1986c). Toward a theory of intergroup communication. In W. Gudykunst (Ed.), *Intergroup communication.* London: Edward Arnold.

Gudykunst, W. (1987a). Cross-cultural comparisons. In C. Berger & S. Chaffee (Eds.), *Handbook of communication science.* Newbury Park, CA: Sage.

Gudykunst, W. (1987b, July). *Cultural variability in ethnolinguistic identity.* Paper presented at the Social Identity Conference, University of Exeter, Exeter, England.

Gudykunst, W. (1988). Uncertainty and anxiety. In Y. Kim & W. Gudykunst (Ed.), *Theory in intercultural communication.* Newbury Park, CA: Sage.

Gudykunst, W. (in press a). *Strangeness and similarity: A theory of interpersonal and intergroup communication.* Clevendon, England: Multilingual Matters.

Gudykunst, W. (in press b). Culture and communication in interpersonal relationships. In J. Anderson (Ed.), *Communication yearbook 12.* Newbury Park, CA: Sage.

Gudykunst, W. (in press c). Uncertainty and anxiety. In Y.Y, Kim & W.B. Gudykunst (Eds.), *Theories in intercultural communication.* Newbury Park, CA: Sage.

Gudykunst, W., Chua, E., & Gray, A. (1987). Cultural dissimilarities and uncertainty reduction processes. In M. McLaughlin (Ed.), *Communication yearbook 10.* Newbury Park, CA: Sage.

Gudykunst, W., & Hammer, M. (in press). The effects of ethnicity, gender, and dyadic composition on uncertainty reduction in initial interactions. *Journal of Black Studies.*

Gudykunst, W., & Kim, Y. (1984a). *Communicating with strangers.* New York: Random House.

Gudykunst, W., & Kim, Y. (Eds.). (1984b). *Methods for intercultural communication research.* Beverly Hills, CA: Sage.

Gudykunst, W., & Lim, T. (1986). A perspective for the study of intergroup communication. In W. Gudykunst (Ed.), *Intergroup communication*. London: Edward Arnold.

Gudykunst, W., & Nishida, T. (1983). Social penetration in Japanese and North American friendships. In R. Bostrom (Ed.), *Communication yearbook 7*. Beverly Hills, CA: Sage.

Gudykunst, W., & Nishida, T. (1984). Individual and cultural influence on uncertainty reduction. *Communication Monographs, 51,* 23-36.

Gudykunst, W., & Nishida, T. (1986a). Attributional confidence in low- and high-context cultures. *Human Communication Research, 12,* 525-549.

Gudykunst, W., & Nishida, T. (1986b). The influence of cultural variability on perceptions of communication behavior associated with relationship terms. *Human Communication Research, 13,* 147-166.

Gudykunst, W., Nishida, T., & Chua, E. (1986). Uncertainty reduction processes in Japanese-North American dyads. *Communication Research Reports, 3,* 39-46.

Gudykunst, W., Nishida, T., & Chua, E. (1987). Perceptions of social penetration in Japanese-North American dyads. *International Journal of Intercultural Relations, 11,* 171-190.

Gudykunst, W., Nishida, T., Koike, H., & Shiino, N. (1986). The influence of language on uncertainty reduction: An exploratory study of Japanese-Japanese and Japanese-North American interactions. In M. McLaughlin (Ed.), *Communication yearbook 9*. Beverly Hills, CA: Sage.

Gudykunst, W., Nishida, T., & Schmidt, K. (1988, May). *Cultural personality and relational influences on uncertainty reduction in ingroup vs. outgroup and same- vs. opposite-sex relationships: Japan and the United States*. Paper presented at the International Communication Association, New Orleans.

Gudykunst, W., Sodetani, L., & Sonoda, K. (1987). Uncertainty reduction in Japanese-American/Caucasian relationships in Hawaii. *Western Journal of Speech Communication, 51,* 256-278.

Gudykunst, W., Stewart, L., & Ting-Toomey, S. (Eds.). (1985). *Communication, culture and organizational processes*. Beverly Hills, CA: Sage.

Gudykunst, W., & Ting-Toomey, S. (1988). Affective communication across cultures. *American Behavioral Scientist, 31,* 384-400.

Gudykunst, W., Wiseman, R., & Hammer, M. (1977). Determinants of sojourners' attitudinal satisfaction. In B. Ruben (Ed.), *Communication yearbook 1*. New Brunswick, NJ: Transaction.

Gudykunst, W., Yang, S., & Nishida, T. (1985). A cross-cultural test of uncertainty reduction theory: Comparisons of acquaintance, friend, and dating relationships in Japan, Korea, and the United States. *Human Communication Research, 11,* 407-454.

Gudykunst, W., Yang, S., & Nishida, T. (1987). Cultural differences in self-consciousness and self-monitoring. *Communication Research, 14,* 7-36.

Gudykunst, W., Yoon, Y., & Nishida, T. (1987). The influence of individualism-collectivism on perceptions of communication in ingroup and outgroup relationships. *Communication Monographs, 54,* 295-306.

Guilford, J. (1959). *Personality*. New York: McGraw-Hill.

Gullahorn, J., & Gullahorn, J. (1966). American students abroad. *Annals of the American Academy of Political and Social Science, 368,* 43-59.

Gumperz, J. (1982a). *Discourse strategies*. London: Cambridge University Press.

Gumperz, J. (Ed.). (1982b). *Language and social identity*. London: Cambridge University Press.

Gumperz, J., Aulakh, G., & Kaltman, H. (1982). Thematic structure and progression in discourse. In J. Gumperz (Ed.), *Language and social identity*. Cambridge: Cambridge University Press.

Guthrie, G., & Bennett, A. (1971). Cultural differences in implicit personality theory. *International Journal of Psychology, 6,* 305-312.

Haire, M., Ghiselli, E., & Porter, L. (1966). *Managerial thinking: An international study.* New York: John Wiley.

Hale, C. (1980). Cognitive complexity-simplicity as determinants of communication effectiveness. *Communication Monographs, 47,* 304-311.

Hall, B., & Gudykunst, W. (1986). The intergroup theory of second language ability. *Journal of Language and Social Psychology, 5,* 291-302.

Hall, E. P. (1985). The etic-emic distinction. In B. Dervin & M. Voigt (Eds.), *Progress in communication science* (Vol. 7). Norwood, NJ: Ablex.

Hall, E. T. (1959). *The silent language.* New York: Doubleday.

Hall, E. T. (1966). *The hidden dimension.* New York: Doubleday.

Hall, E. T. (1976). *Beyond culture.* New York: Doubleday.

Hall, E. T. (1983). *The dance of life.* New York: Doubleday.

Hamilton, D. (1979). A cognitive-attributional analysis of stereotyping. In L. Berkowitz (Ed.), *Advances in experimental social psychology* (Vol. 12). New York: Academic Press.

Hamilton, D., & Bishop, G. (1976). Attitudinal and behavioral effects of initial integration of white suburban neighborhoods. *Journal of Social Issues, 32*(2), 47-67.

Hamilton, D., Carpenter, S., & Bishop, G. (1984). Desegregation of suburban neighborhoods. In N. Miller & M. Brewer (Eds.), *Groups in contact.* New York: Academic Press.

Hammer, M., & Gudykunst, W. (1987). The influence of ethnicity and sex on social penetration in close friendships. *Journal of Black Studies, 17,* 418-437.

Hammer, M., Gudykunst, W., & Wiseman, R. (1978). Dimensions of intercultural effectiveness. *International Journal of Intercultural Relations, 2,* 382-393.

Hammers, J., & Blanc, M. (1982). Towards a social-psychological model of bilingual development. *Journal of Language and Social Psychology, 1,* 29-49.

Harnet, D., & Cumming, L. (1980). *Bargaining behavior: An international study.* Houston, TX: Dane.

Harris, M. (1968). *The rise of cultural theory.* New York: Crowell.

Hartman, P., & Husband, C. (1972). The mass media and racial conflict. In D. McPhail (Ed.), *Sociology of mass communication.* Harmondsworth, England: Penguin.

Harvey, Q., Hunt, D., & Schroder, H. (1961). *Conceptual systems and personality organization.* New York: John Wiley.

Hays, R. (1985). A longitudinal study of friendship development. *Journal of Personality and Social Psychology, 48,* 909-924.

Hecht, M. (1978). The conceptualization and measurement of communication satisfaction. *Human Communication Research, 4,* 253-264.

Hecht, M. (1984). Satisfying communication and relationship labels: Intimacy and length of relationship as perceptual frames of naturalistic conversations. *Western Journal of Speech Communication, 48,* 201-216.

Hecht, M. L., & Ribeau, S. (1984). Ethnic communication: A comparative analysis of satisfying communication. *International Journal of Intercultural Relations, 8,* 135-151.

252 *Culture and Interpersonal Communication*

Henley, N., & LaFrance, M. (1984). Gender as culture: Difference and dominance in nonverbal behavior. In A. Wolfgang (Ed.), *Nonverbal behavior: Perspectives, applications, intercultural insights.* Lewiston, NY: C. J. Hogrefe, Inc.

Herman, S., & Schield, E. (1961). The stranger group in a cross-cultural situation. *Sociometry, 24,* 165-176.

Herskovits, M. (1955). *Cultural anthropology.* New York: Knopf.

Hewes, D., Graham, M., Doelger, J., & Pavitt, C. (1985). "Second-guessing": Message interpretation in social networks. *Human Communication Research, 11,* 299-334.

Hewstone, M. (1985). Social psychology and intergroup relations: Cross-cultural perspectives. *Journal of Multilingual and Multicultural Development, 6,* 209-215.

Hewstone, M., Bond, M., & Wan, K. (1983). Social facts and social attributions: The explanation of intergroup differences in Hong Kong. *Social Cognition, 2,* 142-157.

Hewstone, M., & Brown, R. (1986). Contact is not enough. In M. Hewstone & R. Brown (Eds.), *Contact and conflict in intergroup encounters.* Oxford: Basil Blackwell.

Hewstone, M., & Giles, H. (1984). Intergroup conflict. In A. Gale & A. Chapman (Eds.), *Psychology and social problems.* Chichester, England: John Wiley.

Hewstone, M., & Giles, H. (1986). Stereotypes and intergroup communications. In W. Gudykunst (Ed.), *Intergroup communication.* London: Edward Arnold.

Hewstone, M., & Jaspers, J. (1982a). Intergroup relations and attributional processes. In H. Tajfel (Ed.), *Social identity and intergroup relations.* London: Cambridge University Press.

Hewstone, M., & Jaspers, J. (1982b). Explanations for racial discrimination. *European Journal of Social Psychology, 12,* 1-16.

Hewstone, M., Jaspers, J., & Lalljee, M. (1982). Social representations, social attribution, and social identity. *European Journal of Social Psychology, 12,* 241-269.

Hewstone, M., & Ward, C. (1985). Ethnocentrism and causal attribution in Southeast Asia. *Journal of Personality and Social Psychology, 48,* 614-623.

Hill, B., Ide, S., Ikuta, S., Kawasaki, A., & Ogino, T. (1986). Universals of linguistic politeness: Quantitative evidence for Japanese and American English. *Journal of Pragmatics, 10,* 347-371.

Hirokawa, R., & Miyahara, A. (1986). A comparison of influence strategies utilized by managers in American and Japanese organizations. *Communication Quarterly, 34,* 250-265.

Hofman, T. (1985). Arabs and Jews, Blacks and Whites: Identity and group relations. *Journal of Multilingual and Multicultural Development, 6,* 217-237.

Hofstede, G. (1979). Value systems in forty countries. In L. Eckensberger, W. Lonner, & Y. Poortinga (Eds.), *Cross-cultural contributions to psychology.* Lisse, The Netherlands: Swets & Zeitlinger.

Hofstede, G. (1980). *Culture's consequences: International differences in work-related values.* Beverly Hills, CA: Sage.

Hofstede, G. (1983). Dimensions of national cultures in fifty countries and three regions. In J. Deregowski, S. Dzuirawiec, & R. Annis (Eds.), *Explications in cross-cultural psychology.* Lisse, The Netherlands: Swets & Zeitlinger.

Hofstede, G. (1984). Hofstede's culture dimensions: An independent validation using Rokeach's value survey. *Journal of Cross-Cultural Psychology, 15,* 417-433.

Hofstede, G., & Bond, M. (1984). Hofstede's culture dimensions: An independent validation using Rokeach's value survey. *Journal of Cross-Cultural Psychology, 15,* 417-433.

Honeycutt, J. (1986, May). *Processing information about others and attributional confidence in initial interaction on the basis of expectancies.* Paper presented at the International Communication Association convention, Chicago.

Hsieh, T., Skybut, J., & Lotsof, E. (1969). Internal vs. external control and ethnic membership: A cross-cultural comparison. *Journal of Counselling and Clinical Psychology, 33,* 122-134.

Hsu, F. (1981). *Americans and Chinese* (3rd ed.). Honolulu: University of Hawaii Press.

Hsu, F. (1983). *Rugged individualism reconsidered.* Knoxville: University of Tennessee Press.

Hsu, F. (1985). The self in cross-cultural perspective. In A. Marsella, G. DeVos, & F. Hsu (Eds.), *Culture and self: Asian and Western perspectives.* New York: Tavistock.

Hu, H. (1944). The Chinese concept of "face." *American Anthropologist, 46,* 45-64.

Hui, C. (1982). Locus of control: A review of cross-cultural research. *International Journal of Intercultural Relations, 6,* 301-323.

Hui, C., & Triandis, H. (1985). Quantitative methods in cross-cultural research: Multidimensional scaling and item response theory. In R. Diaz-Guerrero (Ed.), *Cross-cultural and national studies in social psychology.* North Holland: Elsevier.

Hui, C., & Triandis, H. (1986). Individualism-collectivism: A study of cross-cultural researchers. *Journal of Cross-Cultural Psychology, 17,* 225-248.

Hulin, C. (1987). A psychometric theory of evaluations of item and scale translations: Fidelity across languages. *Journal of Cross-Cultural Psychology, 18,* 115-142.

Hur, K. (1982). International mass communication research. In M. Burgoon (Ed.), *Communication yearbook 6.* Beverly Hills, CA: Sage.

Hwang, J., Chase, L., & Kelly, C. (1980). An intercultural examination of communication competence. *Communication, 9,* 70-79.

Hwang, K. (1983). *Face and favour: Chinese power games.* Unpublished manuscript, National Taiwan University.

Hymes, D. (1972). Models of the interaction of language and social life. In J. Gumperz & D. Hymes (Eds.), *Directions of sociolinguistics.* New York: Holt, Rinehart & Winston.

Ickes, W. (1984). Compositions in black and white: Determinants of interaction in interracial dyads. *Journal of Personality and Social Psychology, 47,* 330-341.

Ickes, W., & Barnes, R. (1977). The role of sex and self-monitoring on unstructured dyadic interaction. *Journal of Personality and Social Psychology, 35,* 315-330.

Ide, S., Hori, M., Kawasaki, A., Ikuta, S., & Haga, H. (1986). Sex differences and politeness in Japanese. *International Journal of the Sociology of Language, 58,* 25-36.

Inkeles, A., & Levinson, D. (1969). National character and sociocultural systems. In G. Lindzey & E. Aronson (Eds.), *Handbook of social psychology* (2nd ed., Vol. 4). Reading, MA: Addison-Wesley.

Insko, C., Nacoste, R., & Moe, J. (1983). Belief congruence and racial discrimination. *European Journal of Social Psychology, 13,* 153-174.

Isen, A. (1984). Toward understanding the role of affect in cognition. In R. Wyler & T. Srull (Eds.), *Handbook of social cognition* (Vol. 3). Hillsdale, NJ: Lawrence Erlbaum.

Ishida, I. (1984). Conflict and its accommodation: "Omote-ure" and "uchi-soto" relations. In E. Krauss, T. Rohlen, & G. Steinhoff (Eds.), *Conflict in Japan.* Honolulu: University of Hawaii Press.

Ishii, S. (1984). Enryo-sasshi communication: A key to understanding Japanese interpersonal relations. *Cross-Currents, 11,* 49-58.

Ishii, S., Klopf, D., & Cambra, R. (1979). Oral communication apprehension among students in Japan, Korea, and the United States. *Current English Studies, 18,* 12-26.

Izard, C. (1968). *The emotions as a culture-common framework of motivational experiences and communicative cues.* Technical Report No. 30, Vanderbilt University, Contract No. 2149(03)-NR 171-6090, Office of Naval Research.

Izard, C. (1971). *The face of emotion.* New York: Appleton-Century-Crofts.

Izard, C. (1980). Cross-cultural perspectives on emotion and emotion communication. In H. Triandis & W. Lonner (Eds.), *Handbook of cross-cultural psychology* (Vol. 3). Boston, MA: Allyn & Bacon.

Jackson, J. (1975). Normative power and conflict potential. *Sociological Methods and Research, 4,* 237-263.

Jahoda, G. (1983). The cross-cultural emperor's conceptual clothes: The emic-etic issue revisited. In J. Deregowski, S. Dzuirawiec, & R. Annis (Eds.), *Explications in cross-cultural psychology.* Lisse, The Netherlands: Swets & Zeitlinger.

Jaspars, J., & Hewstone, M. (1982). Cross-cultural interaction, social attribution, and inter-group relations. In S. Bochner (Ed.), *Cultures in contact.* Elmsford, NY: Pergamon.

Jaspars, J., & Warnaen, S. (1982). Intergroup relations, social identity, and self-evaluation in India. In H. Tajfel (Ed.), *Social identity and intergroup relations.* Cambridge: Cambridge University Press.

Johnson, C. (1977). Interdependence, reciprocity and indebtedness: An analysis of Japanese American kinship relations. *Journal of Marriage and the Family, 39,* 351-364.

Johnson, C., & Johnson, F. (1975). Interaction rules and ethnicity. *Social Forces, 54,* 452-466.

Johnson, F. (1985). The Western concept of self. In A. Marsella, G. DeVos, & F. Hsu (Eds.), *Culture and self: Asian and Western perspectives.* New York: Tavistock.

Johnson, J. (1983). A test of a model of magazine exposure and appraisal in India. *Communication Monographs, 50,* 148-157.

Jones, E., & Nisbett, R. (1972). *The actor and the observer.* Morristown, NJ: General Learning Press.

Jones, J. (1988). Cultural differences in temporal patterns. In J. McGrath (Ed.), *The social psychology of time.* Newbury Park, CA: Sage.

Jones, T., & Remland, M. (1982, May). *Cross-cultural differences in self-reported touch avoidance.* Paper presented at the Eastern Communication Association convention, Hartford, CT.

Jöreskog, K., & Sörbom, D. (1981). *LISREL V: Users guide.* Chicago: National Educational Resources.

Jourard, S. (1960). Knowing, liking, and the "dyadic effect" in men's self-disclosure. *Merrill Palmer Quarterly of Behavior and Development, 6,* 178-186.

Jung, C. (1933). *Psychological types.* New York: Harcourt, Brace.

Kagan, S., Knight, G., & Martinez-Romero, S. (1982). Culture and the development of conflict resolution style. *Journal of Cross-Cultural Psychology, 13,* 43-59.

Kagan, S., & Madsen, M. (1971). Cooperation and competition of Mexican, Mexican-American, and Anglo-American children of two ages under four instructional sets. *Developmental Psychology, 5,* 32-39.

Kagan, S., & Madsen, M. (1972a). Experimental analyses of cooperation and competition of Anglo-American and Mexican children. *Developmental Psychology, 6,* 49-59.

Kagan, S., & Madsen, M. (1972b). Rivalry of Anglo-American and Mexican children of two ages. *Journal of Personality and Social Psychology, 24,* 214-220.

Kahn, A., Lamm, H., & Nelson, R. (1977). Preferences for an equal or equitable allocation. *Journal of Personality and Social Psychology, 35,* 837-844.

Kalin, R., & Tilby, P. (1978). Development and validation of a sex-role ideology scale. *Psychological Reports, 42,* 731-738.

Kashima, Y., & Triandis, H. (1986). The self-serving bias in attributions as a coping strategy: A cross-cultural study. *Journal of Cross-Cultural Psychology, 17,* 83-97.

Katriel, T. (1986). *Talking straight: Dugri speech in Israeli Sabra culture.* Cambridge: Cambridge University Press.

Keenan, E. (1974). Norm-makers, norm-breakers: Uses of speech by men and women in a Malagasy community. In R. Bauman & J. Sherzer (Eds.), *Explorations in the ethnography of speaking.* Cambridge: Cambridge University Press.

Keesing, R. (1974). Theories of culture. *Annual Review of Anthropology, 3,* 73-97.

Kellerman, K. (1985). Memory processes in media effects. *Communication Research, 12,* 83-131.

Kellerman, K. (1986). Anticipation of future interaction and information exchange in initial interaction. *Human Communication Research, 13,* 41-75.

Kerr, C., Dunlop, R., Harbison, F., & Meyers, C. (1964). *Industrialism and industrial man* (2nd ed.). New York: Oxford University Press.

Kim, K. (1975). Cross-cultural differences between Americans and Koreans in nonverbal behavior. In H-M Sohn (Ed.), *The Korean language: Its structure and social projection.* Honolulu: University of Hawaii Press, Center for Korean Studies.

Kim, Y. (1977a). Communication patterns of foreign immigrants in the process of acculturation. *Human Communication Research, 41,* 66-76.

Kim, Y. (1977b). Inter-ethnic and intra-ethnic communication. In N. Jain (Ed.), *International and intercultural communication annual* (Vol. 4). Annandale, VA: Speech Communication Association.

Kim, Y. (1978). A communication approach to the acculturation process. *International Journal of Intercultural Relations, 2,* 197-224.

Kim, Y. (1979). Towards an interactive theory of communication-acculturation. In D. Nimmo (Ed.), *Communication yearbook 3.* New Brunswick, NJ: Transaction.

Kim, Y. (1986a). *Current research in interethnic communication.* Beverly Hills, CA: Sage.

Kim, Y. (1986b). Social networks in intergroup communication. In W. Gudykunst (Ed.), *Intergroup communication.* London: Edward Arnold.

Kim, Y. (in press). *Communication and cross-cultural adaptation.* Clevendon, England: Multilingual Matters.

Kim, Y., & Gudykunst, W. (Eds.). (1987). *Current research in cross-cultural adaptation.* Newbury Park, CA: Sage.

Kim, Y., & Gudykunst, W. (Eds.). (1988). *Theory in intercultural communication.* Newbury Park, CA: Sage.

Klopf, D. (1984). Cross-cultural apprehension research: A summary of Pacific Basin studies. In J. Daly & J. McCroskey (Eds.), *Avoiding communication: Shyness, reticence, and communication apprehension.* Beverly Hills, CA: Sage.

Klopf, D., & Cambra, R. (1979). Communication apprehension among college students in America, Australia, Japan, and Korea. *Journal of Psychology, 102,* 27-31.

Klopf, D., & Cambra, R. (1981). A comparison of communication styles of Japanese and American college students. *Current English Studies, 20,* 66-71.

Klopf, D., Cambra, R., & Ishii, S. (1983, July). *The typical Japanese university student as an oral communicator: A preliminary profile.* Paper presented at the Japanese Communication Association Convention, Tokyo.

Kluckhohn, F., & Strodtbeck, F. (1961). *Variations in value orientations.* New York: Row, Peterson.

Knapp, M. (1978). *Social intercourse: From greetings to goodbye.* Boston: Allyn & Bacon.

Knapp, M. (1983). Dyadic relationship development. In J. Wiemann & R. Harrison (Eds.), *Nonverbal interaction.* Beverly Hills, CA: Sage.

Knapp, M. (1984). The study of nonverbal behavior vis-à-vis human communication theory. In A. Wolfgang (Ed.), *Nonverbal behavior: Perspectives, applications, intercultural insights.* Lewiston, NY: C. J. Hogrefe, Inc.

Knapp, M., Ellis, D., & Williams, B. (1980). Perceptions of communication behavior associated with relationship terms. *Communication Monographs, 47,* 262-278.

Kochman, T. (1982). *Black and white: Styles in conflict.* Chicago, IL: University of Chicago Press.

Koike, H., Gudykunst, W., Stewart, L., Ting-Toomey, S., & Nishida, T. (1986, May). *Communication openness, job satisfaction, and length of employment in Japanese organizations.* Paper presented at the International Communication Association Convention, Chicago.

Koltuv, B. (1962). Some characteristics of intrajudge trait intercorrelations. *Psychological Monographs, 76*(33), Whole No. 552.

Koontz, H. (1969). A model for analyzing the universality and transferability of management. *Academy of Management Journal, 12,* 415-429.

Korte, C., & Milgram, S. (1970). Acquaintance networks between racial groups. *Journal of Personality and Social Psychology, 15,* 101-108.

Korzenny, F., & Farace, V. (1977). Communication networks and social change in developing countries. In N. Jain (Ed.), *International and intercultural communication annual* (Vol. 4). Annandale, VA: Speech Communication Association.

Krampen, G., & Wieberg, H. (1981). Three aspects of locus of control in German, American, and Japanese university students. *Journal of Social Psychology, 113,* 133-134.

Kroeber, A., & Kluckhohn, C. (1952). *Culture: A critical review of concepts and definitions.* Cambridge, MA: Peabody Museum.

Kumagai, F., & Straus, M. (1983). Conflict resolution tactics in Japan, India, and the United States. *Journal of Comparative Family Studies, 14,* 377-387.

LaFrance, M., & Mayo, C. (1976). Racial differences in gaze behavior during conversations. *Journal of Personality and Social Psychology, 33,* 547-552.

LaFrance, M., & Mayo, C. (1978a). Cultural aspects of nonverbal communication. *International Journal of Intercultural Relations, 2,* 71-89.

LaFrance, M., & Mayo, C. (1978b). Gaze direction in interracial dyadic communication. *Ethnicity, 5,* 167-173.

LaFrance, M., & Mayo, C. (1979). A review of nonverbal behaviors of women and men. *Western Journal of Speech Communication, 43,* 96-107.

Lakatos, I. (1970). Falisification and the methodology of scientific research programs. In I. Lakatos & A. Musgrave (Eds.), *Criticism and the growth of knowledge.* Cambridge: Cambridge University Press.

Lalljee, M., & Cook, M. (1973). Uncertainty in first encounters. *Journal of Personality and Social Psychology, 26,* 137-141.

Lambert, R. (Ed.). (1966). Americans abroad. *Annals of the American Academy of Political and Social Science, 368.*

Lambert, W. (1967). The social psychology of bilingualism. *Journal of Social Issues, 23,* 91-109.

Lammers, C. (1978). The comparative sociology of organizations. *Annual Review of Sociology, 4,* 485-510.

Landis, D., & Brislin, R. (Eds.). (1983). *Handbook of intercultural training: Vol. 1. Issues in theory and design; Vol. 2. Issues in training methodology; Vol. 3. Area studies in intercultural training.* Elmsford, NY: Pergamon.

Langer, E. (1978). Rethinking the role of thought in social interaction. In J. Harvey et al. (Eds.), *New directions in attribution research* (Vol. 2). Hillsdale, NJ: Lawrence Erlbaum.

Lasch, C. (1979). *The culture of narcissism.* New York: Warner.

Lazarus, R. (1982). Thought on the relations between emotion and cognition. *American Psychologist, 37,* 1010-1024.

Lebra, T. (1976). *Japanese patterns of behavior.* Honolulu: University of Hawaii Press.

Lebra, T. (1984). Nonconfrontational strategies for management of interpersonal conflict. In E. Krauss, T. Rohlen, & G. Steinhoff (Eds.), *Conflict in Japan.* Honolulu: University of Hawaii Press.

Leclezio, M., Louw-Potgeiter, & Souchon, M. (1986). The social identity of Mauritian immigrants in South Africa. *Journal of Social Psychology, 126,* 61-69.

Leff, J. (1977). The cross-cultural study of emotion. *Culture, Medicine, and Psychiatry, 1,* 317-350.

Leichty, G., & Applegate, J. (1987, May). *Social cognitive and situational influences on the use of face-saving persuasive strategies.* Paper presented at the International Communication Association Convention, Montreal.

Lennox, R., & Wolfe, R. (1984). Revision of the self-monitoring scale. *Journal of Personality and Social Psychology, 46,* 1349-1364.

Lerner, D. (1958). *The passing of traditional society.* New York: Macmillan.

Lerner, M. (1974). The justice motive: Equity and parity among children. *Journal of Personality and Social Psychology, 29,* 539-550.

Leung, K., & Bond, M. (1982). How Chinese and Americans reward task-related contributions: A preliminary study. *Psychologia, 25,* 32-39.

Leung, K., & Bond, M. (1984). The impact of cultural collectivism on reward allocation. *Journal of Personality and Social Psychology, 47,* 793-804.

Leung, K., & Bond, M. (1987). *On the search for cultural dimensions: Some methodological considerations.* Unpublished paper, Chinese University of Hong Kong.

Leung, K., & Lind, E. A. (1986). Procedural justice and culture: Effects of culture, gender, and investigator status on procedural preferences. *Journal of Personality and Social Psychology, 50,* 1134-1140.

Lévi-Strauss, C. (1971). *Mythologiques, IV: L'homme nu.* Paris: Plon.

Levine, D. (1985). *The flight from ambiguity.* Chicago: University of Chicago Press.

LeVine, R. (1973). *Culture, behavior, and personality.* Chicago: Aldine.

LeVine, R. (1988). The pace of life across cultures. In J. McGrath (Ed.), *The social psychology of time.* Newbury Park, CA: Sage.

LeVine, R., & Campbell, D. (1972). *Ethnocentrism: Theories of conflict, ethnic attitudes, and group behavior.* New York: John Wiley.

Levy, R. (1984). Emotion, knowing, and culture. In R. Shweder & R. LeVine (Eds.), *Culture theory: Essays on mind, self, and emotion.* Cambridge: Cambridge University Press.

Lewin, K. (1936). *Principles of topological psychology.* New York: Harper & Row.

Lewin, K. (1948). *Resolving social conflicts.* New York: Harper & Row.

Lin, Y. T. (1968). *My country and my people.* Taipai, Republic of China: John Day.

Lin, N., Dayton, P., & Greenwald, P. (1977). The urban communication network and social stratification. In B. Ruben (Ed.), *Communication yearbook 1.* New Brunswick, NJ: Transaction.

Lindgren, H., & Marrash, J. (1970). A comparative study of intercultural insight and empathy. *Journal of Social Psychology, 80,* 135-141.

Lipset, S. (1963). The value patterns of democracy. *American Sociological Review, 28,* 515-531.

Little, K. (1968). Cultural variations in social schemata. *Journal of Personality and Social Psychology, 10,* 1-7.

Lloyd, K., Paulsen, J., & Brockner, J. (1983). The effects of self-esteem and self-consciousness on interpersonal attraction. *Personality and Social Psychology Bulletin, 9,* 397-403.

Lomranz, J., & Shapira, A. (1974). Communication patterns of self-disclosure and touching behavior. *Journal of Psychology, 88,* 223-227.

Lonner, W. (1979). Issues in cross-cultural psychology. In A. Marsella, A. Tharp, & T. Cibrowski (Eds.), *Perspectives in cross-cultural psychology.* New York: Academic Press.

Lonner, W. (1980). The search for psychological universals. In H. Triandis & W. Lambert (Eds.), *Handbook of cross-cultural psychology* (Vol. 1). Boston, MA: Allyn & Bacon.

Lonner, W., & Berry, J. (Eds.). (1986). *Field methods in cross-cultural research.* Beverly Hills, CA: Sage.

Lukens, J. (1978). Ethnocentric speech. *Ethnic Groups, 2,* 35-53.

Lukens, J. (1979). Interethnic conflict and communicative distance. In H. Giles & R. Saint-Jacques (Eds.), *Language and ethnic relations.* Elmsford, NY: Pergamon.

Lustig, M., & Myers, S. (1983, February). *Compliance-gaining strategy selection: A comparison of six countries.* Paper presented at the Western Speech Communication Association Convention, Albuquerque.

Lutz, C. (1982). The domain of emotion words on Ifaluk. *American Ethnologist, 9,* 113-128.

Madsen, M. (1971). Developmental and cross-cultural differences in the cooperation and competitive behavior of young children. *Journal of Cross-Cultural Psychology, 2,* 365-371.

Madsen, M., & Shapira, A. (1970). Cooperative and competitive behavior of urban Afro-American, Anglo-American, Mexican-American, and Mexican village children. *Developmental Psychology, 3,* 16-20.

Mahler, I. (1974). A comparative study of locus of control. *Psychologia, 17,* 135-139.

Mahler, I., Greenberg, L., & Hayashi, H. (1981). A comparative study of rules of justice: Japanese versus Americans. *Psychologia, 24,* 1-8.

Majeed, A., & Ghosh, E. (1982). A study of social identity in three ethnic groups in India. *International Journal of Psychology, 17,* 455-463.

Malpass, R. (1977). Theory and method in cross-cultural psychology. *American Psychologist, 32,* 1069-1079.

Mann, L. (1980). Cross-cultural studies of small groups. In H. Triandis & R. Brislin (Eds.), *Handbook of cross-cultural psychology* (Vol. 5). Boston, MA: Allyn & Bacon.

Mann, L., Radford, M., & Kanagawa, C. (1985). Cross-cultural differences in children's use of decision rules. *Journal of Personality and Social Psychology, 49,* 1557-1564.

Marin, G. (1981). Perceiving justice across cultures. *International Journal of Psychology, 16,* 153-159.

Marsella, A. (1980). Depressive experience and disorders across cultures. In H. Triandis & J. Draguns (Eds.), *Handbook of cross-cultural psychology* (Vol. 6). Boston: Allyn & Bacon.

Marsella, A., DeVos, G., & Hsu, F. (Eds.). (1985). *Culture and self: Asian and Western perspectives.* London: Tavistock.

Marwell, G., & Schmidt, D. (1967). Dimensions of compliance-gaining behavior. *Sociometry, 30,* 350-364.

Maslow, A. (1970). *Motivation and personality* (2nd ed.). New York: Harper & Row.

Matsumoto, D., & Kishimoto, H. (1983). Developmental characteristics in judgments of emotion from nonverbal vocal cues. *International Journal of Intercultural Relations, 7,* 415-424.

Matsumoto, D., Wallbott, H., & Scherer, K. (in press). Emotion in intercultural communication. In M. Asante & W. Gudykunst (Eds.), *Handbook of intercultural and development communication.* Newbury Park, CA: Sage.

Mayer, P. (1961). *Townsmen and tribesmen.* Cape Town: Oxford University Press.

Mayo, C., & LaFrance, M. (1977). *Evaluating research in social psychology.* Monterey, CA: Brooks/Cole.

McAndrew, F. (1986). A cross-cultural study of recognition thresholds for facial expressions of emotion. *Journal of Cross-Cultural Psychology, 17,* 211-224.

McBride, S., et al. (1980). *Many voices, one world.* Paris: UNESCO.

McCall, G., & Simmons, J. (Eds.). (1966). *Issues in participant observation.* Reading, MA: Addison-Wesley.

McCroskey, J. (1978). Validity of the PRCA as an index of oral communication apprehension. *Communication Monographs, 45,* 192-203.

McCroskey, J. (1984). The communication apprehension perspective. In J. Daly & J. McCroskey (Eds.), *Avoiding communication: Shyness, reticence, and communication apprehension.* Beverly Hills, CA: Sage.

McCroskey, J., & Daly, J. (Eds.). (1987). *Personality and interpersonal communication.* Newbury Park, CA: Sage.

McGinn, N., Harburg, E., & Ginsburg, G. (1973). Responses to interpersonal conflict by middle-class males in Guadalajara and Michigan. In F. Jandt (Ed.), *Conflict resolution through communication.* New York: Harper & Row.

McGinnies, E., Nordholm, L., Ward, C., & Bhanthumnavin, D. (1974). Sex and cultural differences in perceived locus of control among students in five countries. *Journal of Counselling and Clinical Psychology, 42,* 451-455.

McGuire, W., McGuire, C., Child, P., & Fujioka, P. (1978). Salience of ethnicity in the spontaneous self-concept as a function of one's ethnic distinctiveness in the social environment. *Journal of Personality and Social Psychology, 36,* 511-520.

McKirnan, D., & Hamayan, E. (1984a). Speech norms and attitudes toward out-group members. *Journal of Language and Social Psychology, 3,* 21-30.

McKirnan, D., & Hamayan, E. (1984b). Speech norms and perceptions of ethnolinguistic group differences. *European Journal of Social Psychology, 14,* 151-168.

McLaughlin, M. (1984). *Conversation: How talk is organized.* Beverly Hills, CA: Sage.

McPhail, T. (1981). *Electronic colonialism: The future of international broadcasting and communication.* Beverly Hills, CA: Sage.

Mead, G. (1934). *Mind, self, and society.* Chicago: University of Chicago Press.

Mehrabian, A. (1972). *Nonverbal communication.* Chicago: Aldine & Atherton.

Melischek, G., Rosengren, K., & Stappers, J. (Eds.). (1984). *Cultural indicators: An international symposium.* Vienna: Akademie der Wissenschaften.

Mikula, G. (1974). Nationality, performance, and sex as determinants of reward allocation. *Journal of Personality and Social Psychology, 29,* 435-440.

Miller, G. (1978). The current status of theory and research in interpersonal communication. *Human Communication Research, 4,* 164-178.

Miller, G., & Steinberg, M. (1975). *Between people.* Chicago: Science Research Associates.

Miller, G., & Sunnafrank, M. (1982). All is for one but one is not for all: A conceptual perspective of interpersonal communication. In F. Dance (Ed.), *Human communication theory.* New York: Harper & Row.

Miller, J. (1984). Culture and the development of everyday social explanations. *Journal of Personality and Social Psychology, 46,* 961-978.

Miller, M., Reynolds, R., & Cambra, R. (1982, November). *The selection of persuasive strategies in multicultural groups.* Paper presented at the Speech Communication Association convention, Louisville, KY.

Miller, N., & Brewer, M. (Eds.). (1984). *Groups in contact: The psychology of desegregation.* New York: Academic Press.

Miller, N., & Brewer, M. (1986). Categorization effects on ingroup and outgroup perception. In J. Dovidio & S. Gaertner (Eds.), *Prejudice, discrimination, and racism.* New York: Academic Press.

Milner, D. (1981). Racial prejudice. In J. Turner & H. Giles (Eds.), *Intergroup behavior.* Chicago, IL: University of Chicago Press.

Min, P. (1984). An exploratory study of kin ties among Korean immigrant families in Atlanta. *Journal of Comparative Family Studies, 15,* 59-75.

Minami, H. (1971). *Psychology of the Japanese people.* Toronto: University of Toronto Press.

Mishra, A. (1982). Discovering connections. In J. Gumperz (Ed.), *Language and social identity.* Cambridge: Cambridge University Press.

Miyahara, A. (1984, May). *A need for a study to examine the accuracy of American observers' perceptions of Japanese managers' communication styles.* Paper presented at the Eastern Communication Association convention, Philadelphia.

Montgomery, B., & Norton, R. (1981). Sex differences and similarities in communicator style. *Communication Monographs, 48,* 121-132.

Morris, D., Collett, P., Marsh, P., & O'Shaughnessy, M. (1979). *Gestures: Their origins and distribution.* New York: Stein & Day.

Morris, M. (1981). *Saying and meaning in Puerto Rico: Some problems in the ethnography of discourse.* Oxford: Pergamon.

Morsbach, H. (1973). Aspects of nonverbal communication in Japan. *Journal of Nervous and Mental Disease, 157,* 262-277.

Morse, S. (1983). Requirements for love and friendship in Australia and Brazil. *Australian Journal of Psychology, 35,* 469-476.

Moscovici, S. (1972). Society and theory in social psychology. In J. Israel & H. Tajfel (Eds.), *The context of social psychology.* London: Academic Press.

Mosel, J. (1973, May). *Status and role analysis.* Lecture presented to Japan and East Asia Area Studies Course, Foreign Service Institute, Washington, DC.

Mowlana, H. (1976). A paradigm for comparative mass media analysis. In H. Fisher & J. Merrill (Eds.), *International and intercultural communication.* New York: Hastings House.

Murata, K. (1984). Formation of interpersonal attraction and causal attribution. *Japanese Journal of Experimental Social Psychology, 24,* 13-22 (in Japanese with English abstract).

Murray, J., & Kippax, S. (1979). From the early window to the late night show: International trends in the study of television's impact on children and adults. In L. Berkowitz (Ed.), *Advances in experimental social psychology* (Vol. 12). New York: Academic Press.

Nadler, L., Nadler, M., & Broome, B. (1985). Culture and the management of conflict situations. In W. Gudykunst, L. Stewart, & S. Ting-Toomey (Eds.), *Communication, culture, and organizational processes.* Beverly Hills, CA: Sage.

Nakane, C. (1970). *Japanese society.* Berkeley: University of California Press.

Nakane, C. (1974). The social system reflected in interpersonal communication. In J. Condon & M. Saito (Eds.), *Intercultural encounters with Japan.* Tokyo: Simul Press.

Nakanishi, M. (1986). Perceptions of self-disclosure in initial interaction: A Japanese sample. *Human Communication Research, 13,* 167-190.

Nakanishi, M., & Johnson, K. (1985, November). *Implications of self-disclosure on conversational logics, perceived communication competence, and social attraction: A comparison of Japanese and American cultures.* Paper presented at the Speech Communication Association convention, Denver, CO.

Naroll, R. (1970). What have we learned from cross-cultural surveys? *American Anthropologist, 72,* 1227-1288.

Neulip, J., & Hazleton, V. (1985). A cross-cultural comparison of Japanese and American persuasive strategy selection. *International Journal of Intercultural Relations, 9,* 389-404.

Newtson, D. A. (1973). Attribution and the unit of perception of ongoing behavior. *Journal of Personality and Social Psychology, 28,* 28-38.

Niit, T., & Valsiner, J. (1977). Recognition of facial expressions: An experimental investigation of Ekman's model. *Tartu Riikliku Ulikooli Toimetised: Trudy po Psikhologii, 429,* 85-107.

Nisbett, R., Caputo, C., Legant, P., & Marecek, J. (1973). Behavior as seen by the actor and the observer. *Journal of Personality and Social Psychology, 27,* 154-165.

Nishida, H. (1981). Value orientations and value change in Japan and the USA. In T. Nishida & W. Gudykunst (Eds.), *Readings in intercultural communication.* Tokyo: Geirinshobo.

Nishida, T. (1977). An analysis of a cultural concept affecting Japanese interpersonal communication. *Communication, 6,* 69-80.

Nishiyama, K. (1971). Interpersonal persuasion in a vertical society—the case of Japan. *Speech Monographs, 38,* 148-154.

Noesjirwan, J. (1977). Contrasting cultural patterns of interpersonal closeness in doctors' waiting rooms in Sydney and Jakarta. *Journal of Cross-Cultural Psychology, 8,* 357-368.

Noesjirwan, J. (1978). A rule-based analysis of cultural differences in social behavior: Indonesia and Australia. *International Journal of Psychology, 13,* 305-316.

Nomura, N., & Barnlund, D. (1983). Patterns of interpersonal criticism in Japan and the United States. *International Journal of Intercultural Relations, 7,* 1-8.

Nordenstreng, K. (1984). *The mass media declaration of UNESCO.* Norwood, NJ: Ablex.

Norman, W. (1963). Toward an adequate taxonomy of personality attributes. *Journal of Abnormal and Social Psychology, 66,* 574-583.

Norton, R. (1978). Foundations of a communicator style construct. *Human Communication Research, 4,* 99-112.

Norton, R. (1983). *Communicator style.* Beverly Hills, CA: Sage.

Ochs, E. (1986). Introduction. In B. Schieffelin & E. Ochs (Eds.), *Language socialization across cultures.* Cambridge: Cambridge University Press.

Oddou, G., & Mendenhall, M. (1984). Person perception in cross-cultural settings. *International Journal of Intercultural Relations, 8,* 77-96.

Okabe, R. (1983). Cultural assumptions of East and West: Japan and the United States. In W. Gudykunst (Ed.), *Intercultural communication theory.* Beverly Hills, CA: Sage.

Okonji, M. (1980). Cognitive styles across cultures. In N. Warren (Ed.), *Studies in cross-cultural psychology* (Vol. 2). London: Academic Press.

Olsen, M. (1978). *The process of social organization* (2nd ed.). New York: Holt, Rinehart and Winston.

Osgood, C., May, H., & Miron, S. (1975). *Cross-cultural universals of affective meaning.* Urbana: University of Illinois Press.

Palmgreen, P. (1984). Uses and gratification: A theoretical perspective. In R. Bostrom (Ed.), *Communication yearbook 8.* Beverly Hills, CA: Sage.

Park, M. (1979). *Communication styles in two different cultures: Korean and American.* Seoul, Korea: Han Shin Publishing Company.

Parks, M., & Adelman, M. (1983). Communication networks and the development of romantic relationships: An expansion of uncertainty reduction theory. *Human Communication Research, 10,* 55-80.

Parsons, O., & Schneider, J. (1974). Locus of control in university students from Eastern and Western societies. *Journal of Counselling and Clinical Psychology, 42,* 456-461.

Parsons, T. (1951). *The social system.* Glencoe, IL: Free Press.

Parsons, T., & Shils, E. (1951). *Toward a general theory of action.* Cambridge, MA: Harvard University Press.

Pascale, R., & Athos, A. (1981). *The art of Japanese management.* New York: Simon & Schuster.

Peabody, D. (1985). *National characteristics.* Cambridge: Cambridge University Press.

Pearce, W., & Cronen, V. (1980). *Communication, action, and meaning.* New York: Praeger.

Pearce, W., & Wiseman, R. (1983). Rules theories. In W. Gudykunst (Ed.), *Intercultural communication theory.* Beverly Hills, CA: Sage.

Pelto, P. (1968, April). The difference between "tight" and "loose" societies. *Transaction, 5,* 37-40.

Peterson, R. (1979). Revitalizing the culture concept. *Annual Review of Sociology, 5,* 137-166.

Pettigrew, T. (1978). Three issues in ethnicity. In Y. Yinger & S. Cutler (Eds.), *Major social issues.* New York: Free Press.

Pettigrew, T. (1986). The intergroup contact hypothesis reconsidered. In M. Hewstone & R. Brown (Eds.), *Contact and conflict in intergroup encounters.* Oxford: Basil Blackwell.

Philbrick, J., & Opolot, J. (1980). Love style: Comparison of African and American attitudes. *Psychological Reports, 98,* 211-214.

Philipsen, G. (1975). Speaking "like a man" in Teamsterville. *Quarterly Journal of Speech, 61,* 13-22.

Pick, A. (1980). Cognition: Psychological perspectives. In H. Triandis & W. Lonner (Eds.), *Handbook of cross-cultural psychology* (Vol. 3). Boston, MA: Allyn & Bacon.

Pike, K. (1966). *Language in relation to a unified theory of the structure of human behavior.* The Hague: Mouton.

Pilkonis, P., & Zimbardo, P. (1979). The personal and social dynamics of shyness. In C. Izard (Ed.), *Emotions in personality and psychopathology.* New York: Plenum.

Planalp, S., & Honeycutt, J. (1985). Events that increase uncertainty in interpersonal relationships. *Human Communication Research, 11,* 593-604.

Poortinga, Y. (1975a). Limitations on intercultural comparisons of psychological data. *Netherlands Tijdschrift voor de Psychologie, 30,* 23-39.

Poortinga, Y. (1975b). Some implications of three different approaches to intercultural comparisons. In J. Berry & W. Lonner (Eds.), *Applied cross-cultural psychology.* Amsterdam: Swets & Zeitlinger.

Poyatos, F. (1983). *New perspectives in nonverbal communication.* Oxford: Pergamon Press.

Price-Williams, D. (1980). Anthropological approaches to cognition and their relevance to psychology. In H. Triandis & W. Lambert (Eds.), *Handbook of cross-cultural psychology* (Vol. 3). Boston: Allyn & Bacon.

Prisbell, M., & Anderson, J. (1980). The importance of perceived homophily, level of uncertainty, feeling good, safety, and self-disclosure in interpersonal relationships. *Communication Quarterly, 28,* 22-33.

Prothro, E. (1970). Arab-American differences in the judgement of written messages. In A. Lutfiyya & C. Churchill (Eds.), *Readings in Arab Middle-Eastern societies and cultures.* The Hague: Mouton.

Putnam, L., & Jones, T. (1982a). The role of communication in bargaining. *Human Communication Research, 8,* 262-280.

Putnam, L., & Jones, T. (1982b). Reciprocity in negotiations: An analysis of bargaining interaction. *Communication Monographs, 49,* 171-199.

Putnam, L., & Wilson, C. (1982). Communication strategies in organizational conflicts: Reliability and validity of a measurement. In M. Burgoon (Ed.), *Communication yearbook 6.* Beverly Hills, CA: Sage.

Rahim, A. (1983). A measure of styles of handling interpersonal conflict. *Academy of Management Journal, 26,* 368-376.

Rahim, A., & Bonoma, Y. (1979). Managing organizational conflict: A model for diagnosis and intervention. *Psychological Reports, 44,* 1323-1344.

Ramsey, S. (1979). Nonverbal behavior: An intercultural perspective. In M. Asante, E. Newmark & C. Blake (Eds.), *Handbook of intercultural communication.* Beverly Hills, CA: Sage.

Ramsey, S. (1984). Double vision: Nonverbal behavior East and West. In A. Wolfgang (Ed.), *Nonverbal behavior: Perspectives, applications, intercultural insights.* Lewiston, NY: C. J. Hogrefe, Inc.

Read, K. (1955). Morality and the concept of the person among Gahuku-kama. *Oceania, 25,* 233-282.

Reitz, H., & Groff, G. (1972). Comparisons of locus of control categories among American, Mexican, and Thai workers. *Proceedings of the Annual Convention of the American Psychological Association, 7,* 263-264.

Reitz, H., & Groff, G. (1974). Economic development and belief in locus of control among factory workers in four countries. *Journal of Cross-Cultural Psychology, 5,* 344-355.

Reynolds, P. (1971). *A primer in theory construction.* Indianapolis, IN: Bobbs-Merrill.

Roberts, K. (1970). On looking at an elephant: An evaluation of cross-cultural research related to organizations. *Psychological Bulletin, 74,* 327-350.

Robinson, W. (1950). Ecological correlations and the behavior of individuals. *American Sociological Review, 15,* 351-357.

Rogers, E. (1983). *Diffusion of innovations* (3rd ed.). New York: Free Press.

Rogers, E., & Kincaid, D. (1981). *Communication networks.* New York: Free Press.

Rohlen, T. (1973). Spiritual education in a Japanese bank. *American Anthropologist, 75,* 1542-1562.

Rohner, R. (1984). Toward a conception of culture for cross-cultural psychology. *Journal of Cross-Cultural Psychology, 15,* 111-138.

Rokeach, M., Smith, P., & Evans, R. (1960). Two kinds of prejudice or one? In M. Rokeach (Ed.), *The open and closed mind.* New York: Basic Books.

Ronen, S., & Shenkar, S. (1985). Clustering countries on attitudinal dimensions: A review and synthesis. *Academy of Management Review, 10,* 435-454.

Rosaldo, M. (1973). I have nothing to hide: The language of Ilongot oratory. *Language in Society, 11,* 193-223.

Rosaldo, M. (1980). *Knowledge and passion: Ilongot notions of self and social systems.* Cambridge: Cambridge University Press.

Rosaldo, M. (1984). Toward an anthropology of self and feeling. In R. Shweder & R. LeVine (Eds.), *Culture theory: Essays on mind, self, and emotion.* Cambridge: Cambridge University Press.

Rosch, E. (1978). Human categorization. In N. Warren (Ed.), *Studies in cross-cultural psychology* (Vol. 1). London: Academic Press.

Rose, T. (1981). Cognitive and dyadic processes in intergroup contact. In D. Hamilton (Ed.), *Cognitive processes in stereotyping and intergroup behavior.* Hillsdale, NJ: Lawrence Erlbaum.

Rosenberg, M. (1979). *Conceiving the self.* New York: Basic Books.

Rosenthal, R., Hall, J., Dimatteo, M., Rogers, P., & Archer, D. (1979). *Sensitivity to nonverbal communication: The PONS test.* Baltimore: Johns Hopkins University Press.

Ross, R., & DeWine, S. (1984, November). *Interpersonal needs and communication in conflict: Do soft words win hard hearts?* Paper presented at the Speech Communication Association convention, Washington, DC.

Ross, R., & DeWine, S. (1986, November). *Cross-cultural conflict management: A comparison between United States and Denmark styles.* Paper presented at the Speech Communication Association convention, Chicago.

Rothbart, M., Dawes, R., & Park, B. (1984). Stereotyping and sampling biases in intergroup perception. In J. Eiser (Ed.), *Attitudinal judgment.* New York: Springer-Verlag.

Rotter, J. (1966). Generalized expectancies for internal versus external control of reinforcement. *Psychological Monographs, 80,* (Whole No. 609).

Ruben, B., & Kealey, D. (1979). Behavioral assessment of communication competency and the prediction of cross-cultural adaptation. *International Journal of Intercultural Relations, 3,* 15-48.

Rubovits, P., & Maehr, M. (1973). Pygmalian in black and white. *Journal of Personality and Social Psychology, 25,* 210-218.

Rummel, R. (1972). *The dimensions of nations.* Beverly Hills, CA: Sage.

Russell, J. (1983). Pancultural aspects of the human conceptual organization of emotions. *Journal of Personality and Social Psychology, 45,* 1281-1288.

Ryan, E., Giles, H., & Sebastian, R. (1982). An integrative perspective for the study of attitudes toward language. In E. Ryan & H. Giles (Eds.), *Attitudes toward language variation.* London: Edward Arnold.

Ryan, E., Hewstone, M., & Giles, H. (1984). Language and intergroup attitudes. In J. Eiser (Ed.), *Attitudinal judgment.* New York: Springer-Verlag.

Saha, G. (1973). Judgment of facial expression of emotion—a cross-cultural study. *Journal of Psychological Research, 17,* 59-63.

Salamon, S. (1977). Family bonds and friendship bonds: Japan and West Germany. *Journal of Marriage and the Family, 39,* 807-820.

Salamone, F., & Swanson, C. (1979). Identity and ethnicity. *Ethnic Groups, 2,* 167-183.

Saleh, S., & Gufwoli, P. (1982). The transfer of management techniques and practices: The Kenya case. In R. Rath, H. Asthana, D. Sinha, & J. Sinha (Eds.), *Diversity and unity in cross-cultural psychology*. Lisse, The Netherlands: Swets & Zeitlinger.

Sarbin, T., & Allen, V. (1968). Role theory. In G. Lindzey & E. Aronson (Eds.), *Handbook of social psychology* (2nd ed., Vol. 1). Reading, MA: Addison-Wesley.

Schaupp, D. (1978). *A cross-cultural study of a multinational company*. New York: Praeger.

Scheier, M. (1976). Self-awareness, self-consciousness, and angry aggression. *Journal of Personality, 44,* 627-644.

Scheier, M., Buss, A., & Buss, D. (1978). Self-consciousness, self-report of aggressiveness and aggression. *Journal of Research in Personality, 12,* 133-140.

Scheier, M., & Carver, C. (1977). Self-focused attention and expression of emotion: Attraction, repulsion, elation, and depression. *Journal of Personality and Social Psychology, 35,* 625-636.

Scheier, M., & Carver, C. (1981). Private and public aspects of the self. In L. Wheeler (Ed.), *Review of personality and social psychology: 2*. Beverly Hills, CA: Sage.

Scheier, M., & Carver, C. (1982). Self-consciousness, outcome expectancy, and persistence. *Journal of Research in Personality, 16,* 409-418.

Scherer, K. (1984). Emotion as a multicomponent process: A model and some cross-cultural data. *Review of Personality and Social Psychology, 5,* 37-63.

Scherer, K., & Ekman, P. (Eds.). (1984). *Approaches to emotion*. Hillsdale, NJ: Lawrence Erlbaum.

Scherer, K., Summerfield, A., & Wallbott, H. (1983). Cross-national research on antecedents and components of emotion. *Social Science Information, 22,* 355-385.

Scherer, K., Wallbott, H., & Summerfield, A. (Eds.). (1986). *Experiencing emotions: A cross-cultural study*. Cambridge: Cambridge University Press.

Schneider, D. (1972). What is kinship all about? In P. Reinig (Ed.), *Kinship studies in the Morgan Memorial Year*. Washington, DC: Anthropological Society of Washington.

Schollhammer, H. (1969). The comparative management theory jungle. *Academy of Management Journal, 13,* 81-97.

Schramm, W., & Lerner, C. (Eds.). (1976). *Communication and change*. Honolulu: University of Hawaii Press.

Scott, R. (1977). Communication as an intentional social system. *Human Communication Research, 3,* 258-268.

Scotton, C., & Ury, W. (1977). Bilingual strategies: The social functions of code switching. *International Journal of the Sociology of Language, 13,* 5-20.

Sears, R. (1961). Transcultural variables and conceptual equivalence. In B. Kaplan (Ed.), *Studying personality cross-culturally*. New York: Harper.

Sechrest, L. (1977). On the dearth of theory in cross-cultural psychology. In Y. Poortinga (Ed.), *Basic problems in cross-cultural psychology*. Amsterdam: Swets & Zeitlinger.

Segall, M. (1983). On the search for the independent variable in cross-cultural psychology. In S. Irvine & J. Berry (Eds.), *Human assessment and cultural factors*. New York: Plenum Press.

Segalowitz, N. (1980). Issues in the cross-cultural study of bilingual development. In H. Triandis & A. Heron (Eds.), *Handbook of cross-cultural psychology* (Vol. 4). Boston, MA: Allyn & Bacon.

Shatzer, M., Funkhouser, A., & Hesse, M. (1984, May). *Selection of compliance-gaining strategies among four culturally diverse groups*. Paper presented at the International Communication Association convention, San Francisco, CA.

Shaver, P., Schwartz, J., Kirson, D., & O'Connor, C. (1987). Emotion knowledge: Further explorations of a prototype approach. *Journal of Personality and Social Psychology, 52,* 1061-1086.

Sherif, M. (1966). *In common predicament: Social psychology of intergroup conflict and cooperation.* New York: Houghton Mifflin.

Shimanoff, S. (1980). *Communication rules: Theory and research.* Beverly Hills, CA: Sage.

Shimanoff, S. (1985). Rules for governing the verbal expression of emotions between married couples. *Western Journal of Speech Communication, 49,* 147-165.

Shimanoff, S. (1987). Types of emotional disclosures and request compliances between spouses. *Communication Monographs, 54,* 85-100.

Shouby, E. (1970). The influence of the Arabic language or the psychology of the Arabs. In A. Lutifiyya & C. Churchill (Eds.), *Readings in Arab Middle Eastern societies and cultures.* The Hague: Mouton.

Shuter, R. (1976). Too close for comfort: Proxemics and tactility in Latin America. *Journal of Communication, 26,* 46-52.

Shuter, R. (1982). Initial interactions of American blacks and whites in interracial and intraracial dyads. *Journal of Social Psychology, 117,* 45-52.

Shweder, R. (1973). The between and within of cross-cultural research. *Ethos, 1,* 531-545.

Shweder, R., & Bourne, E. (1984). Does the concept of the person vary cross-culturally? In R. Shweder & R. LeVine (Eds.), *Culture theory: Essays on mind, self, and emotion.* Cambridge: Cambridge University Press.

Shweder, R., & LeVine, R. (Eds.). (1984). *Culture theory: Essays on mind, self, and emotion.* Cambridge: Cambridge University Press.

Siegman, A., & Reynolds, M. (1983). Self-monitoring and speech in feigned and unfeigned lying. *Journal of Personality and Social Psychology, 6,* 1325-1333.

Sillars, A. (1980a). Attributions and communication in roommate conflicts. *Communication Monographs, 47,* 180-200.

Sillars, A. (1980b). The sequential and distributional structure of conflict interactions as a function of attributions concerning the locus of responsibility and stability of conflict. In D. Nimimo (Ed.), *Communication yearbook 4.* New Brunswick, NJ: Transaction.

Simard, L. (1981). Cross-cultural interaction. *Journal of Social Psychology, 113,* 171-192.

Simmel, G. (1950). The stranger. In K. Wolff (Ed. and Trans.), *The sociology of Georg Simmel.* New York: Free Press.

Simmons, S., Vom Kolke, A., & Shimizu, H. (1986). Attitudes toward romantic love among American, German, and Japanese students. *Journal of Social Psychology, 126,* 327-336.

Simonetti, S., & Weitz, J. (1972). Job-satisfaction: Some cross-cultural effects. *Personnel Psychology, 25,* 107-118.

Smith, F., & Crano, W. (1977). Cultural dimensions reconsidered: Global and regional analyses of the ethnographic atlas. *American Anthropologist, 79,* 364-387.

Smith, H. (1981). Territorial spacing on a beach revisited: A cross-national exploration. *Social Psychology Quarterly, 44,* 132-137.

Smith, S. (1979). Effects of cultural factors on mass communication processes. In N. Jain (Ed.), *International and intercultural communication annual* (Vol. V). Annandale, VA: Speech Communication Association.

Smith, S., & Whitehead, G. (1984). Attributions for promotion and demotion in the United States and India. *The Journal of Social Psychology, 124,* 27-34.

Snyder, M. (1974). Self-monitoring of expressive behavior. *Journal of Personality and Social Psychology, 30,* 526-537.

Snyder, M. (1979). Self-monitoring processes. In L. Berkowitz (Ed.), *Advances in experimental social psychology* (Vol. 12). New York: Academic Press.

Snyder, M. (1987). *Public appearances, private realities.* New York: Friedman.

Snyder, M., & Gangestad, S. (1986). On the nature of self-monitoring: Matters of assessment, matters of validity. *Journal of Personality and Social Psychology, 51,* 125-139.

Snyder, M., Gangestad, S., & Simpson, J. (1983). Choosing friends as activity partners. *Journal of Personality and Social Psychology, 45,* 1061-1072.

Snyder, M., & Monson, T. (1975). Persons, situations, and the control of social behavior. *Journal of Personality and Social Psychology, 32,* 637-644.

Sodetani, L., & Gudykunst, W. (in press). The effects of surprising events on intercultural relationships. *Communication Research Reports.*

Solomon, R. (1984). Getting angry: The Jamesian theory of emotion in anthropology. In R. Shweder & R. LeVine (Eds.), *Culture theory: Essays on mind, self, and emotion.* Cambridge: Cambridge University Press.

Sorenson, E. (1975). Culture and the expression of emotion. In T. Williams (Ed.), *Psychological anthropology.* The Hague: Mouton.

Spates, J. (1983). The sociology of values. *Annual Review of Sociology, 9,* 27-49.

Spielberger, C., & Diaz-Guerrero, R. (Eds.). (1976). *Cross-cultural anxiety.* Washington, DC: Hemisphere.

Spitzberg, B., & Cupach, W. (1984). *Interpersonal communication competence.* Beverly Hills, CA: Sage.

Stephan, W. (1985). Intergroup relations. In G. Lindzey & E. Aronson (Eds.), *Handbook of social psychology* (3rd ed., Vol. 2). New York: Random House.

Stephan, W., & Brigham, J. (Eds.). (1985). Intergroup contact. *Journal of Social Issues, 41*(3), whole issue.

Stephan, W., & Stephan, C. (1985). Intergroup anxiety. *Journal of Social Issues, 41,* 157-166.

Stephenson, G. (1981). Intergroup bargaining and negotiation. In J. Turner & H. Giles (Eds.), *Intergroup behavior.* Chicago: University of Chicago Press.

Stewart, J. (Ed.). (1977). *Introduction. Bridges not walls* (2nd ed.). Reading, MA: Addison-Wesley.

Street, R., & Giles, H. (1982). Speech accommodation theory. In M. Roloff & C. Berger (Eds.), *Social cognition and communication.* Beverly Hills, CA: Sage.

Suddenfield, P. (1967). Paternal absence and the overseas success of Peace Corp volunteers. *Journal of Consulting Psychology, 31,* 424-425.

Sunnafrank, M. (1986). Predicted outcome value during initial interactions: A reformulation of uncertainty reduction theory. *Human Communication Research, 13,* 3-33.

Sussman, N., & Rosenfeld, H. (1982). Influence of culture, language and sex on conversational distance. *Journal of Personality and Social Psychology, 42,* 66-74.

Swidler, A. (1986). Culture in action: Symbols and strategies. *American Sociological Review, 51,* 273-286.

Szalay, L., & Deese, J. (1978). *Subjective meaning and culture.* Hillsdale, NJ: Lawrence Erlbaum.

Tafoya, D. (1983). The roots of conflict: A theory and a typology. In W. Gudykunst (Ed.), *Intercultural communication theory.* Beverly Hills, CA: Sage.

Tajfel, H. (1978). Social categorization, social identity, and social comparison. In H. Tajfel (Ed.), *Differentiation between social groups.* London: Academic Press.

Tajfel, H. (1981a). *Human categories and social groups.* Cambridge: Cambridge University Press.

Tajfel, H. (1981b). Social stereotypes and social groups. In J. Turner & H. Giles (Eds.), *Intergroup behavior*. Chicago: University of Chicago Press.

Tajfel, H. (Ed.). (1982a). *Social identity and intergroup relations*. Cambridge, MA: Cambridge University Press.

Tajfel, H. (1982b). Social psychology of intergroup relations. *Annual Review of Psychology, 33,* 1-39.

Tajfel, H., & Turner, J. (1979). An integrative theory of intergroup conflict. In W. Austin & S. Worchel (Eds.), *The social psychology of intergroup relations*. Monterey, CA: Brooks/Cole.

Tanaka-Matsumi, J., & Marsella, A. (1976). Cross-cultural variations in the phenomenological experience of depression: I. Word association studies. *Journal of Cross-Cultural Psychology, 7,* 379-396.

Tannen, D. (1979). What's a frame? Surface evidence for underlying expectations. In R. Freedle (Ed.), *New directions in discourse processing* (Vol. 2). Norwood, NJ: Ablex.

Tannenbaum, A. (1980). Organizational psychology. In H. Triandis & R. Brislin (Eds.), *Handbook of cross-cultural psychology* (Vol. 5). Boston, MA: Allyn & Bacon.

Tannenbaum, A., Kavcic, B., Rossner, M., Vianello, M., & Weiser, G. (1974). *Hierarchy in organizations*. San Francisco: Jossey-Bass.

Tardy, C., & Hoseman, L. (1982). Self-monitoring and self-disclosure flexibility: A research note. *Western Journal of Speech Communication, 46,* 92-97.

Taylor, D. (1968). The development of interpersonal relationships: Social penetration processes. *Journal of Social Psychology, 75,* 79-90.

Taylor, D., & Altman, I. (1966). *Intimacy-scaled stimuli for use in studies of interpersonal relations* (Report No. 9). Naval Medical Research Institute.

Taylor, D., Dubé, L., & Bellerose, J. (1986). Intergroup contact in Quebec. In M. Hewstone & R. Brown (Eds.), *Contact and conflict in intergroup encounters*. Oxford: Basil Blackwell.

Taylor, D., & Guimond, S. (1978). The belief theory of prejudice in an inter-group context. *Journal of Social Psychology, 105,* 11-25.

Taylor, D., & Jaggi, V. (1974). Ethnocentrism and causal attribution in a South Indian context. *Journal of Cross-Cultural Psychology, 5,* 162-171.

Taylor, D., & Simard, L. (1975). Social interaction in a bilingual setting. *Canadian Psychological Review, 16,* 240-254.

Tedeschi, J. (1986). Private and public experiences and the self. In R. Baumeister (Ed.), *Public and private self*. New York: Springer-Verlag.

Tessler, M., O'Barr, W., & Spain, D. (1973). *Transition and identity in changing Africa*. New York: Harper & Row.

Thibaut, J., & Kelley, H. (1959). *The social psychology of groups*. New York: John Wiley.

Thomas, K., & Kilman, R. (1978). Comparison of four instruments for measuring conflict behavior. *Psychological Reports, 42,* 1139-1145.

Thorndike, E. (1939). On the fallacy of inputting the correlations found for groups to the individual or smaller groups composing them. *American Journal of Psychology, 3,* 122-124.

Timaeus, E. (1968). Untersuchungen zum sogenannten konformen Verhatten. *Zeitschrift für Experimentelle und Angewandte Psychologie, 15,* 176-194.

Ting-Toomey, S. (1980). Talk as a cultural resource in the Chinese-American speech community. *Communication, 9,* 193-203.

Ting-Toomey, S. (1981). Ethnic identity and close friendship in Chinese-American college students. *International Journal of Intercultural Relations, 5,* 383-406.

Ting-Toomey, S. (1983). Coding conversation between intimates: A validation study of the intimate negotiation coding system. *Communication Quarterly, 31,* 68-77.

Ting-Toomey, S. (1985). Toward a theory of conflict and culture. In W. Gudykunst, L. Stewart, & S. Ting-Toomey (Eds.), *Communication, culture, and organizational processes.* Beverly Hills, CA: Sage.

Ting-Toomey, S. (1986a). Conflict styles in black and white subjective cultures. In Y. Kim (Ed.), *Current research in interethnic communication.* Beverly Hills, CA: Sage.

Ting-Toomey, S. (1986b). Japanese communication patterns: Insider versus the outsider perspective. *World Communication, 15,* 113-126.

Ting-Toomey, S. (1987, May). *A comparative analysis of the communicative dimensions of love, self-disclosure maintenance, ambivalence, and conflict in three cultures: France, Japan, and the United States.* Paper presented at the International Communication Association convention, Montreal.

Ting-Toomey, S. (1988). A face-negotiation theory. In Y. Kim & W. Gudykunst (Eds.), *Theory in intercultural communication.* Newbury Park, CA: Sage.

Tobey, E., & Tunnel, G. (1981). Predicting our impressions on others: Effects of public self-consciousness and acting, a self-monitoring subscale. *Personality and Social Psychology Bulletin, 7,* 661-669.

Tomeh, A., & Gallant, C. (1984). Familial sex role attitudes: A French sample. *Journal of Comparative Family Studies, 15,* 389-405.

Tönnies, F. (1961). *Community and society.* New York: Harper.

Törnblom, K., Jonsson, D., & Foa, U. (1985). Nationality, resource class, and preferences among three allocation rules: Sweden vs. USA. *International Journal of Intercultural Relations, 9,* 51-78.

Tracy, K., Craig, R., Smith, M., & Spisak, F. (1984). The discourse of requests: Assessment of a compliance-gaining approach. *Human Communication Research, 10,* 513-538.

Trew, K. (1986). Catholic-Protestant contact in Northern Ireland. In M. Hewstone & R. Brown (Eds.), *Contact and conflict in intergroup encounters.* Oxford: Basil Blackwell.

Triandis, H. (1961). A note on Rokeach's theory of prejudice. *Journal of Abnormal and Social Psychology, 62,* 184-186.

Triandis, H. (1967a). Interpersonal relations in international organizations. *Organizational Behavior and Human Performance, 7,* 316-328.

Triandis, H. (1967b). Toward an analysis of components of interpersonal attitudes. In C. Sherif & M. Sherif (Eds.), *Attitude, ego-involvement, and change.* New York: John Wiley.

Triandis, H. (1968). Some cross-cultural studies of cognitive consistency. In R. Abelson et al. (Eds.), *Theories of cognitive consistency.* Chicago: Rand McNally.

Triandis, H. (1972). *The analysis of subjective culture.* New York: John Wiley.

Triandis, H. (1976). On the value of cross-cultural research in social psychology. *European Journal of Social Psychology, 6,* 331-341.

Triandis, H. (1977). *Interpersonal behavior.* Monterey, CA: Brooks/Cole.

Triandis, H. (1978). Some universals of social behavior. *Personality and Social Psychology Bulletin, 4,* 1-16.

Triandis, H. (1980a). Values, attitudes, and interpersonal behavior. In M. Page (Ed.), *Nebraska symposium on motivation 1979* (Vol. 27). Lincoln: University of Nebraska Press.

Triandis, H. (1980b). Introduction to handbook. In H. Triandis & W. Lambert (Eds.), *Handbook of cross-cultural psychology* (Vol. 1). Boston, MA: Allyn & Bacon.

Triandis, H. (1984). A theoretical framework for the more efficient construction of culture assimilators. *International Journal of Intercultural Relations, 8,* 301-330.

Triandis, H. (1986). Collectivism vs. individualism: A reconceptualization of a basic concept in cross-cultural psychology. In C. Bagley & G. Verma (Eds.), *Personality, cognition, and values: Cross-cultural perspectives of childhood and adolescence.* London: Macmillan.

Triandis, H. (1987). Personal communication, February 4.

Triandis, H., & Berry, J. (Eds.). (1980). *Handbook of cross-cultural psychology: Vol 2: Methodology.* Boston, MA: Allyn & Bacon.

Triandis, H. C., Bontempo, R., Betancourt, H., Bond, M. H., Leung, K., Brenes, A., Georgas, J., Hui, H. C., Marin, G., Setiadi, B., Sinha, J.B.P., Verma, J., Spangenberg, J., Touzard, H., & deMontmollin, G. (in press). The measurement of etic aspects of individualism and collectivism across cultures. *Australian Journal of Psychology.*

Triandis, H., Bontempo, R., Villareal, M., Asai, M., Lucca, N., Betancourt, H., Bond, M., Leung, K., Brenes, A., Georgas, J., Hui, C., Marin, G., Sinha, J., Verma, J., Setiadi, B., Spangenberg, J. Touzard, H., & de Montmallin, G. (1986). *Individualism and Cross-cultural perspectives on self-ingroup relationships.* Unpublished manuscript, University of Illinois.

Triandis, H., & Davis, E. (1965). Race and belief as determinants of behavioral intentions. *Journal of Personality and Social Psychology 2,* 715-725.

Triandis, H., & Draguns, J. (1980). *Handbook of cross-cultural psychology: Vol. 6. Psychopathology.* Boston: Allyn & Bacon.

Triandis, H., & Marin, G. (1983). Etic plus emic versus pseudo-etic. *Journal of Cross-Cultural Psychology, 14,* 489-500.

Triandis, H., Hui, C., Albert, R., Leung, S., Lisansky, J., Betancourt, H., & Loyola-Cintron, C. (1984). Individual models of social behavior. *Journal of Personality and Social Psychology, 46,* 1389-1404.

Triandis, H., Leung, K., Villareal, M., & Clack, F. (1985). Allocentric vs. idiocentric tendencies. *Journal of Research in Personality, 19,* 395-415.

Triandis, H., Malpass, R., & Davidson, A. (1973). Cross-cultural psychology. *Biennial Review of Anthropology, 24,* 1-84.

Triandis, H., Vassiliou, V., & Nassiakou, M. (1968). Three cross-cultural studies of subjective cultures. *Journal of Personality and Social Psychology, 8,* (Monograph Supplement No. 4), 1-42.

Tseng, W., & Hsu, I. (1980). Minor psychological disturbances of everyday life. In H. Triandis & J. Draguns (Eds.), *Handbook of cross-cultural psychology* (Vol. 6). Boston: Allyn & Bacon.

Tsujimura, A. (1987). Some characteristics of the Japanese way of communication. In D. Kincaid (Ed.), *Communication theory from Eastern and Western perspectives.* New York: Academic Press.

Tu, W. (1985). Selfhood and otherness in Confucian thought. In A. Marsella, G. DeVos, & F. Hsu (Eds.), *Culture and self: Asian and Western perspectives.* New York: Tavistock.

Tuan, Y. (1982). *Segmented worlds and self: Group, life and individual consciousness.* Minneapolis: University of Minnesota Press.

Turner, J. (1982). Towards a cognitive redefinition of the social group. In H. Tajfel (Ed.), *Social identity and intergroup relations.* Cambridge: Cambridge University Press.

Turner, J. (1987). *Rediscovering the social group: A self-categorization theory.* Oxford: Basil Blackwell.

Turner, J., Shaver, I., & Hogg, M. (1983). Social categorization, interpersonal attraction and group formation. *British Journal of Social Psychology, 22,* 227-239.

Van Dijk, T. (1984). *Prejudice in discourse: An analysis of ethnic prejudice in cognition and conversation.* Amsterdam: John Benjamins.

Varonis, E., & Gass, S. (1985). Miscommunication in native/nonnative conversation. *Language in Society, 14,* 327-343.

Vaughan, G., Tajfel, H., & Williams, J. (1981). Bias in reward allocation in an intergroup and an interpersonal context. *Social Psychology Quarterly, 44,* 37-42.

Vinacke, W., & Fong, R. (1955). The judgment of facial expressions by three national-racial groups in Hawaii: II. Oriental focus. *Journal of Social Psychology, 41,* 184-195.

Walker, H., & Cohen, B. (1985). Scope statements: Imperatives for evaluating theory. *American Sociological Review, 50,* 288-301.

Wallbott, H., Ricci-Bitti, P., & Banninger-Huber, E. (1986). Non-verbal reactions to emotional experiences. In K. Scherer, H. Wallbott, & A. Summerfield (Eds.), *Experiencing emotions.* Cambridge: Cambridge University Press.

Wallbott, H., & Scherer, K. (1986). The antecedents of emotional experiences. In K. Scherer, H. Wallbott, & A. Summerfield (Eds.), *Experiencing emotions.* Cambridge: Cambridge University Press.

Warr, P., & Haycock, V. (1970). Scales for a British personality differential. *British Journal of Social and Clinical Psychology, 9,* 328-337.

Waterman, A. (1984). *The psychology of individualism.* New York: Praeger.

Watson, O. (1970). *Proxemic behavior: A cross-cultural study.* The Hague: Mouton.

Watson, O., & Graves, T. (1973). Quantitative research in proxemic behavior. *American Anthropologist, 25,* 6-14.

Wegner, D., & Vallacher, P. (1977). *Implicit psychology.* New York: Oxford University Press.

Weick, K. (1979). *The social psychology of organizing* (2nd ed.). Reading, MA: Addison-Wesley.

Wells, A. (Ed.). (1974). *Mass communications: A world review.* Palo Alto, CA: Mayfield.

Werner, C., Altman, Z., & Oxley, D. (1985). Temporal aspects of homes: A transactional perspective. In I. Altman & C. Warner (Eds.), *Home environments.* New York: Plenum.

Westen, D. (1985). *Self and society.* Cambridge: Cambridge University Press.

Wetherell, M. (1982). Cross-cultural studies of minimal groups: Implications for the social identity theory of intergroup relations. In H. Tajfel (Ed.), *Social identity and intergroup relations.* Cambridge: Cambridge University Press.

Wiemann, G. (1983). The not-so-small world: Ethnicity and acquaintance networks in Israel. *Social Networks, 5,* 289-302.

Wiemann, J., Chen, V., & Giles, H. (1986, November). *Beliefs about talk and silence in a cultural context.* Paper presented at the Speech Communication Association convention, Chicago.

Wiemann, J., & Harrison, R. (Eds.). (1983). *Nonverbal interaction.* Beverly Hills, CA: Sage.

Wigand, R. (1982). Direct satellite broadcasting. In M. Burgoon (Ed.), *Communication yearbook 6.* Beverly Hills, CA: Sage.

Wilder, D. (1986). Social categorization. In L. Berkowitz (Ed.), *Advances in experimental social psychology* (Vol. 19). New York: Academic Press.

Williams, R. (1947). *Reduction of intergroup tensions.* New York: Social Science Research Council.

Williams, R. (1975). *Television: Technology and cultural form*. New York: Schocken Books.

Winkelmayer, R., Exline, R. V., Gottheil, E., & Paredes, A. (1978). The relative accuracy of U.S., British, and Mexican raters in judging the emotional displays of schizophrenic and normal U.S. women. *Journal of Clinical Psychology, 34*, 600-608.

Witkin, H., & Berry, J. (1975). Psychological differentiation in cross-cultural perspective. *Journal of Cross-Cultural Psychology, 6*, 4-87.

Witkin, H., Dyk, R., Faterson, H., Goodenough, D., & Karp, S. (1962). *Psychological differentiation*. New York: John Wiley.

Wolfgang, A. (Ed.). (1984). *Nonverbal behavior: Perspectives, applications, intercultural insights*. Lewiston, NY: C. J. Hogrefe, Inc.

Wolfson, K., & Norden, M. (1984). Measuring responses to filmed interpersonal conflict: A rules approach. In W. Gudykunst & Y. Kim (Eds.), *Methods for intercultural communication research*. Beverly Hills, CA: Sage.

Wolfson, K., & Pearce, W. (1983). A cross-cultural comparison of the implications of self-disclosure on conversational logics. *Communication Quarterly, 31*, 249-256.

Wolfson, N. (1981). Compliments in cross-cultural perspective. *TESOL Quarterly, 15*, 117-124.

Won-Doornink, M. (1979). On getting to know you: The association between stage of relationship and reciprocity of self-disclosure. *Journal of Experimental Social Psychology, 15*, 229-241.

Won-Doornink, M. (1985). Self-disclosure and reciprocity in conversation: A cross-national study. *Social Psychology Quarterly, 48*, 97-107.

Wood, M. (1934). *The stranger*. New York: Columbia University Press.

Wright, G., & Phillips, L. (1980). Cultural variation in probabilistic thinking. *International Journal of Psychology, 15*, 239-257.

Wright, G., Phillips, L., Whalley, P., Choo, G., Ng, K., Tan, I., & Wisudha, A. (1978). Cultural differences in probabilistic thinking. *Journal of Cross-Cultural Psychology, 9*, 285-299.

Wright, G., Phillips, L., & Wisudha, A. (1983). Cultural comparisons on decision-making under uncertainty. In J. Deregowski, S. Dzuirawiec & R. Annis (Eds.), *Expications in cross-cultural psychology*. Lisse, The Netherlands: Swets & Zeitlinger.

Wright, P. (1978). Toward a theory of friendship based on a conception of self. *Human Communication Research, 4*, 196-207.

Wuthnow, R. (1987). *Meaning and moral order: Explorations in cultural analysis*. Berkeley: University of California Press.

Wyer, R., & Srull, T. (1980). The processing of social stimulus information. In R. Hastie et al. (Eds.), *Person memory: The cognitive basis of social perception*. Hillsdale, NJ: Lawrence Erlbaum.

Yamazaki, T. (1965). *Shiroi Kyoto* (in Japanese). Tokyo: Shinchosha.

Yang, K. (1981a). Social orientation and individual modernity among Chinese students in Taiwan. *Journal of Social Psychology, 113*, 159-170.

Yang, K. (1981b). The formation and change of Chinese personality: A cultural-ecological perspective. *Acta Psychologica Taiwanica, 23*, 39-56 (in Chinese).

Yang, K., & Bond, M. (1983, March). *The Chinese orientation towards the description of personality*. Paper presented at the Conference on Modernization and Chinese Culture, The Chinese University of Hong Kong.

Yang, K., & Lee, P. (1971). Likeability, meaningfulness, and familiarity of 557 Chinese adjectives for personality trait description. *Acta Psychologica Taiwanica, 13*, 36-57 (in Chinese).

Yoshida, M., Kinase, R., Kurokawa, J., & Yashiro, S. (1970). Multidimensional scaling of emotion. *Japanese Psychological Research, 12,* 45-61 (in Japanese with English abstract).

Young, L. (1982). Inscrutability revisited. In J. Gumperz (Ed.), *Language and social identity.* Cambridge: Cambridge University Press.

Young, L., Giles, H., & Pierson, H. (1986). Sociopolitical change and perceived vitality. *International Journal of Intercultural Relations, 10,* 459-469.

Young, L., Pierson, H., & Giles, H. (in press). The effects of language and academic specialization on perceived group vitalities. *Linguistic Berichte.*

Yu, D. (Ed.). (1982). *Ethnicity and interpersonal interaction: A cross-cultural study.* Singapore: Maruzen Asia.

Yum, J. (1983). Social network patterns of five ethnic groups in Hawaii. In R. Bostrom (Ed.), *Communication yearbook 7.* Beverly Hills, CA: Sage.

Yum, J. (1987a). Korean philosophy and communication. In D. Kincaid (Ed.), *Communication theory from Eastern and Western perspectives.* New York: Academic Press.

Yum, J. (1987b). The practice of uye-ri in interpersonal relationships in Korea. In D. Kincaid (Ed.), *Communication theory from Eastern and Western perspectives.* New York: Academic Press.

Zajonc, R. (1980). Feeling and thinking: Preferences need no inferences. *American Psychologist, 35,* 151-175.

Zavalloni, M. (1975). Social identity and the recoding of reality. *International Journal of Psychology, 10,* 197-217.

Zavalloni, M. (1980). Values. In H. Triandis & R. Brislin (Eds.), *Handbook of cross-cultural psychology* (Vol. 5). Boston, MA: Allyn & Bacon.

Zimbardo, P. (1977). *Shyness: What it is, what to do about it.* Reading, MA: Addison-Wesley.

Zung, W. (1972). A cross-cultural survey of depressive symptomatology in normal adults. *Journal of Cross-Cultural Psychology, 3,* 177-183.

Zurcher, L. (1968). Particularism and organizational position: A cross-cultural analysis. *Journal of Applied Psychology, 52,* 139-144.

INDEX

ABOUT THE AUTHORS

WILLIAM B. GUDYKUNST is Professor of Communication at Arizona State University. His major interest is in developing a theory that explains interpersonal and intergroup communication and incorporates cultural variability. An initial statement of the theory appears in *Theory in Intercultural Communication* (Sage, 1988), a volume he coedited with Young Yun Kim. A more complete formulation of the theory will be presented in *Strangeness and Similarity: A Theory of Interpersonal and Intergroup Communication* (Multilingual Matters, in progress). He recently coedited the *Handbook of Intercultural and Developmental Communication* (Sage, in press) with Molefi Asante.

STELLA TING-TOOMEY (Ph.D., University of Washington) is Associate Professor of Communication at Arizona State University. She is the series coeditor of the *International and Intercultural Communication Annual,* volumes XIII-XVI. Her recent work includes coediting *Language, Communication, and Culture* and *Culture and Communicating for Peace: Diplomacy and Negotiation Across Cultures* (both with Felipe Korzenny). In addition, she has contributed numerous articles to leading academic journals, including *Human Communication Research, Communication Monographs,* and *International Journal of Intercultural Relations.* Her program of research focuses on cross-cultural conflict styles in interpersonal relationships.

ELIZABETH CHUA completed her M.A. in Communication at Arizona State University with a focus on culture and communication. She has contributed articles to *Communication Yearbook, International Journal of Intercultural Relations,* and *Communication Research Reports.*